READING
NATIONAL
GEOGRAPHIC

READING NATIONAL GEOGRAPHIC

Catherine A. Lutz and Jane L. Collins

The University of Chicago Press
Chicago and London

The University of Chicago Press, Chicago 60637
The University of Chicago Press, Ltd., London
© 1993 by The University of Chicago
All rights reserved. Published 1993
Printed in the United States of America

04 03 02 01 00 99 98   6 7 8 9 10

ISBN: 0-226-49724-0 (paper)

Library of Congress Cataloging-in-Publication Data

Lutz, Catherine.
    Reading National Geographic / Catherine A. Lutz and Jane L. Collins.
        p.   cm.
    Includes bibliographical references and index.
    1. National Geographic.   2. American periodicals—History—20th century. 3.
Books and reading—United States—History—20th century.   I. Collins, Jane Lou,
1954–   .   II. Title.
    G1.N275L88   1993
    910'.5—dc20   92-40698
                                                                    CIP

⊛ The paper used in this publication meets the minimum requirements of the American
National Standard for Information Sciences—Permanence of Paper for Printed Library
Materials, ANSI Z39.48-1984.

For
Michael
and
for
Bobby

Contents

Illustrations

Preface

O ur parents and grade-school teachers led us to *National Geographic* magazine, and there we found immense pleasure in the views of fantastically decorated forest people, vivid tropical fish and flowers, and the expansive sense of a world large, diverse, and somehow knowable. From the early 1960s onward, we avidly looked through each of the issues as they came into our homes, and went back to many of them again and again. Few of the specific ideas, images, or elements of text-based knowledge that we encountered thirty years or so ago remain with us, but of those that do, a significant proportion are from that magazine. In our childhood, this multitude of photographs suggested an enticing world beyond the relatively homogeneous, suburban American one we knew. They posed the possibility of an alternative to cultural sameness and of places where—as Gregory Bateson would say—people did things in ways that were marvelously different. Donna Haraway has argued that those who work in cultural studies should avoid critiquing practices in which they are not implicated. Both of us were implicated deeply and early in the seductive representations of the third world produced by *National Geographic*. In fact, like many anthropologists who have described to us the effect of the magazine on them, we can, in part, root our life's work in our early reading of it.

The impulse for this book came many years later. We both had lived through and watched on television the reverberations in the United States of the escalation and the end of the Vietnam War. We had been trained in anthropology and had traveled to do fieldwork, one of us in Micronesia and the other in the Peruvian Andes. As young professors at a state university, we were struggling to teach about cultural differences in ways that were meaningful to undergraduates in the 1980s. One day in 1983, while eating lunch in the campus pub, we watched students burst into cheers as a TV newscaster announced that the United States had invaded Grenada. Troubled and perplexed, we wondered what reality the wounded and dying Grenadians had for those students. Had they heard of Grenada before that day? Did they know anything of the history of U.S. intervention in the Caribbean? What preexisting understandings about America and the third world did they hold that allowed for that reaction? What role in forming those understandings was played by a mass media that on this day, as on most others, was uncritical—even celebratory—of American military intervention? We began to feel the need to understand the models of the third world and of cultural difference, broadly shared by white, middle-class Americans, that many of our undergraduate students brought to the classroom and that we ourselves struggled with and against. After much consideration, we turned to the examination of *National Geographic* photographs as one of the most culturally valued and potent media vehicles shaping American understandings of, and responses to, the world outside the United States.

The reality we chose to investigate was not overseas, then, but was in the homes and offices where *National Geographic* is read and produced. Our interest was, and is, in the making and consuming of images of the non-Western world, a topic raising volatile issues of power, race, and history. We wanted to know what popular education tells Americans about who "non-Westerners" are, what they want, and what our relationship is to them. *National Geographic* is certainly not alone in forming these ideas. The magazine exists in a complex system of artifacts and communication devices: newspapers and newsmagazines, television news and special reports, museums and exhibitions, geography and world history textbooks, student exchange programs, travelogues, and films from *Rambo* and *Raiders of the Lost Ark* to *El Norte*. Yet these diverse contexts are in communication with one another, purveying and contesting a limited universe of ideas about cultural difference and how

[handwritten margin note: — central question —]

[handwritten margin note: (Purpose/why)]

it can or should be interpreted. To study *National Geographic,* then, is to study not a single cultural artifact but a powerful voice in an ongoing cultural discussion of these issues. The history, culture, and social reality of North–South relations is primarily written, of course, in corporation boardrooms, government agency offices, and encounters between tourists, bankers, military personnel, and State Department employees, on the one hand, and the people of Southern nations on the other. The role of a cultural institution like the *National Geographic* and its readers might seem small by comparison. But its role is not simply to form an "educated public," nor is it simply to mislead or err in describing those relations; it can also provide support for American state policies and for voting and consumer behavior.

While the *National Geographic* photograph is commonly seen as a straightforward kind of evidence about the world—a simple and objective mirror of reality—it is in fact evidence of a much more complex, interesting, and consequential kind. It reflects as much on who is behind the lens, from photographers to magazine editors and graphic designers to the readers who look—with sometimes different eyes—through the *Geographic*'s institutional lens. The photograph can be seen as a cultural artifact because its makers and readers look at the world with an eye that is not universal or natural but tutored. It can also be seen as a commodity, because it is sold by a magazine concerned with revenues. The features of the photographs, and the reading given them by others, can tell us about the cultural, social, and historical contexts that produced them. This book traces how the magazine has floated in American cultural and political-economic currents of the post–World War II period and asks what the photographs tell us about the American-fashioned world.

The fundamentally critical perspective we take on the magazine and its social context is thus linked in a range of ways to deeply personal concerns. These concerns—with how to imagine and value difference, how to foster both empathetic forms of understanding and historically grounded perceptions—emerge out of our own childhood and adolescent experiences and out of our choice of adult work. As our own early encounters with *National Geographic* attest, its photos do not occupy a fixed place in American culture, teaching generation after generation the same things about the world. They are weighted in certain directions and repeat certain themes, but they have changed over time, and they can be read differently by individuals with different backgrounds and concerns and in different historical periods. They have formed part of a larger cultural discussion of who Americans are and who others might be. Our goal is not to pass judgment but to intervene in—perhaps disrupt for a moment—that discussion. It is to bring to awareness the ways these photographs have operated, to point to some of the prevailing cultural ideas about others through which any photograph of the non-Western world has often been filtered, and to raise questions about what a politically empowering and progressive photography focused on cultural difference might be.

Acknowledgments

The many people who worked on this book should feel it is partly their handiwork. The confrontation of ideas in joint research is the key to creating something at least a bit beyond the sum of the authors' abilities. Even more, collaborative work has a multiplying effect on the pleasures and challenges already inherent in the privilege of solitary research and writing.

We would like to begin by thanking the people at *National Geographic* magazine. A large number of people throughout the institution helped us, often by graciously consenting to long and thoughtful interviews. Others generously granted us permission to reprint their photographs. What interpretation we have placed on those interviews and on these reprinted and other photographs can only be partial, given the limits of time and ability. Nonetheless, it is our hope that the critical eye we have turned on the magazine contributes to debates at the National Geographic Society. Anthropologists' writing culture has some of the same difficulties as photojournalists' photographing culture, and we hope that recognition is reflected in these pages.

We drew a number of graduate students into the pages of the *Geographic* over the several years this book has been germinating, and their enthusiastic and creative labors are at the core of the book. We would especially like to thank

Tammy Bennington, Tamara Bray, Deedee Joyce, and Karla Slocum, as well as Marcia Anne Dobres, Shadman Habibi, Kathleen Roe, Maria Clara Saraiva, Carolyn Steele, and LouAnn Wurst. And to the family of Daniel Lipsman—he is here too. For careful transcribing of the interview tapes, we are grateful to Michael and Tina Brewster-Wray and to Andrea Lain.

Our thanks to John Kirkpatrick, Dawn Richards, and Amy Hamilton for the very productive interviews they held for us with readers in Hawaii. Thanks especially to John for his good advice and support.

The people we and our Hawaii colleagues met as we were conducting interviews on the impact of the photographs have generously allowed us to share their spontaneous readings of the photos. We apologize that the limited space of this book merely allowed us to hint at the rich and imaginative work they did in those interviews.

A number of people gave fundamental help in leading us part way out of the ignorance with which we began this project. Maureen Turim and Margaret Conkey have been learned tutors on the questions of art, artifact, and society as well as steadfast friends. We have also been led to many useful materials and insights by Barbara Abou-al-Haj, Albert Dekin, Susan Sterett, and John Tagg. Very helpful readings of one or more chapters of this book were provided by Lila Abu-Lughod, Whitney Davis, Phoebe Ellsworth, Faye Harrison, William Kelley, John Kirkpat-rick, John MacAloon, Lawrence Rosen, Daniel Rosenberg, Marilyn Strathern, Lucien Taylor, and two anonymous readers for the University of Chicago Press. We had the opportunity to read portions of the manu-script in progress and to benefit from helpful rejoinders, sources, and ideas from audiences at the University of Chicago, the University of California at Berkeley, the University of Heidelberg, the School of American Research, Duke University, Hunter College, the University of North Carolina at Chapel Hill, and New York University.

The research described here was funded by the National Science Foun-dation and the State University of New York Research Foundation. The research benefited as well from the research design suggestions of Stuart Plattner and several anonymous reviewers for NSF. Sabbatical leaves from the State University of New York at Binghamton provided both of us some of the time needed for writing.

As authors writing together, it seems important to acknowledge the tremendous support we have provided one another over the course of this project. Beginning the work as close friends and colleagues, we emerged from the process even closer. The project itself was a collaboration in the best sense—we learned from each other, worked through challenging material together, disagreed, and resolved differences, all within a framework of respect for each other's knowledge, approach to learning, and style of presentation. The excitement that we both felt about the project during its various stages was multiplied by sharing it with each other.

Finally, we are indebted to the thousands of people in and behind the *National Geographic* photographs that are our subject. While we have looked at their images as evidence about American culture and history, we recognize that to them these images mean something else again.

One

Comfortable Strangers: The Making of National Identity in Popular Photography

There they all flock to see, not really a world brought to their
door, but themselves in every foreign and domestic disguise;
themselves as they might be, convincingly photographed
where they are not.

(Wescott 1928:18)

O ver the course of the past century, *National Geographic*
magazine has come to be one of the primary means by
which people in the United States receive information and
images of the world outside their own borders. While *National Geographic* covers a range of topics—including the
geographic and cultural wonders of the United States,
wildlife and nature stories, and accounts of exploration of
space, the oceans, and the polar ice caps—a good portion
of its text and photographs is devoted to images of the
peoples and cultures of the third world. *National Geographic* identifies itself as a scientific and educational institution, and it is also located in a long tradition of travelogue
as it sends its staff on expeditions to bring back stories and
photos of faraway people and places. While these photographs and stories of curious and exotic practices can be
perused and marveled at by readers in the privacy of their
own homes, they draw people into contact with a much
wider set of cultural ideas. More than simple documents,

both text and (to a less obvious extent) photographs call up and then reinforce or challenge shared understandings of cultural difference.

Each issue of *National Geographic* magazine is seen by an estimated thirty-seven million people worldwide. Its subscription rate is the third largest for magazines in the United States—following *TV Guide* and *Reader's Digest*. The magazine is used by schools as a teaching tool; it is subscribed to by middle-class parents as a way of contributing to the education of their children; its high prestige value affords it a place on coffee tables; its high-quality printing and binding and its reputation as a valuable reference tool mean that it is rarely thrown away, more frequently finding its way into attics and secondhand bookstores.

This book is concerned with *National Geographic's* contribution to one particular arena of popular culture—the promulgation of images of the world outside United States boundaries. It starts, not from the proposition that there is a "real" third world out there that better documentarians could find, but from the understanding that identity formation draws on images of the other. As Clifford has emphasized, the content of categories such as the non-Western or the "primitive" change over time as they are used to "construct a source, origin, or alterego, confirming some new 'discovery' within the territory of the Western self" (1988:212). The term "non-Western," which bounds this project, is admittedly awkward. We use it in line with the evidence that all non-European peoples seem to play a similar self-contrastive role in a fundamental process of identity formation in middle-class, Euroamerican readers. In using this category to examine how cultural difference is construed, we follow the important ideological line that Europeans have drawn through the Mediterranean Sea (Amin 1989), separating themselves from all others. Nineteenth-century "Hellenomania," which claimed Greece as the source of Western culture, has helped solidify the line, as has the postwar NATO alliance. The category non-Western is not meant to erase the diversity and complexity of cultures that actually exist or to discount the important distinctions that white, Western readers can and do make within the category.

In this sense, our book is not at all about the non-Western world but about its appropriation by the West, and *National Geographic's* role in that appropriation. It is not about how "realistic" Western images of that world are but about the imaginative spaces that non-Western peoples occupy and the tropes and stories that organize their existence in Western minds. The question then becomes, How do the images purveyed by *National Geographic* affect this space? Do they congeal popular paradigms of evolutionary ascendancy? Do they emphasize contrastive work and evaluation? Or do they compel empathy and identification? Do they in some cases do both, drawing attention with an exotic element, and then—having captured their readers' attention—inviting them to imagine how they might feel in the setting depicted? We are further concerned with the *varieties* of identification that may be evoked. Does the identification rely on static humanistic principles that assert universal sameness across boundaries of race, class, gender, language, and politics, or on a progressive humanism that seeks to understand and historicize the differences that separate interconnected human beings?

As outlined in the preface, the concerns that motivated these questions were practical and political. They originated in a search for ways of teaching about the third world that did not objectify and were not paternalistic but that fostered both a sense of how lives around the globe are interconnected and a capacity for empathetic understanding. These and other issues have sparked interest across the social sciences and humanities in the question of how people represent various kinds of human differences—racial/ethnic, gender, historical and class—to themselves and each other. Most important is the fact that those understandings or strategies for describing human differences have helped create and reproduce social hierarchies. At the least, those hierarchies have created small humiliations and rejections, and have lessened opportunities. At the worst, they have abetted wars of extermination, lynchings, and rape. Representations may be deployed for or against such horrors or indifferently in relation to them, but they are never irrelevant, never unconnected to the world of actual social relations. Images of the non-Western world draw on and articulate ideas and thus, like all conceptual work, become cultural and historical, mutable and political in intent and/or effect. There are, we will argue, more or less harmful ways of viewing differences.[1]

Coming to political consciousness through the period of the Vietnam War, we were acutely aware of the power of photographic images to

1. An impressive literature on ethnocentrism first helped us to formulate our ideas about interethnic understanding, including Adorno, Frenkel-Brunswik, Levinson, and Sanford (1950); Forbes (1985); Lambert and Klineberg (1967); LeVine and Campbell (1972); and Preiswerk and Perrot (1978). We have also learned much from more recent studies that take a more textual and interpretive approach to examining difference, including those by Bhabha (1983); Gates (1985); Gilman (1985); Haraway (1989); Tiffany and Adams (1985); and Trinh (1989).

evoke both ethnocentric recoil and agonizing identification. Malcolm Browne's famous photo of a Buddhist monk's self-immolation in Saigon was profoundly disturbing to Western viewers, who could not fathom the communicative intent of such an act. Huynh Cong Ut's 1972 photograph of children fleeing a napalm attack evoked both anguish and a sense of responsibility. Close-ups of individual soldiers and interpersonal acts transformed the war for many Americans from an abstract conflict over principles into a human nightmare—the My Lai massacre, a police chief executing an alleged terrorist at point-blank range, a mother holding a blood-drenched, jet-strafed child (see Moeller 1989). It was our awareness of the power of these photographs to mobilize and raise questions that led us to ask about the impact on popular consciousness of the steady, continual, accessible flow of images from an institution like *National Geographic*.

Whose Representations? Power and Geographic Knowledge

A long line of commentators, among them Debord (1983) and Ewen (1988), have argued that the image is central to contemporary society, that photograph and film have taken over from written texts the role of primary educator. To understand how people are acculturated to a particular set of views about the third world, these commentators might suggest, one should look first to television, film, and mass circulation photographs in magazines and textbooks for their content and their effect on readers. Images have been important in the cultural construction of ethnic/racial difference from the earliest periods of European contact with others (Bucher 1981; B. Smith 1985), but never more so than now, when people give more time to television news than to newspapers, when newspapers have less text and more images than in the past, and when Hollywood films (often with ethnic or racial subthemes) have become more spectacular and more widely and frequently viewed than ever before. Other examples include the immense popularity of the picture magazines *Life* and *Look* in midcentury and of the *National Geographic,* whose subscription rate grew from two to ten million subscribers from the mid-1950s through the 1980s.

Taking the photograph as a central feature of contemporary life, we can go on to ask *how* photographs signify. Rejecting the idea that photos are simply objective documents that signify no differently than does any unmediated experience of the visual world, we find that a number of major works by art historians and others have described the intricate, subtle, and fascinating ways in which photographs can communicate or evoke ideas—ideas replete with feelings. We draw extensively on the insights of those theorists, including Benjamin (1985); Geary (1988); Sekula (1981); Sontag (1977); and Tagg (1988). Our perspective on the photograph attends to formal features of the shot such as composition and point of view, but we interpret them in the historical and cultural context that gives the photograph and its elements their meaning and significance.

The National Geographic Society, which produces *National Geographic* magazine, is a powerful institution. Located in Washington, D.C., it cultivates ties to government officials and corporate interests. It justifies its self-image as a national institution on the basis of its reputation for purveying important scientific knowledge about "the world and all that is in it" and for safeguarding important American values and traditions. The latter include an informed or knowledgeable citizenry, particularly in an epoch in which many have been devoted to the idea of America's global responsibilities. In fact, however, *National Geographic* magazine is no forum for the free exchange of ideas about or from the third world. It is a glossy, stylized presentation of a highly limited number of themes and types of images. As such, it is clearly located within what theorists of the Frankfurt School called mass culture—materials created and disseminated by powerful interests for the consumption of the working classes. In categorizing the magazine as mass culture, we are not counterposing popular ideas about the non-Western world to a more legitimate set of high cultural or elite ideas. We are pointing to the nature of its photographs as mass-produced images sold to a reading (viewing) public.

Since the writings of the Frankfurt School in the 1930s and 1940s, the term mass culture has been used to refer to the commercial production of art and entertainment by powerful culture industries. The reputation of the *National Geographic* as a vehicle for scientific information makes it less obviously a member of this set of cultural products, but examination of its connection to prevalent and historically specific ideas will make clear the relevance of the concept of mass culture for an understanding of its relationship to power and culture.

Far from representing the voices and tastes of the popular classes, or even registering their desires, mass culture was seen by Frankfurt theorists as degenerate and manipulative. To the extent that people accepted and participated in the products of mass culture, they were duped and misled, encouraged to develop a false understanding of their situation in a capitalist society. For adherents of such a view, mass culture represented production *for* the masses by dominant classes, while popular culture referred to the remnants of autonomous culture produced by working-class communities.

A number of theorists have questioned the absolute terms in which mass culture was thus cast. Enzensberger (1974) argued against the claim that mass culture uniformly imposes false consciousness. Its strategies succeed, he contends, because they appeal to the real needs and desires of the popular classes. While these desires may be distorted by the "consciousness industries" of advertising and mass media, Enzensberger argued that they are real, autonomous bases for political behavior.

Fredric Jameson (1983) took the position that mass culture is neither entirely manipulative nor entirely authentic. Rather, in his view, it operates by arousing fantasies and desires within structures that defuse them. Mass culture could not do its ideological work, he argued, if it were not at some level utopian. It could not manage desires and anxieties about the social order if it did not deal in fears and fantasies that are recognizable. As Stuart Hall has said, "Alongside the false appeals, the foreshortenings, the trivialization and short-circuits, there are also elements of recognition and identification, something approaching a recreation of recognizable experiences and attitudes, to which people are responding" (1981:233). For theorists like Jameson and Hall, mass culture becomes an arena of struggle—a battleground for the hearts and minds of the working classes. While culture industries seek to purvey dominant ideologies, the people to whom their messages are directed sometimes struggle to appropriate, subvert, and use the commercially produced images to their own ends. At the least, the works remain subject to their consumers' interpretations.

More fine-grained analyses of culture industries have been concerned to specify which classes, or fragments of classes, use the industries to express their perspective, who the proposed audience is, and who responds. We argue that while the messages contained in *National Geographic* photos are highly specific in terms of the world view they encode—that of the white, educated, middle class—they speak to, and draw into their vision, a far larger group, extending from highly educated professionals and managers through white-collar clericals and technicians into the working class and lower ranks of the service sector. The magazine claims to articulate a *national* vision, addressing the concerns and curiosity of all U.S. citizens.

Clearly, as Bourdieu (1984:21) has noted, the fact that a wide range of classes and groups adopt a social product may conceal the diversity of uses to which it is put by these groups. Upper-middle-class professionals may approach the magazine with the critical confidence of those who have traveled and thus possess independent sources of verification (available to the working classes most often through tours of duty in the military). Still, the upbeat and magnanimous style of the magazine hails these diverse readers and invites them to look out at the rest of the world from the vantage point of the world's most powerful nation. For the National Geographic Society, creating this sort of national vision both expands its market and increases its clout as a scientific-educational establishment. It also makes it a worthy object of study.

The place of *National Geographic* in American culture is unique in several respects. There are now many mass media products that play with the ideological line between fact and fun, including the so-called infotainment programs, dramatic "re-creations" of news events, gonzo journalism, but none has the cultural legitimacy of the *Geographic*. This legitimacy, given it by its connections to the state, national identity, and science, has also been achieved by the stability maintained in the size, format, and appearance of the magazine. And the costliness of the paper and binding almost pushes the *Geographic* out of the category magazine (with its somewhat lowbrow connotations) and into the category book or encyclopedia. *Do you agree?*

Among popular magazines, the *National Geographic* sits near the top of the hierarchy of taste or status. Among all cultural artifacts, it would be considered high middlebrow, according to the culturally constructed taste hierarchies that Bourdieu (1984), Levine (1988), and B. H. Smith (1983), among others, have described for French and American society. Those hierarchies assert that some cultural artifacts are intrinsically more valuable than others (for example, classical music over pop, oil painting over photography), when in fact the value of the artifact can be seen as the complex outcome of its histories of use, the class and gender (Morley 1986) of those who consume it, and so on. The hierarchy shifts over time—Shakespeare was in the nineteenth century considered popular fare (Levine 1988)—and is context-sensitive, for people can disagree about details of hierarchical arrangement. Still, there is broad, if not universal agreement over its nature. Most important, it affects who reads the *Geographic,* how they read it, and how the makers of the magazine proceed with their job.

The special cultural niche occupied by the *Geographic* is also indexed by the degree to which the magazine has been *ignored* by academics and other writers on the subject of photography, mass media, or culture in general. The silence is striking. Histories of photography or even of photojournalism in America typically fail to mention it. Research on mass media has focused on single Hollywood movies or soap operas with smaller audiences than the *Geographic*. Why should this be? We can begin to answer the question by looking at Frith's (1986) typology of cultural artifacts (see fig. 1.1), which makes useful distinctions in focusing on the social class of consumers and on whether the primary self-image of the artifacts' producers is in art or in profit making.

| | PRODUCERS | |
	Artists	Profitmakers
Middle and upper classes	A High culture: Mozart C.D.	B Middlebrow: CBS News
		National Geographic
Working classes	D Popular culture: street musicians	C Mass culture: Roseanne

CONSUMERS (to the left, spanning both rows)

Figure 1.1. Typology of cultural artifacts (adapted from Frith 1986)

National Geographic is produced by a group whose identity is in neither art nor profit, although it is obviously concerned with both in some sense. The scientific and educational thrust of the institution makes it straddle the significant boundary between art and profit. Its consumption by a spectrum of Americans that runs more toward the upper part of the social hierarchy (the subscribers are wealthier and better educated than the average American) places it in the middlebrow category or somewhat higher—between, say, Dan Rather and Mozart. This is evidenced by the respected place it has in professional waiting rooms and its frequent role as a symbol of good taste and wealth in advertising scenes. Each of the boxes in the chart has a kind of gender as well as a class status, with mass culture being associated with the feminine because—in stereotype—it is sentimentalized, it is merely consumed, and it requires less intellect (Modleski 1986a), and high culture with the masculine for the opposite reasons. The *Geographic*'s gender associations are masculine, both because of its content (adventure, science) and its cultural power and position.

Analysts of popular culture have tended to study material lowest on the cultural hierarchy of objects, such as popular television comedies or romance novels, while traditional sociology of culture has focused on

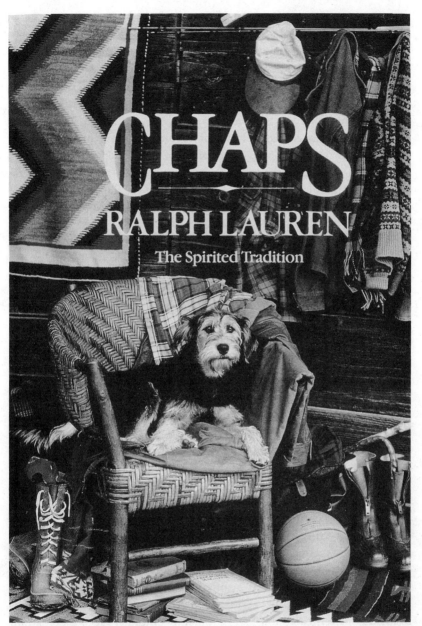

An advertisement for Ralph Lauren, inside front cover of the *New York Times Magazine*, October 28, 1990—one of a number of ads we found in which the *National Geographic* is used as a marker of good taste and upper-middle-class lifestyle. (Photo: Bruce Weber, courtesy Ralph Lauren)

the culture that is seated squarely within box A (Frith 1986). The lack of attention to the *Geographic* may be accounted for by the fact that it is neither an academic observer's "us" nor a "them," neither the "self" nor the "other" for those academic commentators who speak about the world of culture from an identity in Box A right next door to the magazine. Critique or celebration of a cultural object often seems to entail a comparable evaluative treatment of the audience for it (Levine 1988:66). Academics seem to have been less ready to accord such treatment to the middle-class readers of the *Geographic*. The power and importance of the magazine and its photographic ideas could not be greater, however.

The post–World War II history of the *National Geographic* speaks to the evolving patterns of culture and social relations in the United States during that period. The National Geographic Society has its own special history, values, and explicit mission, which we will detail, but the magazine staff applies a range of values that have matched and changed significantly with those of their readers. The turbulence and promise of the second half of the twentieth century in the United States run through the pages of the magazine, although sometimes in studied reaction against its historical context rather than a mere reflection of it. In international relations, the period is one, above all, of the rise, consolidation, and partial thwarting of American hegemony. The cold war, decolonization, Vietnam, and the rise of the officially sanctioned anxieties about foreign terrorists have clear implications for how the third world is portrayed. So, too, does the domestic history of the civil rights and women's movements, of American religiosity, and of the Reagan administration's relegitimation of a view of the class system as the survival of the fittest. The *Geographic* has responded to these events and associated cultural ideas, and it has helped shape the way its readers think about them. Changes in the social experiences of the magazine's readership have also helped give the photographs their qualities and their popularity—changes relating to the rapid expansion of international tourism, rising education and income levels in one period followed by stagnation in the next, residential patterns of suburbanization and continued racial segregation.

Denning (1990) has argued that in late capitalism there is very little cultural production other than in the form of commodities. Thus the drawing of dichotomies between mass and popular culture, between the ideological and the utopian, misses the point. What becomes important, in this highly commercialized world, is not so much the contrast between mass culture and authentic culture as the analysis of how particular cultural forms operate in their social context. Denning criticizes research that simply links or associates a particular form with a social class or movement, seeing it as reflecting in an unproblematic way the interests and concerns of that class. While it is important to understand the class interests and political agendas that shape production of a work, this understanding is rarely adequate to account for the content of the work itself. Denning also criticizes students of mass culture, such as Pierre Bourdieu (1984), who interpret cultural products mainly as markers in class conflict or as symbolic capital. In such approaches, he argues, the content of cultural products and activities evaporates.

The National Geographic Society may be assigned a position within the class structure and foreign policy interests of the United States, as will be demonstrated in chapter 2. Yet the photographs it circulates through the American public are not perfect reflections of these interests. They derive some of their content from the autonomous concerns of the photographer and some from the situations photographed. They are viewed by readers with diverse preoccupations, who understand and interpret the pictures in a variety of ways. Some readings reinforce American illusions of cultural superiority and paternalism, while others entail an engagement with the subject photographed, an identification across cultural boundaries, the awakening of a curiosity that may be politically invigorating.

The Complex Life of Images

This study takes as a starting point the Gramscian notion that hegemony is not so much a structure as a process. Cultural products have complex production sites; they often code ambiguity; they are rarely accepted at face value but are read in complicated and often unanticipated ways. For these reasons, we have structured our study of *National Geographic* photographs so as to gain insight into the process by which its images are formed, selected and controlled, purveyed and read. Our approach contrasts with previous work on cultural artifacts that has focused on one of three areas. (1) Some studies focus mainly on the production site itself and the intentions and struggles within media and other organizations, from those making television news and documentaries (Gans 1979; Silverstone 1985) to the multiple sites at which the Olympics are put together (MacAloon 1987) or the worlds in which art is produced (Becker 1982). (2) Other analysts take their own reading of the significance of the artifact both in and of itself and in relation to its historical or cultural context. These studies have ranged from Hollywood films (Traube 1992; Modleski 1988) to advertisements (Goffman 1979) to journalism (Parenti 1986). (3) Still others focus on reader or consumer response to a wide range of cultural artifacts from individual television programs such as *Dallas* (Liebes and Katz 1990) to romance novels (Radway 1984). Our attempt to examine the *Geographic* from all three perspectives has meant that our work—and the chapters that follow—have been divided into three distinct phases.

The Process of Producing Images of the Non-Western World. Chapters 2 and 3 focus on the National Geographic Society as a social institution. Chapter 2 reviews the history of the organization and its relationship to some aspects of the changing American scene of the twentieth century, the way it has defined itself in various historical periods, and its construction of a particular audience for itself. It examines the complex ways in which the Society has framed its mission: as science, but also entertainment, and as a quasi-official educational enterprise. It looks at how the Society's work fits within a set of other genres and practices that structure our understanding of "otherness"—museums, exotic collections, the midways and expositions of the late nineteenth century. Finally, it looks closely at some of the negotiations and struggles that have gone on within the Society over what its mission ought to be.

Chapter 3 looks at the contemporary practices of producing photographic imagery at the National Geographic Society. Based largely on interviews conducted with photographers, editors, and other staff members, it details the production process from the inception of an idea for a story, through its photography, layout, printing, and other critical junctures. Here we argue that though *National Geographic* photographers often have an independent and critical vision, both the charge they are given regarding what to produce and the subsequent editing processes mean that what is printed in the magazine has only an indirect and attenuated relationship to the photographer's original intent. Producing pictures, captions, and layout is a social and creative act in which negotiation and unacknowledged struggle result in the ultimate artifact, rather than a singular plan deliberately followed through.

The Structure and Content of the Images. A second set of our research activities focused on the attributes of the cultural products—the *National Geographic* photographs themselves. We looked at them analytically in relation to the larger wholes of the genre and its sociocultural context. To learn what the pictures could signify about the third-world peoples they portrayed, we examined closely six hundred randomly selected photographs from 1950 to 1986. We focused on this period in search of the ways that the social upheaval surrounding the escalation and end of the Vietnam War, as well as the civil rights and women's movements at home, affected the images produced at *National Geographic*. We did not believe that the representations generated by the institution would be invariant; we wanted to know how they changed in response to events that affected the lives of readers both directly and through their experience of other media. Through processes described in chapter 4, we chart the tendency of the magazine to idealize and render exotic third-world peoples, with an accompanying tendency to downplay or erase evidence of poverty and violence. The photographs show these people as either cut off from the flow of world events or involved in a singular story of progress from tradition to modernity, a story that changes with decolonization.

In chapter 5 we look at differences in the amount and kind of photographic coverage of particular regions and countries. There we argue that a complex of strategic and cultural factors combine to create a waxing and waning of American and *Geographic* interest in particular groups. The special place of the Pacific in American geography is examined in some detail, as is the power of racial feelings and ideas evident in the photographic treatment of Melanesia and Micronesia. Chapter 6 looks at the particular ways that racial and gender ideologies are deployed, particularly the complex messages the photographs send about how sexuality, gender, and color are involved in the struggle for social progress that is one of the magazine's favorite themes. An American postwar history of race and gender relations is a valuable reference point for what was done in the magazine during the same period. Chapter 7 bridges the three parts of the book, examining the intersections between the structure of the photograph and the "looking practices" of the magazine staff and the readers. These looking practices are highly conventionalized, and some aspects of photographic structure and viewing may be contradictory in their implications.

How Readers View the Photographs. A third set of research activities is concerned with the practices through which *National Geographic* photographs are read or understood. Chapter 8 turns to the analysis of interviews with *Geographic* readers, actual and potential, from New York and Hawaii; it focuses particularly on the responses of these readers to a randomly selected set of *Geographic* photographs. We watch for the degree to which readers' responses accept or parallel the communicative intent of the *Geographic*. When photos are presented to them without captions, do they, on their own, find evolutionary chronicles embedded in the photographs? Do they draw conclusions about the universal humanity that underlies superficial human difference? We also examine the use of evaluative strategies, cases of empathy and identification with those photographed, and the attribution of feeling to the subjects of the photos. In chapter 9 we explore the implications of a critically and politically informed understanding of how *National Geographic* photographs circulate in this society. We discuss further what the pleasures of the magazine consist of, what makes some photographs critical of and others supportive of existing arrangements, what kinds of representations encourage understanding and empathy and what kinds foreclose it, and how some photographs can awaken curiosity about unfamiliar ways of life while others foster categorized stereotyping.

Two

Becoming America's Lens on the World: *National Geographic* in the Twentieth Century

> We must all be of one and the same mind when we look upon the photographic evidence. It is in these photographs that all Americans can meet on the common ground of their beloved traditions. Here we are all united at the shrine.
>
> Francis Trevelyan Miller, *Photographic History of the Civil War* [1912] in Trachtenberg (1989)

The National Geographic Society has been in existence for over a hundred years, in that time constituting itself as an important and reliable interpreter of third-world realities. The Society has employed a number of strategies in constructing its authoritative position and its particular status and place in American culture. It has always been private, but has powerful ties to government; it is a "scientific" institution, yet dependent on the sales and popularity of its magazine; its photographs are realistic, yet highly stylized. Through its long history, the National Geographic Society has strategically deployed realist codes and has fashioned claims to objectivity in order to secure its position as both "scientific" and "popular." Particularly in the period since World War II, it has sought to strike a balance between piquing the public's interest in countries unknown but worthy of exploration and presenting the world as a safe, well-ordered place.

The Evolutionary Chronicle in an Era of New Global Responsibilities

The history of the National Geographic Society and *National Geographic* magazine as generally told is an epic of success: an amateur scientific organization begun by Gardiner Greene Hubbard in 1888 goes on to become the largest scientific-educational organization in the world; a publication that started out as a "slim, dull and technical" journal for gentleman scholars evolves into a glossy magazine whose circulation is the third largest in the United States. *National Geographic*'s success, in these accounts, is attributed to its editors' accurate reading of the American people and "what they want to know" about the world; to its adoption of innovative photographic technologies; and to its ability to secure a reputation for itself as an impartial, accurate, and genteel source of information about the world and its inhabitants (Abramson 1987; Bryan 1987; Buckley 1970; Hellman 1943; Ross 1938).

A more complex reading of the emergence of the National Geographic Society is given by Pauly (1979), who suggests that the organization's structure and mission were conditioned by several significant historical trends converging at the end of the nineteenth century: the emergence of mass journalism, the development of photoengraving technology, the emergence of distinct academic disciplines, and the awakening of Americans' interest in foreign lands that came with the end of the Spanish-American War and the acquisition of new territorial possessions. The convergence of these trends created the space for an organization that could operate effectively on the boundary between science and entertainment and whose subject matter was America's place in the world.

Mass circulation magazines with a national distribution did not exist prior to 1850. The possibilities for their development were enhanced by the completion of intercontinental rail linkages in 1869 and by the Postal Act of 1879, which made cheap distribution possible. But it was not until the 1880s that publishers began to seek profits from advertising rather than from newsstand sales. Adopting a strategy pioneered by women's magazines and "cheap weeklies," the publishers of upscale monthlies such as *Harper's, Century,* and *Atlantic* dropped their prices— dramatically increasing circulation—and began to sell advertising space at rates based on that circulation (Ohmann 1987:139–40). Ohmann relates the tremendous growth of mass circulation magazines in the period 1893–1905 to industry's need to establish a stable clientele in order to enhance demand for its products and to the emergence of advertising as a separate business.

By 1905, according to Ohmann, monthly magazines had become the major form of repeated cultural experience for the United States population. While widespread, their readership was clearly not universal: "It was not the 20 percent who were immigrants or children of immigrants; not the 12 percent who were black; not the poorest Anglo-Saxon farmers and workers; but probably a full half of the white, 'native' stock and something like a third of all the people." (1987:142). While these people shared aspirations of professional standing, most would have been characterized as middle class business owners, clerks, tradespeople, farmers, and so on. And while most of the monthly magazines sold themselves as being of "general interest," each hearkened to a somewhat different segment of this population, characterized by what Ohmann refers to as particular "interests or strategies for living in society" (142). By focusing their appeal in this way, magazines were able to deliver to advertisers a set of consumers who were likely to share aspirations, needs, and consumer habits.

National Geographic's strategy differed markedly from those of other monthlies. It defined itself as a scholarly rather than a profit-oriented enterprise, and initially it obtained a stable income from subscriptions rather than from advertising. Its initiation in 1888 predated the magazine revolution of 1893, when the major monthlies dropped prices precipitously and in return won massive increases in circulation. But its growth, in the early years, was linked to the increasing popularity of monthly magazines and to the expectation that they would be found in middle-class homes. And its readership was similar to that of the other monthlies, appealing largely to families whose current realities were middle-class but whose aspirations tended toward the educated, "cultured" life-style of upper-middle-class professionals.

If the rise of mass circulation magazines provided the vehicle for the *Geographic's* mission, the growing economic and political dominance of the United States provided the issues to be addressed. Many historians have described the late nineteenth century as a period when Americans developed new confidence in their status among nations. In the words of John Higham, "The jingoism of the early and mid-nineties culminated in an exhilarating little war with Spain. The victory, won swiftly and in a holiday spirit, required few strains or sacrifices" (1955:108). Following actions in the Caribbean and the Philippines in 1898, the United States acquired dependencies without encountering significant opposition from other imperialist powers. According to Higham, "the summons to take up the white man's burden, preached by a few before 1898, was accepted in a genial, light-hearted mood. What a dazzling field for American achievement opened now among 'backward' island peoples" (1955:108). The early National Geographic Society touted its research in political and economic geography as a notable contribution to the nation in an era of new global responsibilities. It published articles on the geographic and commercial possibilities of America's new possessions, discussed the benefits of colonialism, and assigned itself a role of arbitrator in determining the proper spellings of parts of the world, hitherto unknown or ignored, and now brought into view by colonialism (Pauly 1979:521).

Encounters with newly colonized peoples, as well as an increasing flow of immigrants, required the Anglo-American imagination to develop some way of accounting for cultural differences. Theories of polygeny and environmental determinism had offered the nineteenth-century public some straightforward ways of explaining difference. But as George Stocking has pointed out, a significant paradox emerged. To the extent that the peoples in question "remained subordinate, exploited, and unfree," they challenged the "myth that 'civilization' was associated with the triumph of liberal principles and the equal freedom of all human individuals" (1987:230). If higher levels of civilization were characterized by equal treatment of all human beings, then colonial domination, racial discrimination, and other forms of oppression became an embarrassment.

According to Stocking, social evolutionary thinking provided the resolution of this paradox for nineteenth-century thinkers. Continuing inequalities could be interpreted as residual effects of uneven biological or cultural development. Those whose status was unequal could be assumed to be lagging behind in the mental or moral development on which equality should be premised, thus requiring the "tutelage" of colonial domination.[1] The "metaphorical extendability" of such assumptions made it possible to apply them to a wide range of situations, encompassing inequalities among nations, races, genders, and classes.

The anthropology of the late nineteenth century dedicated itself to the search for evidence of the evolutionary backwardness of subaltern peoples, inventing a wide range of biological and sociocultural indices for the purpose. From craniometry to the cataloging of marriage principles, the study of difference was directed toward the creation of hierarchy.

---

1. Compare Slotkin (1985:236–38) on attempts to reconcile notions of tutelage and guardianship (of Native Americans and African-American slaves) with democratic ideals in the mid-nineteenth century.

By the first and second decades of the twentieth century, psychologists and biologists were attempting to link evolutionary schemes to abstract, yet unilinear, measures of development, such as IQ (Gould 1981). An emerging understanding of genetic principles, combined with social evolutionary thought, fueled the eugenics movement, efforts to limit immigration, and restrictive racial codes.

The National Geographic Society emerged in the midst of this context and positioned itself as a key actor in presenting "primitive" peoples for western perusal. The Society's brand of evolutionism was not the pessimistic social Darwinism of the nativist and eugenics movements, the kind that worried about a presumed tendency of lower-class and primitive peoples to outmultiply their betters. Rather, they advanced what Stocking has called a more classical social evolutionism, an optimistic brand of the doctrine that focused on the "evolutionary guarantee" of progress through the increasing triumph of rationality over instinct even as it continued to justify residual inequalities of sex, class, and race (Stocking 1987:233). *National Geographic* reinforced America's vision of its newly ascendant place in the world by showing "how far we've come." While its photographs detailed, and occasionally lingered on, one or another aspect of native life, its underlying story was always the evolutionary chronicle, with its contrastive work, its encoding of hierarchy and power relations, and its projection of an inevitable outcome.

An Amateur's View of the World

If social evolutionary thought and imperialist adventures formed a precondition for *National Geographic*'s emergence and success, a changing view of science formed another part of the context. By the late nineteenth century, the full impact of positivism as an intellectual development had been felt in the United States. The new scientists held the world—both natural and social—to be orderly and knowable. They rejected the search for ultimate causes as a remnant of religion and metaphysics, embracing instead attempts to discern regularities and "laws" in the world around them. The new science was becoming a profession, supported and housed by universities, government, and industry. "Amateur" became a pejorative term, and the gentleman scholar conversant with a wide range of fields was seen as a quaint remnant of past eras. Concomitant with a rise in specialist fields of study, there was a decline in such eclectic and broadly defined areas as natural history.

Geography lagged behind in this process of academic specialization. In the 1880s, it was still a genteel social activity. No academic graduate departments existed before 1903, and the American Geographic Society was dominated by elderly amateurs. In Pauly's words, "It seemed likely that in America the more technical geographical research might be divided up among departments of geology, anthropology, economics, and engineering, while geographical societies would turn into ineffectual adventurers' clubs without substantial links to science" (1979:519). The formation of the National Geographic Society reflected the tensions intrinsic to this larger process of professionalizing science, tensions which were played out over some years in interactions between board members and editorial staff.

The National Geographic Society was formed in 1888 by Gardiner Greene Hubbard, a lawyer, a member of a prominent Boston family, and a patron of science. The initial meetings, held at Washington, D.C.'s Cosmos Club, brought together thirty-three distinguished geographers, most of whom held positions in federal bureaus such as the Geological Survey, the Coast and Geodetic Survey, and the Weather Bureau. Many of these men, including John Wesley Powell, William Morris Davis, W. J. McGee, Cleveland Abbe, Grove Karl Gilbert, C. Hart Merriam, Henry Gannett, and A. W. Greely, were prominent in efforts to define an independent subject matter for geography and to professionalize the field. While from its inception the National Geographic Society was designed to have "as broad and liberal" a membership base "as is consistent with its own well-being and the dignity of the science it represents," its original goals were both the diffusion and sponsorship of geographic research (Abramson 1987:33).

The *Geographic's* founders belonged to the traditional elite. Their interest in diffusing knowledge could be seen as of a piece with other educational philanthropy (in the form of museums and public libraries) of that class at that time. But the practical bent of its early leaders, their increasing isolation from the university-based centers of science, and the growth of its circulation into the twentieth century gave the magazine more middlebrow associations. The very notion of the middlebrow was meant to distinguish the cultural products of the nineteenth-century Brahmin elite on the one hand and those of the uneducated masses on the other. This process is detailed for a similar institution by Radway (1988), who sees the emergence of the middlebrow Book-of-the-Month Club in 1926 as related to class fracture between older moneyed families and those immigrant businessmen who were no longer maintaining the

The National Geographic Society board meets with discoverers of the North and South Poles at Society headquarters, January 11, 1913. Also present were the ambassadors of France and Great Britain and the U.S. attorney general. (Photo: Harris and Ewing, © National Geographic Society)

proper boundary between commerce and culture preserved by the older nonimmigrant elite. While the *National Geographic* attempted to hold that boundary through separating advertising from text in its pages and through its tax-exempt status, its popularity over the years has placed it in too many hands for it to escape middlebrow connotations.

Gardiner Greene Hubbard had a history of backing practical science, most notably in the person of Alexander Graham Bell (who married Hubbard's daughter in 1877). Though membership increased under his leadership from just over two hundred in 1888 to nearly fourteen hundred ten years later—the core of an evolving national professional geographic society—the organization was not yet a financial success story (Pauly 1979). It was approximately $2,000 in debt at the time of Hubbard's death in 1897. yikes!

Change in the nature of the society began to occur when Bell took over in 1898. A renowned and successful inventor, he had been trained as a teacher of speech, and he saw his scientific work as a gentlemanly avocation. The wealth generated by his invention of the telephone ensured that he could pursue his scientific interests independently. Bell seemed much more attuned to the Society's mission to disperse geographic knowledge rather than to promote new research, and he believed that people would read geography only if it were light and entertaining. It was Bell who hired Gilbert Hovey Grosvenor (who later became *his* son-in-law) to help build circulation in 1899. He encouraged Grosvenor to study popular magazines of the time, particularly *Harper's* and *Century*, in order to glean ideas for the *National Geographic*. He also directed him to study "popular geographers" from Herodotus to Darwin, noting that the success of such works was due to the fact that they were "accurate, eyewitness accounts; simple and straightforward" (Abramson 1987:48).

Grosvenor's first innovations were in promotion and marketing. Membership in the Society had always been by nomination. Grosvenor began actively developing lists of individuals who could be nominated, drawing names from friends and from membership lists of other organizations. He also began rejecting articles provided by the editorial committee when he found them to be too technical or difficult. Board members who resented the new popular thrust of the magazine sought to divest Grosvenor of his position during his honeymoon in Europe in 1900, but were unsuccessful because Bell kept control of the money. By 1902, Grosvenor had not only regained his former authority but was appointed editor.

As a result of Grosvenor's innovations, the *Geographic* style became more similar to that of other popular monthlies, marked by "a realism full of pep and information," and a mode of direct address to the reader that was "colloquial, forceful, direct, and seemingly personal" (Wilson 1983:55). *National Geographic* also shared with other turn-of-the-century magazines a sense of "endless possibilities": phrased in a consumer rhetoric in the women's magazines, the *Geographic's* version focused on a wider world of possibilities. Unlike most other magazines of the period, however, it was not centered in New York or Boston, did not yet have a professional journalistic staff, and was not run by the immigrant WASPs who dominated the other magazines.

Increasing freedom of the organization from its semiprofessional roots gave it the ability to create its peculiar and powerful position as an arbiter of national culture. Two elements were crucial in carving out this niche. The first was the recapturing and revitalization of the declining field of natural history. Defunct as an intellectual arena by the late nineteenth century, it obtained a new lease on life through the institutions of mass culture. In Bell's hands and Grosvenor's, the magazine became such an institution. Grosvenor "was extending the life of the old rubric of natural history at a time when it was rapidly being parceled up among the various specialities. . . . The *Geographic* was the direct and lively descendant of the cabinet of curiosities, a close cousin of the natural history diorama" (Pauly 1979:527).

The National Geographic Society was founded within two decades after the inauguration of the American Museum of Natural History and in a period of expansion of the Smithsonian Institution. In these contexts, photographic or material traces of the colonized world were relocated to new spaces in the industrialized West. Once appropriated and transferred, they provided the materials out of which new stories about the world could be created. As Clifford has demonstrated, collecting and displaying are crucial processes in forming Western identity, and cultural description itself is a kind of collecting that selectively accords "authenticity" to human groups and their institutions and practices (Clifford 1988). *National Geographic,* like the great natural history museums, took images of Africa, Asia, and Latin America from their historical contexts and arranged them in ways that addressed contemporary Western preoccupations. Haraway (1989) demonstrates how the African Hall of the Museum of Natural History encodes Western preoccupations with manhood, virile defense of democracy, and connection (or loss of connection) with nature. In choosing systems of classification or explanation, both magazine editors and museum directors provided an illusion of adequate representation and an opportunity to construct stories about otherness.

Regardless of what stories were told, the very acts of collecting and presenting were significant. They created illusions of possession, of a stable and complete "humanity," and of the possibility of ordering the exotic and the foreign (Baudrillard 1968). As Susan Stewart (1984) has forcefully argued, in collections "desire is ordered, arranged, and manipulated, not fathomless" (163). "Like Noah's Ark, those great civic collections, the library and the museum, seek to represent experience within a mode of control and confinement. One cannot know everything about the world, but one can at least approach closed knowledge through the collection" (161). The knowledge thus produced is necessarily ahistoric. The context of the collection "destroys the context of origin," and the order imposed by the collector obscures the histories of production and acquisition of the artifacts or photographs themselves (1984:165). *Na-*

tional Geographic, like other collections, has been a kind of souvenir: it collects the world between its covers, it is collected by subscribers, and it relies heavily on the photograph, a technology that necessarily miniaturizes the real world.

On the Boundary between Science and Pleasure

The second element of the niche *National Geographic* carved out for itself also went against the grain of the new nineteenth-century positivist science. This was the attempt to combine scholarship and entertainment. The *Geographic* sought, on the one hand, to be a potent force in exploration and scientific research that was independent of national scientific organizations and their ideologies of specialized research, and on the other to win the attention of large masses of people.

What was to be gained by successfully achieving such a combination? First, it placed the *Geographic* in the powerful position of being both a broker and a maker of scientific knowledge. In the prevailing atmosphere of scientific specialization and the consequent denigration of amateurs and lay practitioners, *National Geographic* could fill the void between academic practitioners and the public by purveying science, while also claiming to foster and practice science in its own right. From the institution's second decade, the funding and conduct of research was always marginal to the institution's main role of popularizing and glamorizing geographic and anthropological knowledge, yet it was sufficient to establish and retain its reputation as a *scientific* and educational organization. This made it possible for the *Geographic* to speak with the voice of scientific authority, while remaining outside of and unconstrained by the scientific community.

Second, there was a tremendous flexibility to be had by manipulating the boundaries between science and entertainment. Editors concerned with market imperatives could justify photographs that glorified the exotic and ritualistic aspects of primitive societies or that sensationalized head-hunting, cannibalism, mutilation, or tattoo, on the grounds that they were picturesque or otherwise piqued interest. Presented in a magazine that claimed to present "true facts" in a judicious manner, these images were given a scholarly veneer, and readers were given reinforcement for old prejudices. Editors tended to choose photographs that were likely to appeal to an American audience; these were then fed back to the reading public as examples of the latest, brightest scientific knowledge. In the process, the reading public's original vision of what was interesting or aesthetically pleasing about the world outside United States borders was validated, elaborated, and heightened by its presentation as scientific fact.

When a new vision of the non-Western world was called for, *National Geographic* did not have to adhere to scientific method in constructing it. Not constrained by scholarly opinion, it could choose images with impunity. Editors could choose a grisly photograph of a headless Ifugao warrior based on its "scientific merit"; they could justify the absence of photographs showing poverty or hunger on grounds of presenting a "positive image"; and they could appeal to aesthetics for their use of multiple photographs of attractive young women and lush landscapes. As Pauly has wryly observed: "The principle of absolute accuracy dictated printing photos of bare-breasted native maidens . . . but the demand of artistry and the uncontroversial meant that these native subjects were young, well-proportioned and often draped like classical nudes" (Pauly 1979:528). Editors were attentive to both the market and the scientific community but slaves to neither. They were free to construct their own particular vision of the non-Western world.

This boundary shifting was not unique to the *Geographic*. Much the same phenomenon has been noted in the international fairs and expositions held in the United States from 1876 to 1916. While the main exposition areas retained a staunchly scientific or technological mode of presentation, the midways became areas where entertainment and educational functions were brought into close proximity. The midway was the major arena for the display and exposition of non-Western cultures—a place where Americans could "study ethnography." This presentation equated the non-Western world in tangible ways with peep shows and freak shows, playing on images of the harem, the overblown sexuality of the East, and the general projection of the forbidden desires of whites onto dark-skinned peoples. It also permitted the exposition directors "to have their ethnological cake and eat it too," by affirming or denying the scientific accuracy of the exhibitions to suit their needs (Rydell 1984:138).

The midways were invariably constructed as evolutionary ladders, where tourists could move from the savagery of Dahomeyan culture to the more civilized Javanese, to the Chinese and Japanese (Rydell 1984:66). They played on notions of the nonwhite world as barbaric and childlike, encouraging comparison with the scientific progress displayed in the main part of the exposition. Because displays involved the participation of members of the culture in question, their status as representations was overwhelmed by the concreteness and concurrence of real human bodies. The significant feature for this discussion, however, was the way that the interpenetration of science and entertainment functions fomented the construction of evolutionary and racist understandings of the United States and its relation to the rest of the world. Most displays were organized by distinguished anthropologists, including Franz Boas, Alice Fletcher, Ales Hrdlicka, Otis T. Mason, and John Wesley Powell. Their work did not necessarily play to themes of cultural evolution and racial superiority, and they may, in other contexts, have adamantly opposed these themes. Nevertheless, the placement of the exhibits, their juxtaposition with nonscientific exhibits that debased nonwhite peoples, and their sensationalization in brochures and promotional materials permitted exposition directors to construct a vision of the relation between the United States and the rest of the world that played to and reinforced popular notions of racial superiority (Rydell 1984).

The juxtaposition of "the West" and "the rest" was also clearly at work in the pages of *National Geographic* magazine. The non-Western world was never the only topic covered in an issue. Stories about wildlife and about life in the United States have always been featured prominently, as were more technical pieces on climate and geomorphology in the early years. Putting articles on the United States side by side with articles on the non-Western world often helped depict progress and cultural evolution. As Joseph Hawley, who presided over the United States Centennial Commission, claimed in 1879: "Comparison is vital to the success of any exposition. . . . You can never discover your success or failure without comparison with other nations. . . . Comparison is essential to show the effects on the industries and arts of climate, race, geography" (Rydell 1984:32). The juxtaposition of articles on New Guinea rituals with articles on orderly farms in New England or shiny new factories in the South underscored evolutionary themes in the articles and photographs themselves.

The progressive, rather than social Darwinist, nature of the *Geographic*'s evolutionism was reflected in Grosvenor's unwillingness to publish overtly hostile or racist material. This policy was made explicit in his "seven principles," announced to the Board of Trustees and published in the magazine in March 1915:

1) The first principle is absolute accuracy. Nothing must be printed which is not strictly according to fact. . . .
2) Abundance of beautiful, instructive, and artistic illustrations.

3) Everything printed in the Magazine must have permanent value. . . .
4) All personalities and notes of a trivial character are avoided. . . .
5) Nothing of a partisan or controversial character is printed.
6) Only what is of a kindly nature is printed about any country or people, everything unpleasant or unduly critical being avoided.
7) The contents of each number is planned with a view of being timely. (Bryan 1987:90)

[handwritten marginal note: Portraying the world with rose colored glasses? — fair?]

Avoiding overtly critical material contributed to an impression of good sportsmanship in the evolutionary struggle. If formerly colonized peoples hadn't quite made it to the levels of civilization of the industrialized nations, they were not condemned; the rhetoric was one of slightly older school chums rooting for them while they gave it their best shot.

The Photograph as Evidence

In *National Geographic's* continuing efforts to locate itself on the boundary between science and entertainment, photographs became an increasingly significant tool. When the first photographs were published in 1896, board policy of the era demanded that they be subordinate to, and illustrative of, the text. Early reproductions were by steel engraving, and though of high quality, were expensive and slow to produce. When photoengraving reduced the cost significantly, Grosvenor was quick to see the potential of this new technology in contributing to his goal of popularizing the magazine. In 1905, without the approval of the board, he published eleven full pages of photographs of Lhasa, Tibet, sent to the magazine by two Russian explorers (Abramson 1987:61–62). While a number of board members were shocked and angry, public response was overwhelmingly favorable. Society membership, which stood at 3,400 at the time the photographs of the "forbidden city" were published, soared to 11,000 by the end of the year. Grosvenor's move and this response served to establish photographs as the mainstay and distinguishing feature of the magazine.

Like the text, pictures were constrained by Grosvenor's principles of fairness, veracity, and positive outlook: they were to be beautiful (aesthetically pleasing), artistic (embodying certain conventions of highbrow forms of art), and instructive (realistic in representation). The magazine relied on sharply focused, easily readable photographs to bolster its claim that it was presenting an unbiased, unmediated view of the world, a claim that went hand in hand with the assertion that all written material was accurate, balanced, and fair. What writers accomplished by an insistently upbeat and uncomplicated style, the erasure of conflicting points of view, and the presentation of names, dates, and numbers, often gratuitous, was reinforced by the codes of photographic realism. Photographs lent to the articles they illustrated what Barthes (1977:21) has called the prestige of the denotation. They created the illusion that the objects presented actually occurred in nature in the ways they were photographed: "Nature [rather than the photographer] seems spontaneously to produce the scene represented" (Barthes 1977:45).

The acceptance of photographs as a form of evidence is the outcome of a historical process that was completed only in the second half of the nineteenth century and that was bound up with new uses for the photograph in the state's practices of social control (Tagg 1988:98). "Photographs were not viewed as metaphors of experience, but rather as sections of reality itself. If photographs showed gigantic trees and awe-inspiring mountains, then all the trees were gigantic and all the mountains awe-inspiring. When photographs depicted Indians as 'savages,' Indians were confirmed as savages" (Lyman 1982:29). The *Geographic* capitalized on this notion of the photograph as evidence and established itself as a source of accurate and timely information on the colonial world.

National Geographic's adoption of realist codes must be understood in relation to photographic trends. In the early part of this century, American photography was dominated by the pictorialist school, which used techniques such as soft focus to create photographs reminiscent of painting. The *Geographic* did not adopt such a style but relied on technically adequate, though naive, prints from travelers. The goal of the editorial staff was to print photographs that were "straightforward." As an editor put it in 1915, *National Geographic* had discovered a "new universal language which requires no deep study . . . one that is understood as well by the jungaleer as by the courtier; by the Eskimo as by the wild man from Borneo; by the child in the playroom as by the professor in the college; and by the woman of the household as by the hurried business man—in short, the Language of the Photograph" (Bryan 1987:133). The implication was that the photograph was a direct transcription of a reality that was timeless, classless, and outside the boundaries of language and culture. The photographer's intent, the photographic product, and the reader's experience were assumed to be one. For this reason, photographs, unlike other cultural texts, were held to be readable by even the simplest among us.

The *Geographic*'s adoption of "straight photography" rather than pictorialist codes was shared with a tradition of documentary photography that was emerging during this period. Nevertheless, its photographs did not greatly interest most documentary photographers, who by the 1920s and 1930s were influenced by surrealism and cubism, and who were actively playing with the codes of realist representation to surprising ends. Documentary photographers attempted to capture "decisive" moments, in which elements came together in ways that were moving and significant and that went beyond the literal transcription of a scene. *National Geographic* photographers, in contrast, were asked to make literal transcription their goal. Until well into the 1970s, picture editors shunned photographic techniques that drew attention to themselves or revealed too clearly a photographer's "point of view." They favored those that permitted the labors and point of view of the photographer and editor to recede into the background, thus encouraging the reader to see his or her contact with the photographed subject as unmediated, if necessarily indirect.

For an artist whose imagination was captured by the possibilities of new realist modes, this was refreshing. The photographer Paul Strand remarked in 1923 that "compared to this so-called pictorial photography, which is nothing more than an evasion of everything truly photographic . . . a simple record in the *National Geographic* magazine . . . or an aerial photographic record is an unmixed relief" (Strand in Lemagny and Rouille 1987:108). Strand was making a point about pictorialism and only tangentially about *Geographic* photographic style, yet his willingness to concede to its photographs the status of a "simple record" is telling. In a sense, he was accepting the editor's judgment that the photos possess self-evident meanings: they can be read by anyone "without deep study."

Recent work on the realist tradition emphasizes not only its distinct stylistic features, but also how absolutely it turns on an image's consistency with, and reinforcement of, cultural expectations. When we speak of photographic realism, "we must historicize the spectator"—that is, we must consider to whom and under what conditions photographic images will appear "realistic" (Tagg 1988:156). Or as Pierre Bourdieu has pointed out, "If the photograph is considered to be a perfect inscription of the visible world, it is above all because the selections that it makes completely conform to [the world's] logic" (1965:109). If the sharp focus and conventional framing of *Geographic* photographs marked them as "records," it was their replication of popular understandings of the third world that made them seem neutral in their presentations and gave them the comforting feel of "commonsense" realities captured on film. In this way, the mass media's images "become mirrors, serving to reflect Americans' feelings, rather than windows to the complex, dynamic realities of foreign societies" (Guimond 1988:68). Images of peasants and tribal peoples confronted with and desiring Western technologies and consumer goods confirmed choices Westerners had made (or felt they had made). Photographs of familylike groups created a sense of order and logic that validated Western family arrangements and familial emotions, regardless of how the people photographed had come together or what their social relationships, in real life, might be.

The National Geographic Society brought this realist style to bear not only on the new territories and interests of the United States but also on unfolding world events. When World War I broke out in July 1914, the society included a map of the "New Balkan States and Central Europe" in its August issue. Every subsequent issue provided war coverage and updates—plenty of facts, figures, and diagrams, consistently upbeat, sympathetic to the Allies, but withholding any openly supportive statements until the United States entered the war in 1917. Partly as a result of this coverage, the *Geographic* was one of only a few magazines that saw its readership increase during World War I, growing from 285,000 in 1914 to 650,000 in 1918. In addition to its reporting, the Society visibly involved itself in the war effort by printing draft notices for the government, organizing a Liberty Loan drive, and collecting socks and sweaters for service personnel (Bryan 1987:128–33; Abramson 1987: 118–19).

Although *National Geographic* took the war in stride, much of the rest of the world did not. Its impact on modern consciousness has been explored by Paul Fussell, who argues that the ironic stance which dominates much of modern literature originated in the "application of mind and memory to the events of the Great War," for the war essentially reversed the idea of progress. Writers like Henry James struggled to understand how a supposed long age of "gradual betterment" could culminate instead in an "abyss of blood and darkness" (1975:35). Modern ethnography, too, took its shape in a world that had been shattered by World War I and that was haunted by nihilism in its aftermath (Clifford 1988:64). Functionalism and other representations of cultures as ordered wholes were the product of a generation of social scientists who were "acutely aware of the possibility of disorder." In Clifford's words,

> With the breakdown of evolutionist master narratives, the relativist science of culture worked to rethink the world as a dispersed whole, composed of distinct, functioning, and interrelated cultures. It reconstituted social and moral wholeness plurally. If synecdochic ethnography argued, in effect, that "cultures" hold together, it did so in response to a pervasive modern feeling, linking the Irishman Yeats to the Nigerian Achebe, that "things fall apart" (1988:64).

The "pervasive modern feeling" did not upset the *National Geographic's* institutional mission to present order in the face of rapid change and perplexing events. The order-seeking impulses of scientific theory confirmed and enriched a *National Geographic* view of the world between the wars and provided a rationale for a vision of third-world locations as safe, cohesive, and well-integrated. *Not true? False Info.?*

The Photograph as Spectacle

The most significant events at *National Geographic* during the 1930s turned on the adoption of color photography. Hand-tinted plates had been introduced to the magazine in 1910; the first autochrome was published in 1916, and tinted photographs were used throughout the 1920s (Abramson 1987:133–39). The first natural color photographs to be published in the *Geographic* were taken at the North Pole in 1926. Through the late 1920s and early 1930s society photographers experimented with several other processes, including Finlay, Agfacolor, and Dufay. Kodak's fast, portable color film in rolls became available in 1936, and while it took more than two years to catch on at *National Geographic,* quickly became the film technology of choice (Bryan 1987:205–13; Vesilind 1977).

Color photography inevitably changes the nature of representation. Color tends to dominate the photograph, often at the expense of line and movement. It affects the mood of the image in ways that may either reinforce or contradict the shape and placement of objects. Because of its high impact, color frequently becomes a consideration in choosing what subject to photograph or selecting among subjects already photographed: "Even though Kodachrome was already unnaturally bright, photographers . . . splashed the strongest possible colors in their pictures so that they would be more effective in print. One result was that the staff photographers—who were constantly being sent to colorful places to slake what was seen as the public's unquenching thirst for colorful scenes—would often find themselves needing more color to take advantage of the color film and would resort to placing the people in costume" (Bryan 1987:294–95). Not surprisingly, this was referred to as the red shirt school of photography.

Color photography began to differentiate the *Geographic* from a growing tradition of photojournalism that continued to rely on black-and-white photographs well into the 1950s. It became possible to render the exotic and picturesque in even more dramatic ways, leading editors to emphasize these traits rather than historical significance and timeliness. Pictures in *National Geographic* were increasingly seen as akin to picture postcards or snapshots taken by tourists and, Guimond says, were valued accordingly:

> Because tourism is so popular and because it is considered a particularly "reliable" way to understand realities, it is not surprising that these magazines' [*Time, Life,* and *National Geographic*] articles and photo-essays are often, in effect, tourist trips with the editors, reporters and photographers acting as tour guides. . . . Similarly, many magazines, particularly the *Geographic,* heavily emphasize the exotic aspects of foreign cultures, even as they also often give their readers . . . simulated, "candid" contacts with their subjects—little conversations with (and pictures of) camel drivers, village schoolteachers, and picturesque peasants—which may occur during tourist trips" (1988:40–41).

The use of color photography also highlighted the magazine's similarity to museum exhibits—with their highly framed, aestheticized tidbits of traditional culture—rather than to starker news reportage or scientific documentation. Like museum exhibits (as well as catalogs and department stores) the *Geographic* laid out the wonders of the world for curious readers (Harris 1978). It selected the most compelling, grouped them in meaningful ways, and explained their qualities and fine points in its captions. Color photographs served to highlight this sense of opulence and the *availability* of what was displayed. As John Berger has observed, color photography makes viewers feel that they can almost touch what is in the image, reminding them that they might, in fact, possess it (1972:141). Though it made all the more uneasy the place of "science" in its mission, the *National Geographic*'s increasing appeal to the popular tastes of its readers was more than compensated for by the attention that its color photographs drew and by the leadership the Society was able to establish in the use of color images.

A Private "National Institution"

The Society fared well in the depression, topping one million members in 1935 and employing over seven hundred workers by the next year. These burgeoning figures must be partly accounted for by the fact that, in keeping with official policy, the human suffering of the decade did not find a place in the pages of the magazine. Articles produced in the late 1930s, most notably those by Douglas Chandler, were openly sympathetic to national socialist agendas. He was dropped as a contributor after it was discovered that he was funded by the Nazi party. John Patric's coverage of Mussolini's Italy, also from the late 1930s, shows the sinister side of a commitment to present "only what is of a kindly nature." Even the Society's quasi-official history represents the early coverage of World War II as a somewhat curious overextension of tact and nonpartisanship: "John Patric's March 1937 'Imperial Rome Reborn' celebrated Italy's new glories, but the photographs were chilling: one of gasmasked uniformed children was captioned 'Weird visitors from another world? No; schoolboys preparing for war.' Another, of children, read, 'Chins high, shoulders squared, boy Black Shirts emulate Il Duce's posture'" (Bryan 1987:219).

With the advent of World War II, the Society had a tradition to uphold—reporting on the war for Americans at home. Its coverage was marked by the same patriotic fervor as in World War I. Once again it published detailed maps, placed one major war-related article in every issue, and established a semiofficial status for its activities through its participation in the war effort. It furnished maps (and elegant map cases) to the President of the United States as well as to the Navy Hydrographic Office, the United States Army Map Service, and the Coast and Geodetic Survey, which in turn prepared maps for the Air Force. Its 1944 map of Japan was used for planning air offensives against Japan (Abramson 1987:176–77). Its spellings of geographic locations were adopted by major wire services in the 1940s.

Just as the Society took advantage of its ambiguous status somewhere between science and entertainment, it took advantage of its connections to government. It traded on its close ties to government officials, and

Gilbert H. Grosvenor, president and editor (second from left), with colleagues, presents President Dwight D. Eisenhower with new *Geographic* maps at the White House in 1953. (Photo: Willard Culver, © National Geographic Society)

the official uses to which its products were put, to create an image of itself as a "national institution"; at the same time, it retained its status as a private, tax-exempt organization that was relatively unconstrained by government.

Editor Grosvenor had always cultivated close personal relationships with a number of individuals in government. William Howard Taft was his second cousin, and he developed a warm working relationship with Theodore Roosevelt over the years. In the 1930s, the Society established a tradition of calling on the president of the United States to present Gardiner Greene Hubbard medals for geographic distinction. By the 1980s, six presidents had contributed articles to the magazine: Theodore Roosevelt, William Howard Taft, Calvin Coolidge, Herbert Hoover, Dwight Eisenhower, and Lyndon Johnson. Members of the Board of Trustees have included former first ladies, chief justices, the chair of the Board of Governors of the Federal Reserve System, the chief of staff of the United States Air Force, an assistant secretary of the Navy, a rear admiral in the Coast and Geodetic Survey, the deputy administrator of NASA, and officials of the National Park Service. Given its nonprofit status, the Society was able to enlist the aid of government officials who could not have supported private commercial enterprises (Abramson

1987:7) and to cultivate connections to industry and finance. Bank presidents and industrialists have regularly had a place on its Board of Trustees.

"Good Eggs" in the Cold War

After World War II and into the 1950s, the Society operated in a national context dominated by the expansion and consolidation of power. Emerging with its economy relatively unscathed, the United States was in a position to finance the reconstruction of a war-devastated Europe.[2] At the same time, it began to usurp the position of European nations in relation to their former colonies, establishing important trade relationships with the new nations of Africa, Latin America, and Asia. International agreements at Bretton Woods and Dumbarton Oaks established the U.S. dollar as the world's currency standard and restructured relationships of lending and patronage in ways that enhanced the nation's power. In the early 1950s, Congress was rechanneling foreign assistance to these newly independent economies. Beginning with the Food for Peace Bill in 1954, concessionary grain sales were used to create food dependency in the third world, increasing the political clout of the United States and securing supplies of strategic metals and other resources needed for industrial expansion. As of 1952, the United States Air Force had 131 bases overseas, and the United States Navy, several dozen; American companies sold arms to countries receiving military aid from the United States; Gulf, Mobil, Texaco, and Exxon were operating in the Middle East; and multinationals were establishing their economic hegemony (Guimond 1988:61).

Still, the United States public tenaciously held to a view of its presence in the newly independent nations as benevolent. The popular press continued to stress kindness and generosity as basic American traits. GIs in Korea were photographed giving chewing gum to children. American leaders traveled abroad with candy bars and soft drinks in their hands to distribute during photo opportunities (Guimond 1988:61–62). And the *Geographic* upheld this image with articles such as "The GI and the Kids of Korea: America's Fighting Men Share Their Food, Clothing and Shelter with Children of a War-torn Land" (1953); photos captioned

2. See Lipsitz (1981:3) for a discussion of the distribution of benefits from wartime industrial expansion and the resulting concentration of capital in U.S. industry.

"Uncle Sam is a good egg: British school children agree" (1943); and articles (slightly more to the point) such as "Cuba—American Sugar Bowl" (1947). United States air bases were touted in captions such as the following from 1950:

> Lunch on his arm, a new rug over his shoulder, this smiling Okinawan symbolizes the new hope that has come to the "doorstep to Japan."
>
> Battles and typhoons have ravaged little Okinawa during the past five years, but today there is cause for cheer among the island's people . . . long-neglected Okinawa is undergoing a face lifting. After the transformation it will be a semi-permanent, well-equipped United States air base similar to Clark Field in the Philippines.

Despite the fact that the cold war period saw the construction of bomb shelters, the stockpiling of nuclear weapons, and the McCarthy hearings, for most of the American public it remained a time of defiant innocence—of optimism, power, and a sense of invulnerability. The *Geographic* contributed to softening the entrance to the nuclear age with articles such as "Nevada Learns to Live with the Atom" and "Man's New Servant, the Friendly Atom." In the meantime, the non-socialist third world continued to be portrayed as simple, childlike, and friendly—in the words of one caption, as "Paradise in search of a future."

Publishing at *National Geographic* was characterized by some strange lacunae in coverage during the cold war. Favorable portrayals of eastern bloc nations would have been unpatriotic; yet to dwell on their evils would violate editorial policy. For this reason, there was no coverage whatsoever of the Soviet Union from 1945 to 1959 (when Vice-President Richard Nixon described his trips to the Soviet Union for *Geographic* readers, including his "kitchen confrontation" with Nikita Khrushchev). China's people, a popular subject before the war and before Communism, were covered rarely between 1950 and 1976, but returned to the pages of the *Geographic* with President Nixon's visit in 1975.[3]

Strong growth in circulation occurred during the 1950s and especially

---

3. To some extent, coverage of eastern bloc nations (particularly China) was influenced by travel restrictions on western journalists (although *National Geographic* has frequently been able to circumvent such restrictions by using European photographers when the U.S. State Department was the restricting party, and by obtaining waivers and special permissions).

the 1960s. There were about 2 million subscribers in 1957, 5.6 million in 1967, and 7.2 million in 1971 (see figure 2.1). While some of this increase in circulation should be seen as a result of the innovations Melville Bell Grosvenor introduced, one can also point to related cultural changes. The 1950s saw the burgeoning of the "white-collar" segment of the work force. Some of these jobs entailed significant managerial responsibilities and led to the formation of a new stratum of workers who acted in many ways as intermediaries "between labor and capital" (Walker 1979). In addition, however, vast numbers of jobs were created in health-related services, sales, teaching and counseling, financial services, and technical and administrative support services. These jobs had many of the attributes of traditional white-collar employment—they involved desk work, required literacy, and often entailed some managerial functions. They did not, however, entail the same levels of power

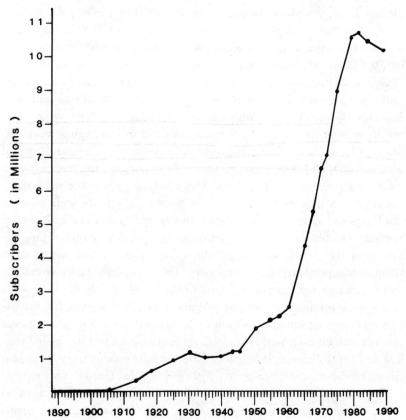

Figure 2.1. Circulation growth, *National Geographic* magazine, 1888–1990

or pay as the more professional white-collar positions. For both the "professional managerial class" (Ehrenreich and Ehrenreich 1979) and less privileged ranks of the service sector, upward mobility was linked to the possession of what Bourdieu (1984) calls educational and cultural capital. Parents of the postwar "baby-boom" generation who desired advancement for their children struggled to provide them with good books, enriching travel experiences, and a college education. Educational levels rose from the 1950s through the 1970s; sales of books to the American public doubled between 1952 and 1961 (Kaledin 1984). National Geographic Society membership was not marketed *only* to members of these classes, but they were responsible for a significant portion of its growth during this period.

In the 1950s and 1960s, as at the turn of the century, the *Geographic* appealed to a middle-class audience with "mid-to-high-brow" aspirations. Membership profiles have consistently revealed a population slightly better educated, wealthier, and older than the population as a whole. *National Geographic* was a recognizable emblem of conservative middle-class taste and of aspirations for education and a measure of sophistication. While the view of American culture it promulgated was raceless and classless, egalitarian and generous, the naiveté of such a view could be ignored only by those on the privileged side of race and class divisions. Generally speaking, *National Geographic* helped white, upwardly mobile Americans to locate themselves in a changing world, to come to terms with their whiteness and relative privilege, and to deal with anxieties about their class position, both national and international.

Other aspects of the 1950s and 1960s helped to fuel the magazine's popularity. A new emphasis on mathematics and science went hand in hand with the national hysteria when in 1957 the Soviet Union launched Sputnik. That event had more impact on the American popular imagination than the decolonization of the third world, which began with Ghana's independence that same year. The immediate postwar era has also been tagged the era of the expert (May 1988), a role the *Geographic* was well positioned to continue playing. Growth in *Geographic* circulation also came simultaneously with phenomenal growth in international tourism, which increased from 71.2 million arrivals in 1960 to 183 million in 1970 (Robinson 1976), and with the mass exodus from American cities and the concomitant breakup of the extended family. This nuclear suburban family, which was also increasingly a unit defined as a member of the nation rather than of any ethnicity, looked to national mass media products to replace the pleasures of the extended family and to find models of that de-ethnicized identity (Budd, Entman, and Clay 1990). The *Geographic* audience came to the magazine through this period increasingly comfortable with mass culture and with seeing itself as synonymous with the larger national whole—some large fraction of which either could not afford or did not care about this particular view of the world.

Erasing the Colonizer

As the United States reached the apex of its postwar power, voices from formerly colonized peoples were reaching the West in louder and more articulate forms. Independence movements and anticolonial struggles in India and Africa challenged both the philosophical basis and the on-the-ground reality of Western power. The negritude movement in Africa and the Caribbean, denying the right of the West to define third-world cultural identity, offered powerful new self-definitions. The United States was attempting to forge and solidify new economic relationships to nations of the South at a time when colonial power relations were being overturned and when evolutionist theory and its corollary—"the white man's burden"—were being contested.

The anticolonial struggles that reverberated through the social sciences, generating new forms of self-examination and challenges to extant theories, only intensified the search for order at *National Geographic*. Images of safety and stability in the third world were not abandoned. On the contrary, images of Westerners were politely removed from colonial and neocolonial contexts, thereby avoiding uncomfortable questions about the nature of their presence, obscuring the contexts and difficulties of the photographic encounter, and creating a vision of the cultures in question as hermetically sealed worlds—captured only in the sense of captured on film.[4] Again, the analogy to collections is instructive: "The point of the collection is forgetting—starting again in such a way that a finite number of elements create, by virtue of their combination, an infinite reverie. Whose labor made [the collection] is not the question: the question is what is inside" (Stewart 1984:152). In the hey-

---

4. An "On Assignment" page, marking the circumscribed reintroduction of the western observer, was added to the magazine in the mid-1980s; it featured the photographer and writer at work, often showing them alone at their work, encountering technical problems, or simply posing. For more details on how these data were generated, and their interpretation, see chapters 4 and 7.

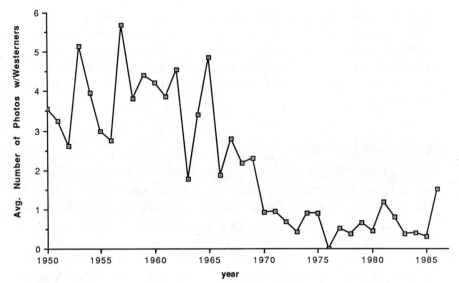

Figure 2.2. Average number per article of photographs with Westerners in non-Western settings, 1950–86

day of colonial culture, the inclusion of Westerners in the photographs of the colonized served to establish a sort of authenticity—to demonstrate that the photographer was "really there." By the late 1960s, however, the colonial and postcolonial relationships that permitted *National Geographic* to photograph the world had become a site of struggle, and reference to them was studiously avoided.

It was also becoming evident that home was not exempt from the anticolonial, antiracist struggles that had been emerging in the third world. The contradictions beneath the peaceful, postwar veneer of the 1950s were revealed by the emergence of struggles for civil rights. With the increasing radicalization of the movement after 1964, race and cultural difference erupted into mass culture and the media in ways that they had not since the last century and with an intensity that far surpassed the struggles over immigration and ethnicity in the late-nineteenth and early-twentieth centuries. *National Geographic* did not report on these issues. The struggles of the period are nonetheless part of the background for its 1950s coverage and the assiduous way the magazine averted its eyes from anything that suggested interracial or intercultural conflict.

Important changes in the leadership of the National Geographic Society occurred during the 1950s but did not portend changes in style. Gilbert Hovey Grosvenor retired as editor-in-chief in 1954, but continued as chair of the board. John Oliver LaGorce, who had worked beside Grosvenor since 1905, was appointed president of the society and editor of the magazine. In 1957, after a preparatory period as associate editor, Gilbert's son Melville Bell Grosvenor took over LaGorce's roles as president and editor. A businessman at heart, Melville Grosvenor kept a close eye on membership figures and readership surveys. He introduced photographs on the cover of the magazine to great acclaim and initiated the society's subsidiary product line with the first atlases and globes. He also greatly increased field budgets, giving editors more shots to select from and consequently more leeway in constructing a particular *Geographic* vision of the world.

Perhaps more important than changes at the top, which were carefully conducted to insure continuity, was the proliferation of staff at other levels during this period. Prior to World War II there had been only two staff writer-photographers. The *Geographic* still relied on diplomats, businessmen, and vacationing educators for many of its stories and photographs. By 1967, fifty full-time writers and fifteen full-time photographers had been employed, providing an opportunity for the staff to shape stories much more directly and to play a more significant role in producing images purveyed by the magazine.

Avoiding Controversy in a World Full of Conflict

Melville Bell Grosvenor stepped down from his positions in 1967; Melvin M. Payne took over the presidency of the National Geographic Society; the editorship went to Frederick Vosburg for three years and then to Grosvenor's son, Gilbert. Memberships had more than doubled during Melville Grosvenor's tenure, but perhaps his greatest contibution had been the hiring of a group of individuals known within the organization as Young Turks—highly acclaimed photojournalists from major Midwestern newspapers, who deviated strongly from the rather effete gentlemanly ethos of previous decades. Key among them was Wilbur Garrett, who was to serve as the editor between 1980 and 1990. This new cohort was interested in modernizing the appearance and content of the *Geographic*. They advocated more use of natural lighting in photographs, more white space in layouts, and all-color issues. They also pushed for coverage of more controversial issues.

As the Vietnam War unfolded, the *Geographic* was caught in a quandary it had not experienced in other wars. Should it honor its tradition of upbeat, fact-filled war reporting? How could it do so in an undeclared, as yet low-key war? Trusting in the past success of its war reportage, it began its coverage in 1961, with a piece by Wilbur Garrett and Peter White entitled "South Viet Nam Fights the Red Tide." In 1962 the society sent photographer Dickey Chappelle to work on an article titled "Helicopter War in South Viet Nam," which was accompanied by the first published photographs of American service personnel in action to be seen by the American public.[5] The difficulties of Vietnam War reportage presaged growing disagreements among National Geographic board members over the coverage of conflict.

While the 1960s had seen some resistance to modest changes in the style and content of the magazine, resistance became more overt in the 1970s. Four articles published in 1977 drew the attention of both the public and the trustees to the magazine's more issue-oriented and critical stance. The first was a story on Cuba by writer-photographer Fred Ward, which drew an angry response from the right-wing media-monitoring organization Accuracy in Media for its lack of criticism of Cuba's political system and its acceptance of a government official's prognostications of economic growth; it also angered board member Crawford Greenewalt, who was Chairman of E. I. du Pont de Nemours & Co., because one of Du Pont's chemical plants had been seized in Cuba (Bryan 1987:389). The second was an article entitled "To Live in Harlem." This story was less controversial for its focus than for its presentation to advertisers as an example of the "new" National Geographic magazine. A call to potential advertisers in the New York Times read: "The geography of Harlem: Poverty, dope, crime and people who wouldn't leave for a million dollars. . . . Isn't it time you took another look [at National Geographic]?" By suggesting that advertisers who took another look would find the Geographic more relevant and interesting, the announcement implied that the magazine had been stodgy and less relevant in the past and that a major shift in editorial policy was occurring. The third article, titled "One Canada or Two," reported on Quebec's explosive separatist movement. Finally, and perhaps most crucially, a spring article titled "South Africa's Lonely Ordeal" drew fire for its overt discussion of apartheid and the situation of black South

5. Ritchin notes that Dickey Chappelle (who was killed covering the war in 1965) also photographed an execution during this trip that was similar to the one with which Eddie Adams riveted the attention of the American public in 1968, but that the photograph was published only in "an obscure magazine" (not National Geographic). "The world was not ready," he said, "to see the brutality of the war, nor searching for such a symbol of it" (1984:24).

Africans and for the disturbing photographs by James Blair of a black child's grave marked by the infant's white doll and a cardboard cross, and of black maids holding the children of a wealthy white couple. Despite the fact that it had been allowed to preview the story and to recommend major changes, the South African government placed advertisements in major American newspapers accusing the society of "anti-white racism" and serious misrepresentation of the facts (Bryan 1987).

In June of 1977, Melvin Payne, chair of the Board of Trustees, formed an ad hoc committee to determine whether the series of topical, controversial articles meant that the magazine's editorial policy was changing. Gilbert Grosvenor saw this move as a direct threat to his prerogatives as editor. He argued that the magazine "had not deviated from its 89-year tradition of factual accuracy, timeliness, and objectivity"; it was not the magazine that was changing, but the world that was (Bryan 1987:390). Grosvenor's actions in publishing the articles were supported by both Melville Grosvenor and Frederick Vosburg.

Changes were occurring, in fact, not only in the world at large but also in the world of journalism, where conflicts within the press over coverage of the Vietnam War had "spilled the blood on the rug" (Moeller 1989:385). In a review of Vietnam War coverage, Moeller has argued that the new style of Vietnam photographs broke with the aesthetic of the century's two world wars. Instead of careful compositions of battles, photographers focused on the plight of the individual soldier and civilian in the context of conflict. This new style personalized the events of the war. It also challenged, and changed, the existing set of journalistic conventions for covering world events.

In this context, Grosvenor and those who supported him believed that a continuing Pollyanna style of reporting would make the *Geographic* look increasingly shallow and out of touch. The public, they said, was becoming accustomed to grisly facts and critical coverage. If *National Geographic* continued to print only "kindly" and noncontroversial stories, they feared the loss of two elements crucial to their earlier success. First, an increasingly sophisticated public would simply find their stories uninteresting—predictable and without punch. Carefully rendered versions of the idealized and exotic third world, which had formerly piqued interest, would offer little competition to stories of the real-life drama and pathos of the Vietnam War. Second, the principle of "kindliness" was found increasingly to be in conflict with the principle of "absolute accuracy." Given media attention to conflicts in places like South Africa, noncontroversial stories about these locations would be open to question. As *Newsweek* observed in its coverage of the controversy, "In any other magazine the articles on South Africa, Cuba under Castro, and life in Harlem would be considered tame—if not belated—attempts to report the issues of the day" (T. Schwartz 1977). *National Geographic's* claim to present a factual representation would be weakened by its studious avoidance of the conflicts and violence that were covered by other sources (Bryan 1987).

In opposition to Grosvenor's view, the ad hoc committee established by Payne decried the "missionary" instinct of the magazine's recent coverage, arguing that "controversy is adequately covered in the daily press" (Abramson 1987:240); it suggested that the correct approach to coverage of controversy was to "state precisely what the current situation is, but . . . don't take sides . . . don't even quote people on either side" (Bryan 1987:395). Editors, perhaps correctly, perceived that even the recognition that multiple points of view existed cast doubt on their claim to present an authoritative and objective account. Coverage of social or political resistance movements not only suggested that the world was unstable but that an omniscient, unbiased stance was not possible. Ultimately, according to Bryan, the committee asked Grosvenor for a statement that the *Geographic* would simply not treat areas or issues "[so emotionally charged] that an objective piece cannot be written." Grosvenor complied by publishing a short editorial statement in 1978 affirming the *Geographic's* rejection of "advocacy journalism" (Bryan 1987:395–96).

That such coverage already appeared naive and "storybookish" to reading audiences of the 1970s is evidenced by the parody of the *Geographic* that appeared in Tim Menees's "Wordsmith" comic strip in 1976, referring to articles on "The Happy Ghetto: Training Ground for the NBA" and "Backpacking on the Ho Chi Minh Trail." It was further evidenced, somewhat ironically, by the *National Review's* defense of the magazine's Cuba story. "*National Geographic* is not ordinarily thought of as a fellow-traveling publication. . . . Indeed, there are few more refreshing magazines, few so beautifully designed to take the reader out of himself and give him an instant vacation from politics and other humdrum distractions." If the *Geographic* flattered Cuba in the article, it was only because "the magazine flatters everyone" (Sobran 1977). For an enterprise that still considered itself a scientific-educational establishment, this defense was almost as damaging as the criticism had been: it labeled the Society's work too definitively as entertainment, if not pablum, and damaged its claims to present a factual account of the world.

Despite the board's rebuff of Grosvenor and renunciations of advocacy in the editorial pages, the magazine continued to publish topical and somewhat controversial pieces. This included a 1986 article on the Ndebele people of South Africa with several strong photographs by the South African photojournalist Peter Magubane. Although the cover shows a woman in traditional dress, including golden, neck-elongating rings, the article opens with a large photograph of a woman in front of her scrap-board and tarpaper house. The "On Assignment" section of the magazine shows Magubane wounded from police gunfire while covering the funeral of a woman in connection with the *Geographic* story.

Environmental conservation also continued to be seen as an important topic at *National Geographic*. Stories on environmental degradation began to be featured in 1970, and the magazine has subsequently published articles on the smuggling of endangered species, on hazardous waste, acid rain, and the destruction of tropical rain forests. Environmental issues received significant coverage in the 1988 centennial issue. Articles on the Underground Railroad and the Vietnam War Memorial treated controversial (but now safely historical) themes.

The increasing tendency to portray other countries in a slightly less positive light might also have been boosted by the shift through the postwar period in the kinds of advertisers who used the magazine. Tourism advertisements, among the most common in the 1950s, by the 1980s were secondary. This shift occurred at least a decade before 1984, when the Geographic introduced *Traveler* magazine, which was to focus much more explicitly on tourism, in both articles and ads. Commercial and editorial interests are occasionally still in conflict, as when the Magubane picture mentioned above occurred across from a full-page ad for a Caribbean cruise line.

Despite the growing editorial independence, it was not long before Garrett came under attack again. His firing in 1990 has been interpreted as the product of long-standing ill will between Garrett and Grosvenor, who served as president of the Society during Garrett's tenure as editor (Truehart 1990). But Garrett's removal also occurred during a time of declining readership and increasing production costs. Gilbert Grosvenor and the board argued that the best strategy was to pay careful attention to market research and to launch a more determined endeavor to "give the public what they want": shorter stories, fewer articles on non-American topics, and less coverage of social problems. Garrett apparently preferred to "give the public what it doesn't know it wants yet"—to play a greater role in shaping public tastes, rather than simply responding to them. Garrett's activist 1970s style did not win over a board of trustees that welcomed the shift to the right of the political sands of the 1980s and 1990s. "Beauty" had to take precedence over "truth." Politeness seemed to be more marketable than politics. Struggles over how to maintain a proper balance between goals such as politeness and realism were not often played out at *National Geographic* through such dramatic moves as those just described. Far more frequently they were negotiated in the interactions between photographers and their editors, between editors and senior staff, and in a multitude of small choices made in diverse contexts of layout and production, to which we turn in the next chapter.

Conclusion

The development of the National Geographic Society can rightly be told as a success story. Its magazine has found a powerful place in American society as a purveyor of the facts worth knowing about the world. It strategically occupies the spaces between science and pleasure, truth and beauty; it presents an idealized and exotic world relatively free of pain or class conflict, a world stumbling or marching on the path to modernity. Through these means, it attracts millions of people to an identity that is highly valued—the educated person, the modern, the friendly American. In contrast with demeaning styles of representing the third world found in the mass media throughout the century, the photographs of the *Geographic* are gracious, sunlit, and smiling. What this style shows is at stake is an American national identity that is rational, generous, and benevolent. That identity, and the class from which it emerged, have found their validation in the *National Geographic* magazine since its inception.

Three

Inside the Great Machinery of Desire

We have to understand—right inside the productive process—
how these difficult modes of address and forms are actually
constructed.

(R. Williams 1986:14)

Hegemonizing is hard work.

(Hall, quoted in Denning 1990:14)

W hile analysts of the 1970s probed the contradictions in popular culture, they left many questions unanswered. If commentators such as Enzensberger (1974) argued that strategies of mass culture succeeded because they satisfied real
needs and desires, they did not take us inside the "great
machinery of desire" to reveal how profit-making enterprises attempted to identify and shape those needs. Thus,
in the 1980s, Raymond Williams (1986) could argue that
the study of the production of texts is one of the most
neglected aspects of mass culture.

It is easy enough to see the work of *National Geographic*
operating in the ways Fredric Jameson (1983) suggests are
common to mass culture. The magazine's photographs, as
later chapters will show, clearly both arouse and assuage
profound social and political anxieties and desires regarding the place of white middle-class privilege in an international class system. Yet these photographs are not the
standardized product of an omniscient industry; they are

generated through a series of complex, and at times contestatory, production practices. Furthermore, they are not inevitably and unambiguously successful—either in arousing or in quelling anxiety. This chapter explores the institutional context within which the photographs are produced; the roles played by photographers, editors, caption writers, and others in their construction; and the policies and accompanying tensions that govern production of photographs. This is, to be sure, only part of the work that goes on at National Geographic. It excludes all operations other than the magazine (research projects, films and videos, book publishing) as well as the work that goes into producing the written text of *Geographic* articles.

This chapter is based on twenty-five interviews conducted at the National Geographic Society in several visits in the summers of 1989 and 1990. During this time we spoke with photographers, picture editors, and the director and associate director of photography; with caption writers, graphic designers, and printing and engraving specialists; and with marketing personnel. In general we were warmly received. We found that many of the staff were delighted to have an opportunity to talk about how they did their work and were generous with their time. Since our visits, friends and associates have expressed surprise at the willingness of the Geographic to open its doors to us. Even as a non-profit enterprise, they said, it might well be concerned about subscriptions and sensitive to criticism. But though its power as an institution might be expected to close it off from outsiders, this power can also produce what an anthropologist who has studied other elite institutions has called "the confidence of class"—a sense that one's position in the culture is assured and unassailable.

Perhaps the best way to convey something of the feeling of day-to-day practice at National Geographic is to describe, in some detail, a weekly planning meeting that we observed on June 14, 1989. Wilbur Garrett, the editor, stood at the front of a small auditorium, surrounded by other men. At the back of the room was a small booth containing a computer with projection capabilities. The meeting began when Garrett, without a call to order, launched into a story about the Mayan archaeological site he had recently visited. The story involved the discovery that the remains of an individual—named "Smoke Jaguar" by the archaeologists—whose age had previously been estimated as eighty-five had the teeth of a thirty-five-year-old. The story evoked much laughter and speculation about how an old man might have a young man's teeth. Garrett then made an announcement about a Geographic employee who had just had

Wilbur Garrett leads a production meeting at National Geographic headquarters. (Photo: James L. Amos, © National Geographic Society)

bypass surgery. He noted, as an afterword, that this was the fourth person from the Society to have undergone such an operation in the past few months and joked that it must be something in the water.

Garrett briefly discussed sales, which appeared to be up slightly and were expected to increase further with the publication of a story on the remains of the battleship *Bismarck*. Garrett observed that new research was showing that mail solicitations were frequently not opened. Three women from membership services confirmed this, and added that promotional materials bound into magazines prove most effective. Garrett teasingly suggested the adoption of new pop-up formats, prompting some groans from the man who handles printing in their Mississippi plant.

Garrett then turned to the question of whether *National Geographic* would face a lawsuit by the Shakers over a recent story. The Shakers—a religious community in the United States—were apparently upset because the article reported their net worth and a rift within the community was described. There was some discussion about whether this was a legal or a "personality" problem.

After about ten minutes, the meeting turned to its main objective—the organization and scheduling of future issues. A projected schedule for the next few months was displayed on the screen in the front of the room. Garrett asked for confirmation that several stories were ready to go, and a young woman altered the graphics on the computer/projector in accordance with the new information. When asking about a story on the Efe in Zaire, he referred to them as "Pygmies" (the term projected on the screen). He corrected himself, with the concurrence of several staff members. There was a suggestion from staff that if the article were ready to go, it might substitute for a scheduled story on East Harlem. Someone asked whether there were Pygmies in East Harlem.

Discussion turned to the difficulties of getting a staff member into Hong Kong to photograph refugees from recent unrest in China. A staff member noted that "their man in China" felt it would not be possible to cover the unrest associated with Tienanmen Square until autumn at the earliest. He had reported to headquarters that dissidents who were not arrested had gone underground and that while it was still possible to talk to people in the streets, this was not a good time to "get into homes and get close to people."

Garrett asked how the printing operation in Mississippi was coming along. The response was "Spoilage down, quality up." In response, someone in the room added "Coronary bypasses up." There was much laughter and some booing. Garrett asked the printer if he could handle musical cards in the binding as well as pop-ups. He groaned again, and the women in membership services reported, tongue in cheek, that these were just on the verge of becoming cost-effective. Garrett, obviously meandering through topics and jumping around to suit himself, asked a man who had recently had bypass surgery if he could prepare a manual on bypasses for the staff.

Garrett returned to business by mentioning that the poster they had produced to promote a special issue on the French bicentennial, showing a kiosk and the Eiffel Tower with Bastille Day fireworks in the background, would appear timely when released in July of this year. Someone in the front row observed that the issue on the bicentennial had been reviewed favorably by the Associated Press and the *Washington Post*. There was a quip about taking the press to lunch at French restaurants through the month of July. With that, the meeting disbanded, as informally as it had come to order and with the same group of men returning to cluster around Garrett.

This brief meeting encapsulated much of what we had learned about the internal workings of the National Geographic Society. First, there was a sense of camaraderie, of working together toward common goals, combined with the strong—almost absolute—prerogative of the editor in setting those goals. This peculiar combination was glossed by at least one staff member during our interview sessions as "a participatory dictatorship." Second, the meeting was dominated by white males, dressed in corporate style. The women present, with one or two exceptions, were clustered in service departments, such as marketing and promotion. Third, there was an action-oriented ethos—an emphasis on first-hand experience—exemplified by Garrett's introductory anecdote about his visit to Guatemala and references to "our man in China" and "getting into people's homes." The rapid-fire coverage of topics, the witty interchange between Garrett and staff, the references to stress and bypasses all created the impression of a fast-paced, state-of-the-art operation. Finally, like so many of the day-to-day decisions made at the Geographic, the underlying agenda structuring the seemingly free-ranging discussion was about balance: between market considerations and content, factual reporting and politeness (the Shaker case), and timeliness and depth of coverage (China). More perniciously, "balance" related to the racial composition of an issue: if the article on the Efe were included, the one on East Harlem should go. How many dark-skinned people could the reading public tolerate in a single copy of the magazine?

Intentionality in a Complex Social Environment

Simple "auteur" (or "artiste") theories of photographic images are inadequate to account for the complex sets of pressures and expectations that confront the individual photographer in an institutional environment such as National Geographic and the complicated processes through which their photographs are transformed through editing, layout, captioning, printing, and—now—computer enhancement. As Sontag and others have shown, the moment of taking the photograph is already complex, a moment in which power is invoked to negotiate a certain kind of intimacy between photographer and photographed. But for *National Geographic* photographers this moment is sandwiched in between other processes that are equally determinative of the final product. On one side is socialization to the organization and the explicit instructions picture editors give photographers before they depart for the field. On

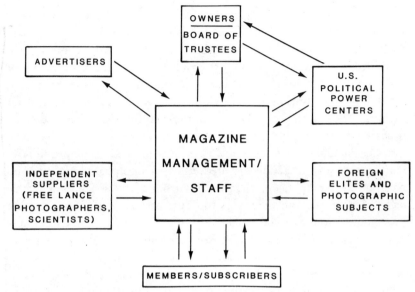

Figure 3.1. The magazine's institutional organization and some participants (after Wallis and Baran 1990:218)

the other is the photo selection process—thirty to forty photos selected out of a set of thousands—and the myriad manipulations of the photograph once it is chosen.

One of the issues raised by the complexity of the photo production process is that of intentionality, or communicative intent. Intentionality is not the same as consequence; an artist's intent may be misapprehended or subverted. Nevertheless, in order to understand the production of a cultural object, we must be able to make some inferences about who are communicating and what they mean to say. Griswold (1987b) has argued that the literature on popular culture has dealt with intentionality in two overly simplified ways. The first reduces the author's intent to "subjectivity—to the agent's individual psychology or consciousness." Intentionality in this psychological sense is also often assumed to be a conscious and unitary phenomenon, with the artist seen as aiming to achieve a certain goal. But the artist, including the photographer, may be unsure or fundamentally ambivalent about what he or she wishes to say by way of the artwork. This first tendency also places intentionality beyond the realm of anthropological or sociological methodology. For Griswold, this conception is too narrow; it prevents us from discussing or understanding the ways that intentionality is shaped by social elements. A second tendency in the literature conceptualizes intentionality too broadly. Located at the level of the entire social order, a hegemonic intentionality is seen as repressing and shaping popular consciousness, without attention to the multiple and ambiguous characteristics of cultural objects themselves.

For Griswold, the type of intentionality that is susceptible to investigation is neither personal and idiosyncratic, nor hegemonic and univocal. Drawing on the work of Baxandall (1985), she suggests that the individual act of production can be linked to a social context through two key concepts: charge and brief. A charge is "a general and immediate prompt for an agent to act," which may be internally generated or may come from a specific external source. In the realm of high culture this may take the form of a commission—to paint a portrait or an altarpiece, to write an opera or a symphony. In these cases, the charge to the artist encompasses a set of expectations about what these forms are, as well as the concerns of wealthy patrons about how they will be realized. Baxandall illustrates the notion of charge with the case of the painter Piero, who was commissioned to paint an altarpiece for the church of Sansepolcro about 1450. The charge to Piero entailed a set of social expectations: "An altarpiece must represent a recognizable scriptural passage, it must be instructive, it must be emotionally moving and able to instill reverence, it must be clear and memorable, and it must reflect the taste and wealth of the client who paid for it" (Griswold 1987b:7). The case of popular culture is not so different—although the taste to be indulged will more often be that of the marketplace, and the commission made by a representative of a profit-oriented industry or enterprise.

For any given charge, Griswold argues, the analyst may reconstruct a brief, which is "a list of constraints and influences that together constitute the artist's probable intention." The brief would include (1) the immediate circumstances, or task at hand—for the *National Geographic* photographer, this would be the photographic assignment; (2) the artist's or producer's training and experience—for the *National Geographic* photographer, once again, this would involve prior training (often in photojournalism) as well as socialization within the enterprise; (3) local conditions or expectations about the form of the product—at the *Geographic* these are based on market research and other, less formal strategies used by editors to imagine their readership and its taste; (4) physical media and constraints—these include the technical limitations within which photography operates, and the techniques and equipment that the National Geographic Society makes available to its photographers and encourages them to use; and (5) aesthetic conventions—at the *Geographic,* this can be most broadly characterized as a realist style, with many more highly delineated conventions encompassed within that style.

Initiating a Story

The initial idea for a story may come from many sources: from photographers, editorial staff, writers, or members of the Board of Directors. An idea that survives initial discussion with colleagues will be developed into a proposal to the Planning Council, the group which votes on the stories that will be moved forward into the planning stages. Ideas for stories need to be grabbers; they need to take familiar, even hackneyed topics and give them a new twist. An idea must include, therefore, not only a topic and area (a Peruvian pilgrimage, for example) but also a way of presenting the topic (changes in the pilgrimage in recent years) or a visually distinct mode of presentation (night photography of the pilgrimage in the snow). An example that we were given of a particularly interesting and in some ways problematic piece was a story on the Crusades in which Moorish Spain was discussed in the text, and photographs from contemporary Morocco were used to illustrate what life would have been like during that period.

An idea for a story may be rejected because it is not innovative enough, because it is too broad or too narrow in conception, because it duplicates something already in the pipeline (there are up to 150 stories in various stages of preparation at any one time) or because something similar has been done too recently. It is often necessary for the person with the idea to develop support for his or her proposal within the organization prior to submitting it. As one editor said, "It is a political thing to get backing for a story." He was referring less to the way in which the story fits the overall politics of the Society (although this is clearly an issue) than to his perception that one had to work strategically to develop this support among the various levels of the decision-making hierarchy.

Once a story is approved, it is assigned a story team of three individuals: the writer, the photographer, and the picture editor. The associate director of photography is responsible for choosing the photographer, a job which entails a careful match between capabilities and sensibilities of the photographer and the subject matter at hand. A photographer with a slick or highly aestheticized style would probably not be sent to do a story on Calcutta; rather, someone perceived to be a good "people photographer" with previous experience in third-world settings and a harder, documentary style would be chosen.

Everyone in the photographic division insists that a writer is not "assigned" a photographer to illustrate the piece. The story is built, they say, on the strength of the pictures, and the pictures must tell a story in their own right. The three-person team meets initially in a story conference. After that point, there may be relatively little contact between writer and photographer, but the photographer works closely with the picture editor to develop the ideas that emerge from the conference.

Picture editors see themselves as responsible for researching the topic, or at least using the materials made available by the research department. They see their role as conceptualizing the story to be told and keeping the photographers on track. They acknowledge that photographers may take issue with this characterization of the division of labor, preferring to see themselves as more independent and self-directed. Because picture editors are or have been photographers themselves, they identify with the artistic side of the endeavor. They feel that they understand the conditions necessary for the photographer to operate as an artist, and they try to provide them. They often portray themselves as providing emotional support or subtly controlling photographers' behavior—encouraging " 'fraidy cats" to try something different or reining in "egomaniacs." In general, however, they view themselves as the brains behind the operation—the ones who give coherence to the photographic endeavor, the control nexus by which the creative work of the photographer is brought into line with the goals and policies of the organization. This separation of conception and execution in photographic work is not unusual; it has been described and critiqued for news and advertising as well (Rosenblum 1978:123–24).

The first step for the picture editor is to provide the photographer with a theme or set of themes that will organize the picture-taking enterprise. An editor working on a recent story on Bolivia, for example, wanted the photographs to show that little had really changed in that country since Independence—that there had simply been a shift in power from Spain to the United States. He wanted the story to convey that there were still tinhorn dictators—a fact of life more important than the politics those dictators might be espousing at the moment. To aid in developing such a theme—in his words, "to focus the photographer"—he provided a story list, or set of potentially photographable subjects, which included photographs of the creole aristocracy; evidence of *caudillismo* in its present form; the prevalence of the black market,

border disputes, and military domination. The editor distinguished between getting the photographer to put a particular spin on a story—in
this case by drawing connections between past and present—and the
more negatively evaluated practice of posing photographs. "We don't
want to pose photographs to make it look like Bolivar's time," he said.
This same editor, however, described a situation in which he wanted to
emphasize connections between past and present in the Middle East, and
to do so in a way that was appealing to Christians (which *National
Geographic* promotional studies have shown to be an important market
segment). In this case, he felt quite comfortable encouraging the photographer to take pictures of fishermen on the Sea of Galilee in postures
that evoked Jesus' words to Saint Peter about fishers of men.

This type of reconstruction and posing was an explicit goal in a story
on Captain Cook's voyages to Tahiti. The picture editor gave the photographer a list of places to visit and a copy of Cook's journal; he in-
structed the photographer to "show the beauty of the island that caused
Cook's soldiers to jump overboard" and to obtain photographs of "non-
[racially] mixed Polynesians." Many of the photos for this piece were
faithful reconstructions of ways of life at the time of Cook's voyage.

The notion of a story told in pictures is crucial to the photographic
process at *National Geographic*. One picture editor said outright, "This
is not travelogue, it is not journalism, it is not an art magazine, it is
storytelling." The ideas and themes that will bind a set of photographs
together and give them coherence do not emerge out of a post-hoc
review of the photographer's work. Rather, they are an a priori charge,
in Griswold's terms, that emerges from the Planning Council and the
editorial staff. Photographers are encouraged to be creative in illustrating
ideas. They are expected to have a sense of scene, a feel for the unusual
and interesting, a sense of drama, an ability to appeal to the senses; but
they are expected to use these capacities in service of the charge they are
given. Photographers may adhere to the charge to different degrees at
different times. As we will see, however, the story is not only written
in a preliminary way through the instructions given to the photographer
but is also reconstructed through the photo selection process.

Clearly the selection and framing of stories is one of the strongest
ways that the National Geographic Society shapes the work of photographers and imposes an ideological line. This is why the process is seen as
highly political, that is, as a site of struggle within the institution. The
process is nominally democratic and open, in that anyone can propose
a story; but for proposals to succeed they must be tailored to perceptions

of "what will fly" with the council. They may be substantially modified to bring them into line, and they may simply be rejected if they are too far off the mark.

The issues are substantial ones. The decision to drop barriers to coverage of formerly shunned nations, such as the Soviet Union, China, and Cuba are among the more visible. But the framing of an article is always significant in terms of what it emphasizes and what it omits. Will an article on South Korea focus on that country's so-called economic miracle or will it be structured in ways that highlight repression and dictatorship? Will an article on South Africa look directly at apartheid ("A Country Divided") or treat it only obliquely? The *Geographic* is, in part, able to honor its commitment to presenting only factual material by deciding, through the selection process and the charge to photographers, exactly what small subsection of the facts it will portray.

The Photographer in the Field

Photography at the *Geographic* is an oddly eclectic enterprise, drawing on a number of photographic traditions but not operating squarely within any of them. The complex nature of the work that is done was expressed to us by photographers and their editors through a series of dichotomies and contrasts. At their broadest, these were contrasts between *National Geographic* photography and other traditions, such as photojournalism, documentary photography, and art photography. On more specific points, photographers drew contrasts that reflected their ways of thinking about the objectivity of the photograph (its status as a record) and about its personal as opposed to its social characteristics. Taken as a whole, their statements represent a fairly complete and explicit theory of photography. The theory occasionally offers a challenge to the goals of the National Geographic Society, but in most instances it is extraordinarily well suited to producing the images of the world that the society desires.

In 1987, there were sixty-six photographers working for National Geographic. Seven of these were on staff, seventeen under long-term contract, twenty-nine operating on a free-lance basis (contracted for particular stories) and thirteen "others" — research grant recipients, expedition photographers, and the like). The Society sees this mix of relationships as important: the use of contract photographers allows the magazine to keep up with changing photographic styles, while a core of staff photographers lends continuity and preserves certain well-established values.

Most photographers at the magazine have previously worked as photojournalists. Many still prize "photography for the record"—pictures valued for their informational content. They are excited by the notion of the photographer in contact with the real world of events and as knowingly (or intuitively) appropriating those bits of life that are most significant.

At the same time, they understand that their work at *National Geographic* diverges from this function of recording events. In discussing the differences, they often refer to photojournalists as producing "spot news" or "point pictures." Spot news photographs simply record an event, and, we were told, in most cases their value is not lasting. This is because, unless they are extraordinarily well done, they have only one dimension—to provide information. Photographers said that *National Geographic* photographs at their best are multidimensional. They are like onions, one editor told us, with many layers that can be peeled back. Though they provide information, they also have an aesthetic dimension that communicates feelings and emotions. One editor made the distinctions:

> Point pictures are pictures that serve to illustrate points; they are very literal and simple, like a declarative sentence. Other pictures have poetry, they give a feel for a thing; they add a whole new dimension to a story. They are not just illustrating the words. Photography can do this especially well—not the facts, but how a thing feels. Not that facts are ignored; photographers have a tremendous knowledge of their subject. But knowledge is not driving everything. The photographer reacts based on this knowledge, but doesn't go out to illustrate it. It is not up here [points to forebrain] but further back.

The editor went on to say that when photographers come in directly from news training, they tend to be event-focused and superficial and have to be encouraged to peel the onion, to go deeper into each situation and event. They are encouraged to find scenes whose significance is not just the event at hand but that say something about the everyday life of the society.

Photographic editors also argued that *National Geographic* photography differs from photojournalism in taking a broader view of what is historically significant. The magazine tries to show "the whole context," one editor said, rather than events at a particular historical moment. Thus, recording certain events may give them undue weight in creating the public's image of a particular part of the world. The editor cited the case of a photographer, in South Korea covering the Olympics, who took the opportunity to photograph student demonstrations and their repression. He was upset when the home office refused to print many of his photos. The editorial staff took the position that while they were real documents in the sense that they reflected events that had actually occurred, the magazine would give a distorted image of life in Korea by giving them prominence. The editor was clear about the fact that the goal was not to demonstrate what happened in Korea at any one time but to give an overall, balanced sense of what life there was like.

Moeller (1989) draws a contrast between "the decisive moment" (Cartier-Bresson's phrase) and "the random moment" in news photography. In most cases, she argues, news photographs concentrate their attention on moments when history is made; they stress connections between the event photographed and those that precede and follow it. They aim to capture the decisive moment, a moment like no other, when things come together in a way that they never have before and are unlikely to again, a moment thus deeply imbued with historical significance. In other cases, photographers may frame an event in order to present it as a random moment: "that instant which could be *any* time and, therefore, can be *every* time" (Moeller 1989:409). Such photographs stress timelessness rather than history; inherence rather than contingency; and enduring human values rather than current human actions. Despite the fact that the magazine's photographers frequently invoke Cartier-Bresson as a photographer whose work they would like to emulate, random or enduring moments are clearly what the magazine's editors are after. One editor played on Cartier-Bresson's language by suggesting that the magazine seeks to portray the "incisive" moment, which he defined as a lull between peak actions. While not wholly random, such a moment focuses more on statements about the values and human qualities that inform the event than on the event itself. It steps outside the contingent and fleeting historical moment to comment on more timeless themes.

Pratt (1985) has described a common strategy for representing differences in travel writing that can suggest how photographs of such random moments work in the consciousness of individuals. The people portrayed in Western travel literature, she argues, are not seen as named individuals involved in a significant historical event. Rather, they are homogenized into a collective "they," which is distilled even further into an iconic "he" (the standardized adult male specimen). This abstracted "he"/"they" is the subject of verbs in a timeless present tense, which characterizes anything "he" is or does not as a particular historical event but as an instance of a pregiven custom or trait (Pratt 1985:139).

This emphasis on timelessness, inherence, and enduring human values is not unique to *National Geographic*. It has provided the underlying logic for a number of museum displays and photographic exhibitions, among them the Family of Man collection, first displayed in the United States in 1955 and thereafter overseas. The organizer, Edward Steichen, was moved to put the exhibit together by his desire to promote peace and his sense that some recent exhibits of horrific war photography were not achieving that goal. "What was needed," he felt, "was a positive statement on what a wonderful thing life was, how marvelous people were, and above all, how alike people were in all parts of the world" (Meltzer 1978:293). As Barthes has noted in his review of the exhibition, the logic of the display operated in two stages: first,

> the difference between human morphologies is asserted, exoticism is insistently stressed, the infinite variations of the species, the diversity in skins, skulls and customs are made manifest, the image of Babel is complacently projected over that of the world. Then, from this pluralism, a type of unity is magically produced: man is born, works, laughs and dies everywhere in the same way; and if there still remains in these actions some ethnic peculiarity, at least one hints that there is underlying each one an identical "nature," that their diversity is only formal and does not belie the existence of a common mould. (1972:100)

Barthes argues that the exhibit, structured as it is, serves "to suppress the determining weight of History." It is true that children are always born, but what does this matter, he asks, compared to whether or not children are born with ease or difficulty, whether or not they are threatened by a high mortality rate, whether or not such and such a type of future is open to them. Of the exhibit's depiction of labor as the universal fate of humanity, Barthes notes:

> That work is an age-old fact does not in the least prevent it from remaining a perfectly historical fact. Firstly, and evi-

dently, because of its modes, its motivations, its ends and its benefits, which matter to such an extent that it will never be fair to confuse in a purely gestural identity the colonial and the Western worker (let us . . . ask the North African workers of the Goutte d'Or district in Paris what they think of the *Great Family of Man*). Secondly, because of the very differences in its inevitability: we know very well that work is 'natural' just as long as it is 'profitable', and that in modifying the inevitability of profit, we shall perhaps one day modify the inevitability of labor. It is this entirely historified work which we should be told about, instead of an eternal aesthetics of laborious gestures. (1972:102)

While classic humanism postulates that beneath thin veneers of difference, one quickly reaches "the solid rock of a universal human nature," Barthes argues that a progressive humanism would instead constantly examine what is purported to be natural and universal "in order to discover History there, and at last to establish Nature itself as historical" (1972:101). Clearly, photographic practice at *National Geographic* is geared to a classic form of humanism, drawing readers' attention through its portrayal of difference, and then showing that under the colorful dress and the skin, as it were, we are all more or less the same.

If its emphasis on everyday life and human nature distinguishes *National Geographic* photography from standard photojournalism, neither does it lie squarely in the tradition of art photography. Staff photographers share with their colleagues in photojournalism a disdain for "personal pictures" (see Gans 1979:186), in which the photographer's own aesthetic vision is seen as interfering with his or her presentation of what is really out there. Viewers are distracted from their perusal of what seems to be an unmediated record by artistic devices which remind them that the photographer did indeed have a point of view.

While pictures should not be unduly personal, most photographers expressed a desire to have some aspects of their style, or personal vision, come through and be recognized. (They clearly recognized, and were willing to characterize, elements of each other's styles). A number of photographers maintained that tolerance for "artsy" or impressionistic pictures had increased at the *Geographic* in recent years. One editor concurred. In the 1960s and 1970s, he observed, photographers understood themselves to be simplifying and clarifying a complex flow of images; they interpreted their job as imposing some sort of organization on a chaotic reality. By contrast, he believed that in the 1980s photographers (and viewers) became more tolerant of ambiguity in images, more willing to portray the complexities and nuances of situations. He characterized this change as a growth in the sophistication of photography at the Society, and as a shift in style to accommodate postmodernism. Photographers saw it as an editorial move rather than a departure in photographic practices. They pointed out that photographers have been turning in "radical, artsy, and impressionistic" photographs for at least twenty-five years, but that editors have only recently begun to use them.

A story illustrating conflict over the right to print personal or more artistic photographs was repeated to us on several occasions. A rather grisly photograph of a sheep's head on a slaughterhouse floor had been submitted in a final carousel of slides for an article on North African immigrants to France. The photograph was interesting in its composition (and very much resembled a similar slaughterhouse photograph by Henri Cartier-Bresson). Both the picture editor and photographer strongly advocated using it, preferring it over another of an immigrant family watching television in the living room, an animal carcass beside them. Wilbur Garrett, the editor, objected—presumably because the photograph was too strong. In a statement that was clearly meant to be his last word he suggested loudly that if people were so fond of the photo they could put it on their wall. It did not appear in the magazine, but it was hanging in at least three offices during our visits.

Photography at the Society thus positions itself midway between art photography and photojournalism.[1] It is more expressive and multidimensional than news photography, yet it performs an educational function by transmitting information about people and places. This is clearly an extension of the strategic occupation of the boundary between entertainment and science. At the *Geographic,* being expressive entails saying things about enduring human truths, about human nature. Despite the fact that these photographic statements about human nature have clearly been commissioned by way of the charge to photographers,

1. Perhaps for this reason, too, photographers at National Geographic so often cite Cartier-Bresson as one whose work they would like to emulate. While sometimes specifically referring to his mastery of mid-range photography, at other times they are expressing admiration for the "spirit" of his work, locating his work, like theirs, on the boundary between art and photojournalism. In this, however, they seem to ignore the fact that his work wrought havoc with the boundary itself, subverting realist codes by using them to surrealist ends and radically questioning the distance between personal and political.

and the story as conceptualized by the Planning Council and picture editor, they are packaged and offered to readers as truths found in the field.

The space between art and news is not the only uncertain territory that *National Geographic* photographers occupy. The truth status of photography has been the subject of long and intense debate. Some critics—Barthes, for example—have argued that the photograph has a strong relationship to a prior, though irretrievable, reality. The special quality of photography stems from the fact that it is almost a direct "inflection" of this prior moment (Barthes 1981). Others have vehemently opposed such a view, arguing that photography entails the production of a new reality that has little or no relationship to the prephotographic situation (Tagg 1988). In discussing the truth status of the work they produce, *National Geographic* photographers often relate their work to the tradition of documentary photography, particularly to the photographic work sponsored by the Farm Security Administration in the 1930s and 1940s. These are "deep" photographs that speak to the human condition, but they are also popularly held to be factual in content. Walker Evans and Dorothea Lange, and in the 1950s Robert Frank, are referenced by *National Geographic* photographers as part of the tradition within which they would locate their work—or the best of it. In invoking these earlier photographs, they involve themselves in the larger debates that have surrounded it (Becker 1978; Tagg 1988). They inevitably raise, for example, the question of objectivity. To what degree does the photographer's theory of what is going on in the world influence his or her pictures? While the motivations for and uses of Farm Security Administration photography were complex (Tagg 1988), it was taken for granted that these artists were involved in social commentary. Most *National Geographic* photographers, in contrast, are uncomfortable with the idea that they are making a social statement with their photographs. Having too strong a social theory, we were told, makes you less objective. A preconceived idea of what the social issues are not only creates bias but interferes with "gut instincts" about what is important in the field. Editors and photographers concur in the view that a single, indisputable objective reality is accessible to the photographer who listens by way of the gut of common sense, rather than the intricacies of theory or the noise of a committed point of view.

In this respect, *Geographic* photographers and their editors are like many journalists in America, who generally subscribe to a view of their work as nonpolitical, nonpartisan, and objective both ideally and actually

(Hallin 1987; Weaver and Wilhoit 1986). That a dislike for politics and partisan conflict characterizes much journalism is evident in, for instance, a 1982 television documentary on Central America, narrated by Bill Moyers, who treated all parties to the conflicts in a negative light. "Only the journalists themselves, 'without an ideology to promote,' appeared to possess real wisdom" (Hallin 1987:18). Hallin notes that the consequences of this distrust of the partisan in journalism include support of the existing social order. Even when journalists are critical of administration policy or a foreign political scene, they will at the same time be critical of the activists working to change it. They will in fact be more critical of the latter, who will make, or appear to make, passionate political appeals while "the elites can often fall back into a quiet 'technocratic' or 'statesmanlike' posture" (Hallin 1987:19).

The ideal of journalistic objectivity can also follow from the need or desire to pursue the largest possible audience. Developed in the nineteenth century, the ideal "allowed the press to cultivate and to accumulate a modern mass public by appearing to present simply *facts,* in such a form and temper as to 'lead men of *all* parties to rely upon its statements,' as the *New York Times* (22 March 1860) put it" (Schiller 1981:87; emphasis added). Analysts of the media have observed that individual firms often feel subject to pressure from sponsors or lobbies. "Production firms that rely on getting a great many of their most important resources (money, authority, personnel, services, and the like) from the mainstream of society (governments, giant advertisers, powerful advocacy organizations, necessarily huge audiences) will likely arrange their activities so as to offend as few of these entities as possible" (Turow 1984:118). This statement clearly applies more to *National Geographic* than to some other kinds of magazines, particularly those that do not have a tax-exempt status granted by the government and those with smaller, more specialized audiences.

If objectivity is threatened by theory, it is served by what *National Geographic* photographers like to call serendipity. Serendipity is invoked in an almost mystical fashion to refer to what makes a good—a deep—photograph. At some level it refers to the coming together of informational content with color, movement, and composition. But it is also understood as the photographer's ability to watch for and take advantage of moments that have significant emotional content or another layer of meaning. These cannot be engineered, and "too strong a theory" reduces the photographer's openness to such moments. As one editor commented:

The control of the photographer can only extend so far. If it goes too far, you get a gimmicky photograph. If it is more relaxed, it is possible for true serendipity to occur. Too much control is counterproductive because taking a photograph *is* a mystical process. It works or it doesn't—it is nonsense to me to *talk* about whether a picture works.

Other photographers, however, explicitly rejected the idea of serendipity. One staff photographer complained: "It assumes you don't know why you're there." From his perspective, *National Geographic* photographers have some of the same responsibilities as photojournalists. They need to understand fully the context in which they are working and to have a sense of what kinds of photos will get to the heart of the issues at hand.

While the topic was not addressed explicitly, it is clear that photographers who enter the field with too strong a notion of what is going on may have difficulty working within the scope of the story outlined by the council and the picture editor. In contrast, sending a photographer to search for serendipitous moments in the context of a well-defined charge should serve to generate a wide array of interesting and compelling photographs loosely grouped around a central theme. For editors, this is obviously preferable to photographs structured around the photographer's own political or aesthetic agenda.

If serendipity is one way that photographers and editors believe they can achieve objectivity, another is through the search for balance. Gans (1979) has described how considerations of balance enter into decision making in journalism. Convinced that diversity is crucial to holding an audience, editors seek to achieve an appropriate mix of serious and light material, negative and positive topics, short and long pieces, and strive for a balanced representation of political views and appropriate amounts of coverage of world areas.

At the *Geographic,* balance is pursued most assiduously in photo selection. This entails balancing focal lengths and subjects, making sure there is an adequate array of portraits, landscapes, and mid-range photographs. It involves balancing positive and negative, upbeat and gloomy, critical versus laudatory themes. As one editor put it, "It behooves us to show reality—and nothing is all bad or all good. If [the photographer] didn't find any happy people, I'd tell him to go back and find them." Photographers accommodate this attitude. One argued that, for their young readers especially, too heavy a focus on negative aspects of a story could be disturbing. "For instance, in a story about volcanoes," he advised, "you should balance the devastation with something good about volcanoes." But at least one photographer was explicitly critical of the notion of balance: "It is a bad word," he said, "because it implies there's another side to the truth."

Closely linked to discussions of objectivity are concerns with the degree to which the subject matter of a photograph can and should be manipulated. In general, photographers and editors believe that it is better to strive for candid shots. This is in keeping with what Becker (1978) has called the naturalist argument in photography: "The value of the picture resides in its truth observation. This value is jeopardized to the extent that the photographer intervenes in the social circumstances, causing a rupture from what naturally would have happened" (1978:43). Photographers feel and express the contradiction between this ethos and the practical need to orchestrate photographs in order to conform to a charge, to enhance colors, or to create interest in other ways. They agree that while some manipulation may be necessary, photographs should not *look* gimmicky. Most also express dismay at new technologies that make possible the enhancement and alteration of photographs after the fact, technologies described by Ritchin (1990). Computer alteration not only undermines the naturalist argument; it also raises powerful questions about the right of photographers to exercise control over their work. Photographers at *National Geographic* have never controlled which of their pictures will be published; the loss of control over what the final product will look like further erodes their authorship.

The photographers rarely suffer from a shortage of resources to do their job. They are provided with the transportation needed to reach even the most remote outposts and the equipment needed to take photographs under virtually any conditions. There is no limit to the number of rolls of film they may shoot on an assignment. As one staff member said: "One thing distinguishes photography and printing at National Geographic from what you find at other places—money, the money to do things right."

An example of photographic practice was observed by one of us (JC) in the late 1970s in the Andes. A *National Geographic* photographer needed an image of the traditional process of freeze-drying potatoes in order to complete a story on potatoes around the world. He and his assistant flew to Lima and then to a southern Andean town, where they hired a taxicab to drive them to a remote village on the Peru–Bolivia border. Knowing that the process of freeze-drying potatoes involves stepping barefoot on the tubers in order to express the moisture, the photographer wanted pictures of children because the size of their feet would be more in keeping with the small Andean potatoes. When he learned that the children were in school, he immediately went with a translator to ask the principal if several could be released to work on the project. Much to his dismay, they emerged not in colorful Andean dress but in gray school uniforms. Piling them into and onto the taxicab, he escorted them long distances (often cross-country) to their homes to change, and then to the site of potato processing. By the time everything was set up, the sun was too low in the sky for shooting pictures. The photographer, who was working on a tight schedule, could not stay to try again the next day. After taking a few Polaroids for the children, he and his assistant headed back to the airport to travel on to the next assignment in the Himalayas. In many other instances as well, much trouble and expense go into seeking to get the right shot.

Certain photographers were especially admired for their problem-solving abilities—their special inventiveness and creativity in devising new ways to get the right shot. Stories of photographers climbing mountains, hanging on ropes from helicopters, or traveling in difficult weather to get particular views are part of the lore of the institution. While the Society itself occasionally exploits these stories as evidence of its commitment to bringing the new and remarkable from the far reaches of the earth, photographers invoke them as a demonstration of their status as resourceful, practical people.

The photographers we talked to stressed the need to establish some sort of rapport with the people they photographed in the field. They emphasized that it takes time to get to know people and to win their confidence, and they spoke of the need to treat those they photographed with respect. A photographer told about approaching a group of men sitting on a bench in Harlan County, Kentucky, and asking them if he could take their picture. At first the men objected because they were dirty and were wearing their work clothes, but eventually they agreed on condition that the caption would explain that they were taking a break from working on their cars. The photographer made sure that it did. This was, he said, a question of ethics, part of what he called an attempt to show people through their own eyes—to portray them so that they would recognize themselves.

Photographers told anecdotes about conflicts with government offi-cials over permission to take photographs. One of them had to do with getting a picture of trekkers along the Yangtse River. The photographer

Photographer Eric Valli hangs suspended from a cliff face, surrounded by swarming bees, in order to photograph honey hunter Mani Lal in Nepal, illustrating the lengths to which magazine personnel will go to "get the picture." (Photo: John Lewis)

found that his guides were unwilling to have him take the picture, probably because it would make their country look underdeveloped, and ultimately he had to threaten to get off the boat and hike back if his guides wouldn't stop. The picture was important, he argued, because the area being traversed was to be flooded by a hydroelectric dam within two years, and the trekkers would be outmoded. Thus, he saw his role as documenting a piece of history. For him, photographing these people was like "going back a thousand years." In this instance, obtaining the photograph took precedence over maintaining rapport with his guides. Because to some extent they view their work as part of a humanistic/scientific endeavor, National Geographic photographers expressed few qualms about their right to photograph whatever they chose in third-world settings.

Within the National Geographic Society, there is a clear distinction between photographers and the rest of the staff. Photographers are seen as renegades, somewhat quirky, and as operating in and responding to a different world from that of the "home staff." One editor spoke of the inherent tension between the two groups. Photographers, he said, want to tell the truth about what they've seen, while editors and home staff may object, protesting that it is radically different from what they assume is out there. This kind of split has been described for the press. During the Vietnam War, it was found, journalists stationed in Southeast Asia were radicalized by their experiences and came to hold views that diverged markedly from those of their supervisors in Washington and New York (Moeller 1989; Gans 1979).[2]

Though perceived as being somewhat apart from the institution as a whole, the Geographic photographers fall into groups that correspond to periods of hiring. A staff member characterized the first period (up until about 1960) as the ascendancy of "the Eastern elite." These were people of Victorian values, graduates of Harvard and Yale, who saw themselves as curators of museum pieces and curiosities from around the world. When they traveled abroad, these gentlemen-adventurers would interact almost exclusively with the elite. They might, for example, "stay with the King of Thailand and be carried around the country in a sedan pulled by slaves—up until the 1950s." They viewed subsequent generations of photographers and writers as "peasants with travel cards" because of their more middle-class backgrounds and their tendency to interact with the common people.

Beginning in the early 1960s, a second generation of fieldworkers was hired by Melville Grosvenor. Their prototype was the Midwestern journalist, fresh from a major Midwest newspaper, who had won several

---

2. National Geographic contrasts with other national and international journals in often conducting its work outside of the capital cities and relying less on government sources, which the media sees as the primary source for information on foreign policy and other matters (Hallin 1987). Photojournalists appear more likely to leave Washington than writers (Moeller 1989), and so the magazine's distinctiveness is accentuated in this way as well.

national or regional awards. This group was described to us as "conservative, with a common man's outlook on life—parochial." They in turn characterized their predecessors as "overly intellectual." Photographers of this cohort sought pictures of "street urchins and prostitutes" because they wanted to show "stark reality." When they traveled abroad they were more likely to work with mid-level government bureaucrats than with the elite.

The photographers hired in the 1970s and 1980s were described to us as more liberal, less ethnocentric, and more interested in social change. Their view of the world has been heavily colored by college demonstrations and the Vietnam War, and they currently play a large role in promoting an environmentalist stance at the magazine. While attitudes from all three groups survive within the institution, all have been reshaped, we were told, through interactions with one another and by the styles and practices dictated by the editor and the board in any given period.

Selecting Photographs: Putting the Story Together

The initial stage in selecting photographs is the film review process, in which home staff members review every frame of film for technical difficulties, such as exposure problems or camera malfunction. Photographers are normally notified quickly about the technical status of the pictures so that they can make adjustments, if necessary, in the field.

One picture editor told us that in his initial review he works "viscerally," reducing thousands of slides to approximately 180. He avoids safe, boring pictures in favor of those that are both visually appealing and packed with information. He looks for photographs that "appeal to a few of your senses," photos that touch the viewer because they are beautiful or because they are shocking. Ideally, he said, a photograph should raise questions. He pointed out a photograph of a young boy in a circumcision ritual and said that readers should ask, What kind of game is this? Why is he crying? What's going on? Another editor echoed this sentiment: "A picture should make you want to study it; if you saw it in real life you'd want to stop and watch."

In making these visceral selections, picture editors take their own reactions as a good indicator of how the average reader will respond. One editor said that if a photograph touched him in some way, it would probably do the same for "some guy in Peoria" or "a lady in Paducah." Gans (1979:237) has also found this criterion prevalent among newspaper editors.

After the first culling, the editor normally has a more cerebral reason for choosing one photograph over another. Photographs need to convey a sense of movement, of building to a point. At least since the 1980s, a literal progression of ideas may be less important than developing a trope or an allegory, or even evoking a particular mood. One editor said, "Today the tendency to put people into situations and set them up is a lot less common. They [the public] are looking for less literal images." He showed us pictures for a story on Chile that he felt were unusual and nonliteral. Instead of presenting a church service to make a point about faith, one showed a woman with a huge bloody crucifix in her home. "Cumulatively, when you put these nonliteral photos together in a way that makes some points, you end up with a sense of texture, smell, taste that you might not have otherwise. A good photographer internalizes goals and knowledge; [he] almost makes personal pictures. You get readers as close to walking down the streets of Santiago as you can and let them put their own spin on the pictures."

Photographers and editors associate this greater ambiguity with greater objectivity. They believe that the ambiguity gives the reader a truer, more unmediated sense of what a place is like, in part because it engages readers *perceptually* rather than *conceptually*, encouraging them to use their senses and judge for themselves rather than accept an editorial evaluation.

Photo selection is the stage where the favored notion of balance is most rigorously imposed. While thematic continuity is important and while certain elements may be repeated to give the story a specific tone, editors seek to achieve balance along a number of dimensions. This includes not just ensuring presentation of positive and negative dimensions of the subject but combining frenetically active pictures with more tranquil shots ("mothers with children" and "men praying in soft light"), and considerations of focal length and portraiture.

Picture editors are also concerned about the "strength" of photographs. They refer to disturbing pictures (of AIDS victims or of drug culture) as strong or tough. Strong pictures are dangerous because they may offend some viewers or may be seen as inappropriate for children. (They are thus likely to generate outraged letters to the editor and canceled subscriptions). There is some sense that strong photographs are what people get in the rest of the media and that National Geographic should be doing something different. It is revealing that among the people we talked to, the inverse of strong photographs was not "weak" but "balanced"—revealing an underlying framework in which the strong portrayal of conflict and pain is inherently unbalanced or "biased."

Strong photographs are also dangerous because they are subject to multiple interpretations. One editor suggested that photographs of people dying of AIDS in Africa could be read in a number of ways: there are those, he said, who might see them and say, "Those damned Africans deserve to get AIDS and die." Photographers have tended to see this reaction as something that they could control through the ways that they framed the subject, perhaps by limiting the variety of spins that viewers can place on a picture. But in the end "a photographer can only produce a story for him- or herself that feels balanced, and then send it out into the world." The editor who said this pulled out a picture of Chile's General Pinochet with his arm around his wife and asked ironically, "He looks like a great person here, doesn't he?"

Disagreements over whether or not to use strong photographs are often framed as a generational rather than a political issue. People influenced in their training by media coverage of Vietnam, for instance, are seen as favoring tough photographs. Differences that emerge are not automatically framed as battles over timeless values, but understandable differences of opinion that are keyed to the training and social experiences of different cohorts. This allows older, more conservative staff members to give in on an issue without conceding they are wrong, chalking it up to "letting the younger generation have their day." And when they are unable to concede, they can assuage those pressing for change by assuring them that ultimately they too will have their day.

The result of the photo selection process is a set of eighty to one hundred photos that are shown to the director of photography for his input and approval. The slides are then shown to the editor in a picture review session, during which the photos are whittled down to twenty-five or so. While discussion is often heated, the editor of the magazine has the final word.

Photo selection continues to be a crucial process after its first purpose has been served. All pictures are archived, many now on videodisc for easy search and retrieval, and a large number are reused in other Geographic publications, such as Bryan (1987), the magazine's hundred-year *Index*, the centennial history issues of 1988. One can get a sense from these reprintings of how the institution evaluates the relative merits (or market value) of its previous work. Images chosen for multiple reprinting tend to be the safer pictures, for example, a cherubic Russian three-year-old holding up three fingers to the camera, as well as the more beautiful ones.

Selection of "the best" from any photographer's work often reveals much about its sociopolitical context, as Bolton (1990) has shown in his brilliant analysis of an exhibition of Richard Avedon's work and its reception. The organizers chose the least "difficult" photograph for the entrance to the exhibit and the cover of the accompanying catalog. A photo of a smooth-faced teenage girl in overalls was pulled ahead of the mass of other photos, which mainly show people who are dirty, heavily made up, angry, or alienated-looking.

Layout: The Art of Juxtaposition

Once pictures are selected they are sent to layout—a process that generally takes a full two weeks for a single article. This job, which entails choosing the size, order, and placement of the photographs, is performed by specialists in consultation with the photographer and picture editor. Photographs are not matched to text, even at this point.

Layout specialists emphasized that their work is content-driven, meaning that the informational content of the photographs takes precedence

After heated internal debate, James Nachtwey's June 1988 photograph of a man scavenging garbage in Guatemala was printed small to offset its harsh subject matter. (Photo: James Nachtwey, Magnum Photos)

over aesthetic content, color, or other considerations in deciding on sequencing. Related to this is layout's decision on how large to print a photograph; each one must be large enough to be "readable"—that is, for the reader to discern and appreciate its detail. Other criteria are aesthetic—photographs with good lines, shapes, and colors; and the highlighting of the new or unusual in style or subject matter through means such as large sizing or isolation on a page. Layout must also be sensitive to the juxtaposition of pictures, both in terms of form and content. Juxtaposition produces the "third effect," or new meanings evoked in viewers by seeing two photos side by side. Layout editors pay close attention to this effect, both in mundane matters, when they avoid repetition of similar landscapes, or when political considerations enter in. As Guimond has noted, photographs of heads of state who are friendly with the United States are rarely seen on the same pages with images of suffering, poverty, and violence, "presumably because such juxtapositions might imply they were having difficulty controlling conditions in their countries" (1988:57).

Layout editors use design principles to enhance the drama of the story. They try to begin an article with a grabber photograph that is visually exciting and contains information and themes relevant to the article, and perhaps an aerial shot in order to orient the viewer. As the story develops, they aim to strike a balance between considerations of design and the thematic concerns prescribed by the picture editor.

Exceptions to these rules prove revealing. A picture editor pointed out to us a 1988 photograph of people scavenging in a garbage dump in Guatemala that had been printed quite small—too small for its detail to be clearly readable. The president and the editor had disagreed about that picture, the editor feeling it was too harsh. The compromise reached was to print it, but in minimal size. Take also the relative sizing of two children photographed in the same article, one poor and sitting in the street, the other at a computer. Perhaps to communicate the rarity of the latter, the photo of the fortunate child is about one-third the size of the other. The photo of the poor girl is beautified by a brilliant sidewalk chalk drawing of a movie star next to where she is sitting.[3]

In another case, we observed the layout of a story on Efe hunters.

3. There are a number of other possible effects of these sizing decisions. Polan (1986a:4–5) makes the point that a large person or item filling the photographic frame has the effect, other things being equal, of inviting the viewer into the frame while a smaller item within a larger frame can do the opposite. Cropping can manipulate the degree of inclusion or exclusion.

For a stylish smile, an Efe teenager (bottom) endured the agony of having her front teeth chipped to points (below). Later she added to her allure by submitting to the age-old ritual of body scarring in the Lese village (right). Following their sexually active teen years, Efe women often marry around age 20 and soon have their first child. Orange hair on children around the time of weaning (opposite) indicates undernourishment, which the Efe and Lese suffer periodically.

STEVEN WINN

Archers of the African Rain Forest 683

By doing this aren't they creating a false reality?

Detailed and difficult to read, photographs of Efe women's bodily ornamentation were printed small and set next to a smiling young girl in order to balance what editors saw as the "grim" tone of the rest of the article. (Photos: Steven Winn and Robert C. Bailey)

The text notes that women provide the bulk of food in this society. In response to our question, the layout editor told us that pictures of men came before pictures of women because the article focused on hunting. It was not clear, however, why the women pictured were adorning themselves or why hunting was the chosen focus.

In this same story, a portrait of a smiling young girl was printed relatively large, while some highly detailed shots of women's bodily ornamentation were much smaller. They layout editor explained that a smiling face may be highlighted in order to balance a focus on work or the economy. In this case, all those involved in the story agreed that they had portrayed the Efe as somewhat grim, and they had made the photograph larger to counteract that effect.

The layout process is where the story that was initially envisioned is given coherence and emphasis. By the time it reaches this point, however, it has had numerous contributors, all of whom feel some investment in the outcome. Photographers wish to see their favorite photos highlighted. Picture editors want to see themes developed coherently. Layout personnel monitor design criteria. And the magazine editor oversees the work based on his calculation of the impact and popularity of the piece. In addition, a recently established design department monitors articles that emerge from layout to ensure continuity throughout an issue. All of these people may visit the layout department throughout the workday, checking on the progress of the article and negotiating changes. Small wonder that disagreements frequently emerge at this point.

Captions: Dipping the Picture in Lyrical Fixative

At *National Geographic,* captioning pictures is separate from both writing and photography, and equally important. Because marketing studies show that 53 percent of subscribers read only picture captions, not the text, editors see captions as a crucial opportunity to give these casual readers a fix on the article—to expose them to its major themes and give them some information to carry away with them. Thus, it has established a separate department charged with legend writing, which employed ten writers in 1989. Each writer is assigned one article each month to research and caption.

Roland Barthes has described the "anchorage" function that captions play for photographs. A caption serves to "rationalize" a multidimensional image; it "loads" the image, "burdening it with a culture, a moral, an imagination" (1977:25–26). The text of the caption directs the reader toward some meanings and away from others, and thus has an inherently repressive value:

> The caption . . . helps me to choose *the correct level of perception*, permits me to focus not simply my gaze, but also my understanding . . . constituting a kind of vise which holds the connoted meanings from proliferating, whether towards excessively individual regions (it limits, that is to say, the projective power of the image) or towards dysphoric values. (1977:39)

An example drawn from the Society's hundredth anniversary volume illustrates how captions anchor photographs. The Geographic's Frederick Vosburgh, along with three white men and a guide, sit in a cart that two Formosan men are pushing across a log bridge. The white men are

While colonial power relationships are clearly depicted in this 1949 photograph of staff writer Frederick Vosburgh in Formosa, the caption directs attention to the dangers of the ride. " 'Many people get killed on this railroad?' Vosburgh asked. 'Not so many' was the answer.' " (Photo: J. Baylor Roberts, © National Geographic Society)

fully dressed, complete with pith helmets. The Formosan men are shirtless, wearing what Americans commonly call coolie hats. The image is striking for the contrast between the obvious comfort and pleasure of the white travelers and the exertion of the Formosan laborers. Colonial power relations are dangerous ground for National Geographic, however. The caption reads: "On assignment in what was then Formosa in 1949, staff writer Frederick G. Vosburgh and companions rode a push car across crude log bridges spanning mountain ravines. 'Many people get killed on this railroad?' Vosburgh asked. 'Not so many,' was the answer." The caption thus seeks to focus the reader's attention on the dangers of the ride and the primitiveness of the technology involved, rather than on the human relations depicted in the photograph. While this may have worked well for the American audience of the late 1940s, it probably strikes most readers perusing the anniversary volume in the 1980s as somewhat odd. The 1988 reprinting left off, however, where the 1950 caption continued in a vein that now reads as more than odd: "Such questions elicited fatalistic replies."

Guimond (1988:42) has remarked on how the Geographic uses captioning in support of a particular view of the world. He describes a 1975 photoessay, "Iran: Desert Miracle," that includes, among its many images of a "modern, emerging nation," a picture of a ragged boy from Baluchistan, standing by his bicycle. Taken by itself, the scene is highly ambiguous. Viewed in the context of other photographs depicting great wealth, it could be construed as saying something about inequality (clearly a "dysphoric value" from the perspective of National Geographic editors). The caption attached to the picture, however, invites readers to interpret it otherwise: "With the prospect of at least a high school education comes a new wealth of opportunities. Tonight he can dream dreams as vast as all Iran, and waking, may find those dreams coming true." These words direct attention away from the boy's ragged clothing and toward a set of opportunities that are not visible, nor in this case—arguably—were they real. While the boy's bicycle formerly rendered the photograph ambiguous and interesting (How does such a poor boy have a bicycle? What does he use it for? Where has he been with it?), the caption forecloses such thoughts, "holds the connoted meanings from proliferating," in Barthes' words. The bicycle becomes nothing more or less than a symbol of the opportunities described in the caption—the physical evidence that "things are getting better" in Iran and that this boy will find a way to escape his poverty.

Legend writers at National Geographic understand that they must balance presenting information about photographs with developing the stories' key themes. They may interview the photographer to learn about the context, the people portrayed, and the photograph's intention. They may contact the people portrayed in the photos or even travel to the field. To determine the themes that must be developed they interview the layout person, asking why the pictures are grouped as they are. They may end up with a list of topics to be covered. The choice of topics will be influenced by the intellectual and political currents of the time.

In the years immediately following World War II captions describing "new-born nations" and "peoples on the verge of progress" proliferated. Third-world spaces were alternatively delivery rooms and kindergartens as age-old civilizations, through the act of declaring their independence, were reborn as untutored children in the mind of the West. The studied juxtaposition of traditional and modern, always a favorite theme of *National Geographic*, increased in the postwar period. Recent instructions to legend writers at *National Geographic* gently parody (and advise writers to steer clear of) such hackneyed themes.

The recaptioning of pictures reprinted, sometimes decades after initial publication, provides insight into changes in the interpreting of other societies and into the general role of the caption. An intense image from January 1974 shows a black South African gold miner undergoing a scientific experiment. He stands naked in a brightly lit chamber, legs splayed and arms outstretched, starkly silhouetted in an outline reminiscent of Leonardo's sketches of the new body of humanism. The caption of 1974 says: "Trapped in technology's nightmare, a naked research volunteer coated with black paint is bombarded by light to determine the total area of his body—a crucial factor in measuring the capacity to withstand heat. Results of the experiment will help South African gold-mine managers compute the amount of ventilation needed at different depths to maintain adequate working temperatures." The caption strongly implies that the nightmare is only a momentary dream en route to better working conditions and a better life. Reprinted seven years later, the picture is recaptioned in terms meant to draw attention to the artistry of the photographer, but the terms are nonetheless more critical, the experiment now treated as unequivocally dehumanizing: "A silhouette awash in golden light . . . the pattern of diagonals and circles . . . a test chamber of its human guinea pig achieve Stanfield's [the photographer's] purpose—to make us question. What? Why?" (National Geographic Society 1981:287).

Caption writers are expected to produce lively, literate, and concise copy aimed at readers of high-school level. They avoid both "academic" writing and highly informal constructions. The *Geographic* captioning style is distinctive, we were told, in comparison with the typically brief art photography captions. The *Geographic* caption is expansive, allowing for the inclusion of much information, and its style is often lyrical, even ornate. A hazy landscape with Zulu homes in the foreground is captioned in 1971: "Crinkled hills freckled with kraals plunge to the Nsuze River. In this region lies the legendary birthplace of a man called Zulu—which means 'heaven.' In the early 1600's he founded a clan that bears his name, and thus became progenitor of the Zulus, the 'People, of Heaven.' " "Called once more to prayer," says the caption to a 1986 photo of Benaras, India, "an old woman clad in the white garb of a widow makes her way down a ghat [stairway] for morning ablutions. Banaras's population is swelled by widows who, faced with a life of penury, live out their days in austere rest houses. Such is the promise of Banaras—a city of timeworn beauty offering release from a world viewed as but a fleeting aspect of eternity." (See also Hunter 1987: 199–200.)

Caption writers must also gauge the information available to *National Geographic* readers. If they are writing a caption for a photograph of ritual in India, they must decide whether readers will know that they are dealing with Hinduism or whether they must provide this information in the captions. While they are expected to draw out nonliteral aspects of photographs in ways that contribute to the story being told, they must also link the pictures to the world in a way that resolves most of their ambiguity.

Caption writers do not consider their work to have a political dimension, although they concede that their word choice may be controversial. While terms like "guerrillas," versus "freedom fighters," can cause problems, they generally feel able to find neutral terms. We observed one case in a mockup, where the word "elite" had been changed to "prestigious" in reference to an African school. While "elite" has connotations of class and exclusionary social practice, "prestige" connotes a status conferred by public opinion based on merit, and thus plays down the issue of inequality.

Once captions are written, they are circulated to personnel who have been involved with the story. The research department "checks them for accuracy, especially the quotes." They may also be sent to host country specialists or to American academics for checking. The captions in a 1990 article on Dominica were sent to "specialists in economic development, Dominican government officials, academic experts, diplomats, and some of the people pictured" for verification. While verification is clearly a goal, this practice is also designed to ensure that the final copy is broadly acceptable. As one person in the legends department claimed, "We're not in the business of offending people."

Printing: A Creative Process

The complexities of printing at *National Geographic* are too great to go into here, particularly as the process is continually being updated and improved. At several critical junctures in the history of the magazine the quality of photographs was so enhanced that within a few years older pictures looked markedly old-fashioned. Such was the case with the shift to color photography in the 1930s. Other differences occurred with the shift from letter press to web offset about 1972 and from web offset to recessed rotagravure (1977–78).

The original photograph is taken as a guide in the printing process. Working with the photographic exposure, the magazine editor's comments, and the proof from layout, the printing staff develops the image that will be published. They start from the proposition that film materials are "far from perfect in reproducing what was really there." Enhancement processes can, they say, create an image that is closer to the prephotographic reality than the photographic exposure itself.

Some of these alterations are designed to "enhance, repair, and delete"—to take care of problems like scratches on film and lens flares. Others seek to compensate for the "compression effect" of the paper print, where size is smaller and a smaller range of bright to dark is available. Electronic color-correction devices allow them to "enhance contrast, add sparkle, and change the density range in order to brighten the picture, or occasionally produce a print that is better than the film." Using computer enhancement, the printing staff can also open up areas of shadow in order to reveal detail not otherwise visible. The ultimate goal is to "put the photograph in the magazine the way the editor wants it to look—this may or may not be the way the photographer took it or wanted it to look."

Computer alteration of photographs is clearly a touchy issue, especially since 1982, when the Egyptian pyramids were moved closer together so that they would both fit on a cover. When readers commented, the editor responded that the new photo was one that the photographer *might* have taken had he been standing in a slightly different spot (Ritchin

1990:30). Officially, substantive alteration does not occur, but photographers, clearly critical, told stories about engravers who wanted to repair tears in the jackets of poverty-stricken Appalachian farmers or to add grass to barren landscapes. The speed and the ease with which such alterations can be made using new technologies vastly increases the temptation to do so.

Alteration of photos at *National Geographic* has a history, however, that predates computer technologies. Airbrushing to remove blemishes and scars has long been observed. Sometimes the goal has been modesty or propriety. Haraway (1989:160) describes a case where baboon urine was discreetly removed from a windowsill and from the wall below it in a photo for an article on primates. Proofs from a 1966 article on the Nuba of the Sudan reveal a number of instructions to the printer, including "even up flesh color," "delete scar," and "delete" (referring to men's penises—five were "deleted" in the course of the article). When a loincloth did not provide quite enough coverage for the magazine's standards of modesty, "shorts to be added by engraver" was penciled in the margins.[4] And Buckley (1970) reports a case in which the skin color of a partially naked Polynesian woman was darkened in order to render her nudity more acceptable to American audiences. Melville Payne, president of the National Geographic Society at the time, explained: "We darkened her down, to make her look more native—more valid, you might say."

National Geographic does not skimp on the printing process. The board has always been willing to invest in the most up-to-date technologies, as well as in the high-quality paper that is a trademark. The printing operation for the magazine (located in Mississippi, where labor costs are low and factory rent cheap) specializes in producing glossy magazines and high-quality advertising circulars.

The Frame of Marketing and Advertising

The marketing department at *National Geographic* conducts different kinds of studies. Some track *National Geographic* readership on a range of socioeconomic and cultural characteristics, partly by using studies conducted by the Marketing Research Institute and partly through primary research of their own. The department regularly monitors reading

4. We are extremely grateful to Jim Faris (University of Connecticut) for providing us with copies of these proofs.

practices. As a follow up to each issue, they consult selected groups of readers to determine the popularity of particular articles, photographs, and covers, and they test the popularity of cover pictures with the population at large. They know which world areas are most popular, the relative popularity of people versus animals, and what topics are likely to attract readers.

From a marketing point of view, *National Geographic* would be best served by limiting its publishing to what one staff member called "little critter" stories—articles on small, endearing animals, or on endangered species. Africa is an unpopular subject, as are social problems. *National Geographic's* willingness to continue publishing such pieces stems from its commitment to occupying the position of commentator and interpreter of phenomena of this type.

The magazine's editor is expected to strike the proper balance between marketing considerations and retaining *National Geographic's* role as an educational institution that provides a window on the world for the American reading public. Conflicts between the magazine editor and the board frequently turn on how to balance these two goals. The firing of editor Wilbur Garrett in 1990 stemmed, at least in part, from the board's perception that marketing considerations should play a larger role in shaping and determining the magazine's content.

Editors have always been careful to ensure that the selection and placement of advertisements in *National Geographic* is in keeping with its reputation as a serious, quasi-scholarly publication. Until the 1980s, advertising material was confined strictly to the front and back of the magazine. In this respect, the magazine emulates scholarly publications rather than *Ladies' Home Journal,* assuming that its readers do not want advertisements to distract them from the serious material presented in the articles. Because the *Geographic* is in the business of selling its own photographs, such placement has traditionally prevented glossy ads from distracting the reader from the main attraction.

But there has been a notable shift in the kinds of advertisements accepted in the *Geographic*. Ads for tourist services were close to the majority of all those published in the 1950s and 1960s. Some time between 1968 and 1971, ads for consumer goods became predominant. Cars, cameras, insurance, watches, fountain pens, and diamonds are only a few of the relatively upscale items purveyed in the magazine over the past few decades. This broadening of items advertised seems to have been made necessary by the growing expense of high-quality paper and printing processes. Still, the companies advertising in the *Geographic* are an exclusive group, focusing on durable or luxury goods and respectable services that slightly overshoot, in terms of class status, the marketing profile of readers of the magazine. The ads are quite traditional in form—aesthetically pleasing but not gimmicky. *Geographic* photography, like all of photojournalism, must operate in an environment conditioned by advertising photography and must often respond to trends that advertising sets. It chooses, however, not to compete openly with innovations in advertisements in its own pages.[5]

Conclusion

Clearly the style and content of *National Geographic* photographs are not simply mandated from above. The influence of the board is felt at all levels, but the content and style of photographic production is not pre-ordained by the trustees. Though not markedly experimental, staff and free-lance photographers generate a wide range of material. Operating within the brief to offer attractive, highly readable, human-interest pictures, they produce substantial quantities of innovative, interesting, and occasionally challenging work.

Once produced, these photographs enter the arena of negotiation. In selecting shots and shaping them into stories, picture editors play a powerful role in imposing an institutional vision, but their power is not absolute. They may also act as advocates for the photographer's vision, presenting his or her case to the director of photography and the magazine editor. The director of photography and his staff have also, at times, played such an advocacy role, supporting the use of "hard" or personal pictures with which senior editors have not been comfortable. Negotiation, veto, advocacy—these processes attend the production of each article. Their outcome is statistically predictable. Most of the time the photos selected will reflect the traditional taste and conservative humanist vision of the magazine. But occasionally the complexities of the process will yield surprises—challenging photographs that may be slightly at odds with standard practice.

5. The use of a hologram to advertise MacDonald's fast-food establishments on the back cover of the 100th Anniversary issue is exceptional both in the low class-status of the product, and the use of gimmickry. In this case, the "high-tech" look of the ad seemed to compensate for its other problems, and to render it worthy of inclusion. It may also be that MacDonald's—like Coca Cola, which advertised on the magazine's back cover for many years—has reached the status of an emblem of America itself, class unspecified.

While the highly negotiated nature of this process of photo selection brings the risk of conflict, senior staff recognize it as essential. To impose too strict a brief on photographers and the editors who work most closely with them would destroy creative impulses and discourage first-rate photographers from working for the *Geographic*. By granting photographers a slightly wider range of creative license than will actually be drawn upon, the editors seek to guarantee a constant supply of what they consider very good pictures—photographs that operate within traditional realist frameworks, yet contain elements of surprise and interest. At the same time, they rely on certain precepts of institutional culture— understandings about serendipity, balance, and objectivity—to ensure that photographers know what is expected and do not go too far afield.

Four

A World Brightly Different: Photographic Conventions 1950–1986

To make an exact image is to insure against disappearance, to cannibalize life until it is safely and permanently a specular image, a ghost.

(Haraway 1984/85:42)

The result of the production practices and institutional history just described is a rich and voluminous corpus of magazine issues and photographs. Even decades-old issues of the magazine have a significant continuing life. Millions of copies are archived in public libraries, and millions more inhabit the bookshelves and attics of private homes. Current copies are scattered liberally across America's coffee tables and doctors' waiting rooms. This corpus has, then, both historical significance and contemporary impact. To understand it, we begin with an analysis of the surface content of the photos. We ask how people in other lands have been depicted, what they have been photographed doing, and how the photo has been composed. The goals of this exploration are to describe the genre, to glean some clues as to the models of difference held by the producers of the magazine, and to relate both of these aspects to historical sociocultural processes and changes of the postwar period.

In the next four chapters, we look at photographs as they relate to each other (that is, the set of *National Geo-*

graphic magazines of the period) and to their historical and social context (the United States since 1950). We develop our own critical sense of the photograph as an artifact that can be analyzed with some reference to—but not reducible to—its makers' institutional context, constraints, intentions, and unconscious motives on the one hand, or, on the other, its readers' construction of meaning. In reading the photographs in this way, we have drawn on the insights of the social historians and theoreticians of images, including especially Benjamin (1985), Gaines (1988), Geary (1988), Graham-Brown (1988), Modleski (1988), Sekula (1981), Shapiro (1988), Sontag (1977), Tagg (1988), Traube (1989), and Williamson (1978).[1] These scholars have drawn our attention to the many ways in which photographs signify—through formal elements such as color, composition, and vantage point; through narrative structure, including what is internal to the shot and what results from setting photographs in a sequence; through specific items in photo and caption that relate directly to cultural ideas and phenomena outside the picture; through their position in a cultural hierarchy that includes art, television, and consumer goods; and through their ability to assume or ignore, to evoke or discount, their readers' social experience and values.

In addition to this kind of analysis of individual *Geographic* photographs, we took a large set from the period 1950 through 1986 and systematically asked a series of questions about each. We chose this period because we wanted to trace effects of the decolonization process and the Vietnam War. Another consideration was that only after World War II did a large number of people contribute to each issue. Photographs before the war reflect individual as much as truly institutional behavior.

Our method consisted of randomly sampling one photograph from each of the 594 articles featuring non-Western people published in that period.[2] Each photo was coded independently by two people for twenty-

---

1. It is perhaps not surprising that much of the most insightful work on the relationship between images and society has been done in the two areas of advertising (among others, Ewen 1988; Goffman 1979; Williamson 1978) and "documentary" photography. In this latter area, the bulk of the work done has been on early documentary photos in the U.S. and Europe (Moeller 1989; Tagg 1988; Trachtenberg 1989) and of tribal peoples (Geary 1988; Green 1984; Graham-Brown 1988; Lyman 1982).

2. "Non-Western" countries were defined as all areas outside of North America and Europe (the latter including Greece and Turkey). While Canada, Alaska, and the Soviet Union were generally excluded from our consideration,

two characteristics (see Appendix A), many of which will be described and analyzed in the following chapters.[3] Although at first blush it might appear counterproductive to reduce the rich material in any photograph to a small number of codes, quantification does not preclude or substitute for qualitative analysis of the pictures. It does allow, however, discovery of patterns that are too subtle to be visible on casual inspection and protection against an unconscious search through the magazine for only those which confirm one's initial sense of what the photos say or do.

An important set of themes runs through all *National Geographic* renderings of the non-Euramerican world. The people of the third and fourth worlds are portrayed as *exotic;* they are *idealized;* they are *naturalized* and taken out of all but a single historical narrative; and they are *sexualized.* Several of these themes wax and wane in importance through the postwar period, but none is ever absent. While each region, country, or ethnic group has received some distinctive treatment, the magazine's global orientation means that readers may be likely to see all regions, even those occasionally not so depicted, as exotic, ideal, and so on. Together these themes establish *National Geographic*'s style of coverage, and they have, over the course of a century, helped to set an important cornerstone of its readers' definitions of the world. By looking more closely at some of these features of the photos, we can begin to see how the process of world definition is achieved.

An Exotic World

The eye of *National Geographic,* like the eye of anthropology, looks for cultural difference. It is continually drawn to people in brightly colored, "different" dress, engaged in initially strange-seeming rituals or inexplicable behavior. This exoticism involves the creation of an other who is

---

we did include articles on indigenous people of these areas. Articles on native peoples in the United States were not included because they constitute a very special group of people for magazine producers and readers alike. In taking our sample, we used only photographs in which a person was visible (more than a dot in a distant landscape).

3. The coders were ourselves and a graduate student in anthropology. Extensive preliminary coding led to revision and expansion of initial versions of the code sheet. After a final code sheet was decided upon, initial agreement between coders occurred for 86 percent of all decisions. Discussion between coders was subsequently used to resolve disagreements. The photographic features coded are described in Appendix A.

strange but—at least as important—beautiful. At other times and in other media outlets, the exoticism of other people has been framed visually and verbally as less beautiful and more absurdly or derisively different. Movies, television news, and other postwar cultural artifacts have frequently trafficked in revolting ethnic difference. Take, for example, the evil penumbra painted around the eventually self-immolating Arabs in "Raiders of the Lost Ark" or the pathos and ugliness communicated by news images of Latin American poverty or Ethiopia's starvation (see also Postone and Traube 1986). These kinds of ugliness are relatively rare in the National Geographic.

The exotic other is by definition attractive, albeit in a special, threefold sense. When the camera looks for the unusual, it ensures a reader whose attention is riveted by the intriguing scene. It draws attention, at least implicitly, to things that define "us" in our unmarked and usual state of humanness, that is, as people who dress and act in "standard" ways. It also creates a distance that the magazine may or may not have attempted to bridge in other ways. The distance is a product of making the pictured person a kind of spectacle, the latter defined as something that both demands attention and "offers an imagistic surface of the world as a strategy of containment against any depth of involvement with that world" (Polan 1986b:63). One of the effects of the emphasis on spectacle is to discredit the significance of the foreign, even to create a sense of its fictitiousness.

A World of Ritual.   No single feature renders the third world exotic more forcefully than the magazine's focus on ritual. Nearly one-fifth of all photographs with non-Westerners in them feature people engaged in or preparing for a ritual—ritual being defined in the narrow sense of sacred and formally organized group behavior. These pictures are among the most dramatic in the magazine, often chosen by the editors to spread across two pages in brilliant polychrome. A director in the photography department explained that all photographers naturally gravitate to ritual events because color and action make for intrinsically more interesting material. The interest also derives from cultural themes and helps reproduce them. The non-Westerner comes to be portrayed as a ritual performer, embedded (perhaps some would read encrusted) in tradition and living in a sacred (some would say superstitious) world. This is an emphasis that National Geographic has shared with earlier photography of the non-Western world, whose focus on ritual "reflected the assumption of Boas's generation that ritual contained distilled history and cultural wisdom, that it was the most conservative and thus the most meaningful remnant of culture" (Banta and Hinsley 1986:106). In other instances, this focus on non-Western ritual can be consistent with a view of the other as superstitious or irrational and might be responsible for contempt for the native mind (Drinnon 1980:442). *National Geographic* appears not to have taken this perspective, at least in the postwar period and in relation to the world's "great religions."

Much of the text accompanying pictures of ritual in the *National Geographic* makes explicit reference to an area's rituals and religion(s) as part of a long, ancient tradition. So the caption to a 1962 photograph of a New Guinea marriage feast notes that "tribal life still lies locked in millenniums-old patterns." Context for a Tibetan shaman at prayer in a 1977 photo is provided by a caption which asserts that "the ancient Tibetan way of life . . . combines animism with the teachings of Buddha." The magazine tends to downplay a ritual's contemporary actuality and the historical changes that preceded its current form, although religious syncretism is often highlighted as a special kind of contrast narrative. Fascination with ritual stems from the sense that it is a key to the past and a sign of the trip through time taken by the photographer and writer. Anthropology has made parallel connections between past time and other people (Fabian 1983; Price 1989). Two primary features of exoticism—living close to the sacred or supernatural and living with the past—are actually combined in many of these pictures. By presenting the ritual as a feature of custom or tradition, these pictures can also have, for many readers, the unintended effect of flattening the emotional life of the people depicted. This is because the ritual procession can be seen as a routine that people follow rather than as an expression of individual and group faith. The funeral becomes a moment of cultural display (of special paraphernalia or dress, as well as custom more generally) rather than a moment of grief (Rosaldo 1989).

Indexical Dress. In more than half of the photographs in the sample set, the non-Westerner is shown in indigenous dress, tribal fashion, and/ or ritual costume. The *National Geographic* searches out native clothing in its most elaborate form. The Indian woman is often dressed not simply in an everyday sari, but in a gold-embroidered one, and she is festooned with jewelry. A Tibetan couple in the July 1955 issue stand, arms down, in a full-front portrait with little in the background or

The narrative structure of photographs is often organized around an undiluted display of indigenous dress, which indexes exotic cultural difference, as in this 1954 photo of a Masai woman. (Photo: W. Robert Moore, © National Geographic Society)

their gestures to distract from their bright silk and brocade outfits. A photograph such as that of a Masai woman (1954) is cropped so as to narrate a story about native styles of dress.

Exotic dress alone often stands for an entire alien life-style, locale, or mind-set. This is true not only of the *National Geographic* but of other Western photographic work on the third world as well. Local costume suggests something about the social stability and timelessness of the people depicted (Graham-Brown 1988), and in a story drawing attention to the social transformation of a people, changes from native to western-style dress are often highlighted by photographs that set locals in the two styles of dress in explicit contrast. A photo from the January 1983 *Geographic* shows young South American Indians dancing, some in native skirts and loincloths, some in jeans and T-shirts. A central story of the picture, told by way of dress, is of an encounter or passage between an exotic cultural pattern and a familiar one. The Western observer is likely to see Western dress as saying something about the mind-set of the person wearing those clothes. The man in Western dress can be understood as desiring social change, material progress, and Westernization in other spheres. Exotic dress can stand for a premodern attitude, Western dress for a forward-looking Western orientation.

The highlighting of native dress contributes not only to a view of others as different, but also to their framing as picturesque and erotic, beautiful and sexually alluring (Graham-Brown 1988:118). The orange silks and fur-trimmed shirts of the local elite wrap whole peoples in an imagined sensuality and luxurious beauty. Because differences in dress can easily be interpreted as questions of style and because they draw attention away from such matters as conflict of interest, they make the entire notion of difference among people easily digestible (Bolton 1990:269). Difference becomes assimilable to the idea of taste, and, like that concept, allows the renaming of poverty as "bad taste" and unlike values as matters of consumer choice.

The focus on native dress in *National Geographic* shows some fluctuations during the postwar period, dropping slowly over two decades to 44 percent of the total in 1970. A sudden reversal of this trend put the figure at 63 percent in the early seventies, but that increase was again steadily eroded through the next fifteen years. It is not until the mideighties that the proportion of native dress found in photographs reached the lower levels of the late sixties. The editors of the magazine now face a substantial challenge in how they will deal with the theme of exoticism as differences in dress play less and less into defining cultural difference and as more and more tourists have already seen the dress and the festivals that have done the work of painting an exotic other.

The Role of Color Photography. Contemporary *National Geographic* photographs display vibrant, striking colors. Advanced printing techniques now allow ink to be laid down in such a way that color virtually hovers above the glossy page. Giving the magazine its allure and self-definition, color has distinctive qualities both for those who take the pictures and those who read them. Polan (1986a) contrasts the glamorous and wish-fulfilling qualities of color with the mundane factuality suggested by black and white. Advertising photos have, since the 1950s, almost always been made in color, while news photography has until recently almost always been reproduced in black and white. Through these practices, color has become the language of consumption and plenty, black and white the conduit of facts, often spare or oppressive. Color is the vehicle of spectacle, black and white of the depth of facts behind the screen. Accordingly, for journalists and some artists, color photography came to be seen as "frivolous and shallow," black and white, with its focus on light and shape, as "more artistic and creative" (Bryan 1987:295).

On the whole, however, color photography has been perfectly suited to the *National Geographic* project of presenting an exotically peopled world. While photographs of animals, geological formations, and American and European subjects are also, of course, presented in color, color in relation to people in exotic places can and does lend different potential meaning to a photograph. The color of an orange shirt on an American man can be absorbed as a visual pleasure in itself, while orange-colored robes on a Buddhist monk might become "saffron" in caption or in the reader's imagination, thereby underlining cultural difference.

Some photos continued to appear in black and white into the period we are examining, particularly through 1960,[4] and it is instructive to note what subjects the editors have tended to portray in black and white when its use was declining. A significant number of these pictures show the Western narrator of the article, often explorer or anthropologist. It is almost as though the black-and-white photo says, "This is a person of a distinct type, standing to his 'colored' brethren as the factual black and white does to the fantasy, multicolor shot." Here, more clearly than elsewhere, the Western observer or explorer is portrayed as scientist, whose presence needs to be reported but whose appearance need not be examined in detail. Rarely treated in black and white are the ritual, the spectacle par excellence; and the portrait, a study of personality, the "colorful" individual.[5] Declining use can also mean that a black-and-

---

4. Of the 568 sample pictures containing non-Westerners, 65 are in black and white.

5. Ritual tends to be depicted in color ($x^2 = 3.008$, df $= 1$, p $= .083$); only three of fifty portraits are shown in black and white.

white photo is likely to be interpreted as an old photo by contemporary readers.

Idealizations: From Noble Savage to a Middle-class World

The American Museum of Natural History bears striking similarities to the *National Geographic* magazine (on the former, see Haraway 1984/85). Both began as scientific institutions in the last third of the nineteenth century, with the aim of collecting natural artifacts from around the world and making them available to a public much wider than an educated or scientific elite. Both made extensive use of photographs, and both were concerned to present nature as highly ordered rather than random, creating, in effect, a world without blemish or handicap. Just as the Museum's dioramas never included old or feeble exemplars of elephants or zebras, so too has *National Geographic* presented, until the late 1970s, photographs that virtually eliminate the ill, the pockmarked, the deformed, or the hungry.

The idealization of the non-Westerner, like the idealization of nature, has its roots in the magazine's explicit editorial policy. More broadly, we can see this beautification of the world's people as linked to a number of themes in American cultural history. The first is the notion that nature represented a spiritual domain in which the ills of civilization could be cured (Nash 1982). Since at least some non-Western people were subsumed under the category natural rather than cultural, their perfection and beauty would be represented. There are in the magazine traces of the nineteenth-century religious scientism in which nature was considered divine. These pieties, once centered in the wilderness concept and now in some kinds of environmentalism, echo Schiller's statement, "Everything that nature achieves is divine" (cited in Monti 1987:80). The ambivalence toward modernity that arose with the new middle class at the turn of the century (Lears 1981) could also be played out in these views of beauty and nature in a simpler, more natural overseas world.

Another factor in idealizing is an anxiety about threats of chaos or decay. An ideal world, free of suffering, does not require work to bring about change. Connectedness and responsibility are downplayed, as the world's peoples become aesthetic objects to appreciate. The act of appreciating them lets the viewer see himself or herself as both humane (because the photographed are still recognized as people) and as cultured (because the photograph is like a museum piece, a work of art). The beauty of these pictures can also be seen, as Haraway (1984/85) points out for nature photography and taxidermy and as Stewart (1984) points out for the souvenir, as the attempt to simultaneously arrest time and decay and to allay elite and middle-class fears that the wealth of the American twentieth century might be lost.

Finally, in looking for and finding perfection, the *National Geographic* camera may prevent the reader from finding the exotic other *too* different. Motivated by its classic humanism, the *Geographic* has cleaned up the culturally different person in the same way that other photographers have created images of gays and lesbians in America, presenting "clean-cut, shiny-haired, Land's End *citizens with a difference*" (Grover 1990:168). The move to create a beautiful image can stir up new problems, however, for the search for beauty can produce an intensification of the "fracture, partial identification, pleasure and distrust" (Rose 1986:227) that might accompany much visual experience.

We can now consider some of the techniques by which the magazine achieves its idealization of others.

The Smile. Though *National Geographic* editors see themselves as documenting naturally occurring behavior, the non-Westerners they photograph often acknowledge and turn to the camera. Twenty percent of all pictures have at least one foreground figure looking at the camera, and almost one-third of all photos show one or more people smiling. The smile, like the portrait, follows cultural conventions in defining and depicting the person. The smiling, happy person evokes the goal of the pursuit of happiness, written into the Declaration of Independence. These conventions stand in marked contrast to other ethnopsychologies (Lutz 1988) and other, more serious modes of composing the self for the photograph (King 1985). The smile is a key way of achieving idealization of the other, permitting the projection of the ideal of the happy life.

Portraiture. The portrait often aims to capture the subject at that person's best; because it is posed, it allows for maximum control by both photographer and subject. Moreover, the goal of humanizing the other—giving the reader a sense that these are real people—is furthered when people are photographed as individuals and encountered as readable faces. *National Geographic* staff, recognizing the value of the portrait, makes it a staple of virtually all articles. Nine percent of the photos we examined show a person close up and often outside of a recognizable context, and this percentage has remained relatively constant.[6] Many of the photographs that *National Geographic* staff have selected as classic examples of photographs of the non-West are portraits. Portraits frequently adorn the walls of editorial offices; they are heavily reproduced in the book *Images of the World* (1981), which was published to define and celebrate *National Geographic* photographers; and they dominate in a centennial article on the magazine's photography (Livingston 1988). Of the twenty photographs in the article, which describes an exhibit in 1988 of *National Geographic* photos at the Corcoran Gallery in Washington, D.C., thirteen were of people, and nine of those were portraits.

The portrait allows for scrutiny of the person, the search for and depiction of character. It gives the ideology of individualism full play, inviting the belief that the individual is first and foremost a personality whose characteristics can be read from facial expression and gesture. In a related, although seemingly incongruous way, the portrait may also communicate a message of universal brotherhood. Many at the Geographic might agree with Cartier-Bresson's assessment of portraits: "They enable us to trace the sameness of man" (Galassi 1987). They do this by stripping away culture and leaving the universal, individual person.

Benjamin (1985:682) notes that portraits were very popular when the camera was first invented as part of a "cult of remembrance," a kind of ancestor worship. The *National Geographic* portrait may likewise be related to what Rosaldo (1989) calls imperialist nostalgia, that is, mourning the passing of what we ourselves have destroyed. But the *National Geographic* portrait, like all close-ups of only a part of the body, leaves us with a fragment of a person. According to Mulvey, the close-up "gives flatness [and] the quality of a cut-out or icon" (1985:809) to the depicted. This can sometimes be amplified by the namelessness and exoticism of the photographed non-Westerners in past *National Geographics*.

The portrait, then, has potentially paradoxical or different effects on viewers, highlighting the other as a personality, that central feature of the Western self, which yet remains unnamed, unapproachable, and fragmented. The portrait humanizes and yet constantly threatens to be ab-

6. The portrait is a popular form of photography in all genres. The portrait in *National Geographic* is relatively *uncommon* in comparison with family and advertising photos, which prominently feature the face or full-body posed portrait. Further research might reveal whether and how these differences in portrait rates occur by subject and genre.

sorbed into a taxonomic outcome—the mode of much previous photo-graphic work on non-Westerners, which has "presented[ed] them as ethnic types rather than individuals" (Geary 1988:50).

Group Size. When going beyond the portrait, the *National Geographic* still prefers to photograph non-Westerners in small groups. Almost sixty percent of the sample photos show people in intimate groups of one to three persons, twenty-five percent in medium-size groups of four to twelve, and less than seventeen percent in large groups. Although *National Geographic's* photographic subjects were rarely named until the 1980s (the exceptions were famous figures such as Imelda Marcos or King Hussein), individuals and small groups are nonetheless often depicted in what might be read as rugged individualist stances. An African man is shown working alone plowing a field; a Japanese couple in their fishing boat reel in a heavy net. By contrast, print and television photojournalism often shows large groups engaged in mass protests and the like, limiting small group photos to celebrities or the elite. Individuals or small groups appearing in other photojournalism often come in "human interest" stories, where they may include families undergoing a calamity such as a fire or earthquake.

Gentle Natives and Wars Without Brutalized Bodies. In keeping with the stated policy of showing people at their best, very few *National Geographic* photographs show their subjects engaged in, being victimized by, or in the obvious aftermath of violent encounters. Only four photographs from the entire sample show local people fighting or threatening to fight or giving evidence of previous violence. This does not necessarily indicate that the American audience for these images sees violence or militarism as negative; it may, though, when the violence is perpetrated or threatened by foreigners. Thus, to show *these* people at their best requires a nonaggressive subject. Western photographers in other periods and genres have also hesitated to record militant non-Westerners, as when German photographers hesitated to depict King Njoya of central Africa in uniform during a period of anticolonial tension after 1909 (Geary 1988:53–59). In fully twelve percent of our sample photographs, however, there is some military presence, particularly men in uniform. In these photos, the military is presented as a regular, not unpleasant part of everyday life in the third world, but is rarely seen in internal or cross-national conflict. The military as an institutional force has been normalized, anger or aggression erased.

The *National Geographic* represses what some other representations of non-Westerners prominently feature—the violent potential of the savage other. Aggressivity could be and has been seen as a sign of regression, a primitive loss of control (Gilman 1985:99). Violent resistance to empire building, American or European, has usually been treated as a personality trait of natives rather than a situational response to the theft of land or other mode of attack (Drinnon 1980). This view of aggression as lack of control has led to non-Westerners being culturally constructed, like women and mental degenerates, as both physically strong and characterologically weak (cf. Taussig 1987). While other cultural venues have portrayed the "violent nature" of the Latin American, Middle Easterner, or Asian through the twentieth century, this is not the *National Geographic* beat.

Its avoidance of depicting violence between persons has not deterred the *National Geographic* from giving extensive coverage to wars, especially those in Korea and Vietnam, and the Cambodian genocide.[7] Korean coverage focuses on American soldiers, with the country treated as an interesting backdrop and Koreans as a group receiving needed American help. As Sontag (1977:18) points out, the audience for Korean war images had not been prepared by other media to see Asians as victims. A significant number of these and other photos in the *Geographic* show GIs feeding, entertaining, or enjoying local children.[8] One photograph in a 1956 article on the U.S. defense of Formosa is cheerfully titled "U.S. Navy gives an ice cream party."

National Geographic's Vietnam war photography has been called innocent by one of its official chroniclers, in contrast to the grimmer standards of *Life* and other publications (Bryan 1987). In fact, the difference is stark. The *Geographic's* wars are shown through the anxious faces of civilians rather than the corpses of soldiers as published in other media outlets (Moeller 1989). An early article in October 1961 shows little

7. Those articles include, among many others, "The GI and the Kids of Korea" (May 1953), "The Mekong, River of Terror and Hope" (December 1968), "Along Afghanistan's War-Torn Frontier" (June 1985). Issues covering the Vietnam War include June 1955, October 1961, November 1962, September 1964, January 1965, June 1965, September 1965, February 1966, February 1967, April 1968, September 1968, and December 1968.

8. Similar photos can be found in the *National Geographic's* (and *Life's*) World War II coverage (e.g., Bryan 1987:248–49).

evidence of the war itself. Only two of its forty-two pictures show soldiers, one of training exercises, the other of a patrol headed through and dwarfed by a magnificently ornate city gate in Hue. Three pictures, on the other hand, focus on beautiful young women, with captions describing one with a "face as radiant as the moon" or generalizing to "the grace and charm of Vietnamese women."

No Vietnam War photograph was ever innocent or apolitical, however, for all images of that country at war, whether graphic or not, emerged out of and circulated in the highly politicized atmosphere of the late 1960s and early 1970s. The claim of innocence itself involves a politics. As in much other American media coverage, the editorial intent was to support the government's version of the goals and values of the war effort and, in line with the "kindly light" policy, to make the war appear less unpleasant than it was.[9]

All war photography can potentially suggest parallels between gun and camera. It can also make visible atrocities that would otherwise be hidden. The former effect may be seen in a *Life* magazine photo published in 1969 (reprinted in Drinnon 1980:453) showing the anguished faces of a small group of people from My Lai village just before they were murdered. It is captioned in the photographer's words, "Guys were about to shoot these people. I yelled, 'Hold it,' and shot my picture. As I walked away, I heard M-16s open up. From the corner of my eye I saw bodies falling, but I didn't turn to look."

Such pictures—with their vivid depiction of suffering and their exposure of the passive, even accepting gaze of the photographer—are absent from the *Geographic*'s Vietnam articles. *National Geographic* photographs rarely show wounded civilians or soldiers. A 1966 photograph of a war victim's funeral has a festive air, owing to the bright colors of the clothing and the absence of obvious grief in the crowd. The armed soldiers who defend the casket, a potentially ominous element, stand small, squeezed to the side of the frame (February 1966).

This soft coverage may or may not contradict Wilbur Garrett's claim that his photographs have been "stripping away romantic notions and

9. Moeller (1989) points out, however, that it has sometimes been in the interest of the state to have more rather than less graphic images of war published. Midway through World War II, government censors changed policy to allow photos of wounded or dead American soldiers in order to "help 'harden' the resolve of the public at home" (1989:227). During less popular wars and during losing wars or phases of wars, apparently, both the military and the press tread more carefully, trying to avoid offending the public with death images.

Ronald Haeberle's photograph of My Lai villagers just before their murder, published in *Life* magazine, December 1969. While this photograph is emotionally challenging, it is in some ways infinitely less so than Haeberle's views of the horrific aftermath. In choosing to reproduce this photo rather than those others, we confronted dilemmas similar to those we have detailed for *Geographic* editors—the physical revulsion of seeing slaughtered bodies versus the sense that they tell the central story of war, the fear of having our young children see the image versus the wish to educate them, the desire to give readers more pleasure than painful truth. (Photo: Ron Haeberle, *Life* magazine, © Time Warner, Inc.)

Characteristic of *National Geographic*'s Vietnam War photographs, this image of a funeral from February 1966 bypasses violence and suffering. Bright colors and ceremonial paraphernalia render grief graceful, even picturesque. (Photo: Dickey Chapelle, courtesy of the State Historical Society of Wisconsin, © National Geographic Society)

exposing war as a horrible, futile depravity" and that they aim to temper, "at least for one generation of readers, the fascination, the excitement, and the glory too often associated with war" (National Geographic Society 1981:317). This rendition ignores, however, the ambiguity of photos (even those of horrifying subjects); given some readers' politics and some historical contexts, most war photos can validate more hatred of and effort against the "enemy." Garrett's comment also ignores the heavily prowar text and captions wrapped around virtually all pictures of American wars in the magazine. In the 1961 "Red Tide" article, for example, captions suggest a subhuman nature in the North Vietnamese through metaphors of "prowling Communists" and "enemy-infested jungle[s]."

And there is no more celebratory set of pictures than those in the September 1968 article showing the resolute, compassionate, and handsome young American men of the Air Rescue unit.

To see the *Geographic* editorial hand at work, one has only to contrast James Nachtwey's images of war published in the magazine (June 1988) with those of his published elsewhere (Nachtwey 1989). Captions also soften the potential impact of his pictures: a line of war captives in Guatemala, whose faces could be read as fearful of state torture, is captioned "Trying on a new life through a government amnesty program, former guerrillas and supporters receive donated clothing at Coban army base, where they will begin indoctrination toward resettlement in government-established villages."

Images of brutalized bodies, a stock-in-trade of much war photography, are missing from *National Geographic*. In Vietnam and Korea, the magazine dealt only through denial with the fact that warfare "is waged on tangible human flesh and inscribed in pain" and agreed with readers on "the living wounded body as the final *untellable* legend" of war (Trachtenberg 1989:118; emphasis added). While wounded bodies proliferate elsewhere in American popular culture, nonfiction family magazines are the last place they will be found. For such pictures to appear in the media, what seems to be required is either the frame of fantasy or adult status in viewers, as well as a certain politics.

When in November 1986 *National Geographic* hesitantly returned to cover the area of the Vietnam War after a hiatus of a decade, it inquired into the MIA question in Laos. Showing the discovery of the wreck of a U.S. jet in the jungle, the local Laotians appear not as enemies, survivors or victims but as helpmates to the U.S. team searching for military remains. One photograph has a U.S. soldier holding up a rusted American handgun, suggesting both the archaeological status of the war rather than its recency and continuing reverberations in, for example, dioxin effects of Agent Orange, and the harmlessness of the American, now standing in civilian clothes amid sun-dappled greenery.

A Middle-Class World.   The *National Geographic* has presented a world that is predominantly middle class, in which there is neither much poverty nor great wealth (see figure 4.1). It is a world comfortable to contemplate. Like the absence of violence or illness, these pictures reflect back to Americans their own self-image as a relatively classless society, one in which most citizens define themselves as either working class or

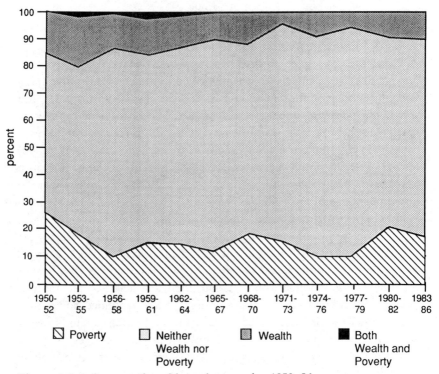

Figure 4.1. Indicators of wealth in photographs, 1950–86

middle class (Davis and Smith 1986:218).[10] At another level, of course, readers know that there are radical gaps between rich and poor in the United States and abroad, and there may be ways that this implicit awareness is addressed by the magazine as well.

There seems to have been a ban on picturing hungry or blemished individuals until the recent past. Exceptions began to appear in the mid-seventies. A 1978 article on smallpox shows its "last victim," a man from Somalia. The picture, small by magazine standards, might show a hint of a smile on the man's lips. Since 1950 a number of articles have focused on famine, including several in 1953, five between 1972 and 1975, and three in the 1980s, but not until a July 1975 article do the first visibly malnourished children show up in our sample of six hundred photos. By the mid-eighties, several articles had focused on hunger or featured some photographic evidence of systemic, non-episodic, hunger.

10. In the NORC-Roper Center 1986 survey, 90 percent of all those surveyed so identified themselves.

In general, a much sharper turn to coverage of human misery has occurred in the 1980s, reflecting the policy divisions and conflicts described
in chapter 2. Many of the strong images of poverty are found in articles
by James Blair on Haiti and South Africa, Steve Raymer on Bangladesh,
and Steve McCurry on several countries. The distress of viewers that is
associated with hunger continues to weigh heavily in editorial decision
making, as in the downsizing of a photo of Guatemalans eating in a
garbage dump.

The *Geographic's* shunning of the poor, the ill, and the hungry
throughout much of the fifties, sixties, and seventies stands in marked
contrast to images in other media portraits of the third world, both
contemporary and historical. Take, for example, *Life* magazine's published review of photography in the 1980s. Looking at all sources, the
editors selected 118 of the "best photographs" of the decade. Of those,
one-third were taken in non-Western settings. More than half of these
depict death, disease, poverty, and war, often in a graphic and wrenching
way, as in the picture of the frozen body of a small girl killed in the
Iran-Iraq war, overlaid by the dead body of what must be her mother,
or that of a dying Colombian girl chest-deep in landslide mud. The
decade's best photos taken in Western settings are much less likely to
show dead, diseased, or physically grotesque bodies.

Gilman (1985) presents evidence that all forms of physiognomic difference between themselves and non-Europeans were objects of intense
interest to Europeans in the nineteenth and twentieth centuries. Both
drawings and photos accentuated the differences, from Chinese men's
queues to the skin color of Africans, often portraying them as patholo-
gies. For many contemporary Americans, the most familiar image of the
non-European commoner is a starving African child. *National Geographic*
images have stood in pointed contrast to such pictures, the ideal set
against the degenerate other found elsewhere. As in the case of violence,
the media present a common cultural pattern of vacillation from angelic
to demonic representation of others (Bhabha 1983; Taussig 1987)—from
National Geographic's unblemished and sunny middle-class smiles to the
television program *Nightline's* more than four hundred hours of angry,
moblike Iranians (often transmitted in black and white or washed-out
color) presented through the 1980s.

This duality can be seen in the context of JanMohamed's (1985) useful
argument (contra Bhabha [1983]) that the ambivalence of colonial representations does not represent genuine confusion within the colonial mind
over the value of the other. Rather, he maintains, "the imperialist is not

fixated on specific images or stereotypes of the Other but rather on the affective benefits proffered by the manichean allegory," which include the ability to create an Other whose goodness and badness seem absolute and not merely social, or so extreme as to be neither human nor historical. Accordingly, "those who have fashioned the colonial world are themselves reduced to the role of passive spectators in a mystery not of their making" (1985:68).

A World of Work.   In a less obvious way, the magazine's photographs also idealize through focusing on people's industriousness. While other historical and contemporary forms of Western representation of the non-Western world frequently show people at rest or engaged in newsworthy behavior, often violent or episodic, the *National Geographic* favors the view of a world at work (see table 4.1). Of the pictures which clearly suggest that people are either at work or play (that is, excluding portraits, shots of ritual, or ambiguous pictures), two-thirds focus on people working at productive tasks. Correspondingly, 63 percent of all pictures were coded as showing people in an active mode, whether walking, engaged in vigorous recreation, or working. The passive or lazy native favored in much colonialist discourse (Gilman 1985) is seldom in evidence. The pragmatic reasons for this emphasis were pinpointed by an editor who noted that photos of people at work provide information on the economy of a country; they allow for more candid shots, as people are absorbed in their tasks; and the fact that they are in action provides more intrinsically interesting photographic material. Such pragmatic incentives, however, do not cancel out the role of the photographs in broader cultural discourses about the industriousness of the native.

Table 4.1. Activity type of main foreground figure in *National Geographic* photos (non-Westerners only)

	%	N
At work or in work context (includes ritual preparation)	37	204
At rest or leisure activity (includes eating)	19	101
Ritual activity	16	88
Portrait	9	48
Neither clearly work nor play or both work and play	18	99
Not ascertainable	1	5
Total	100	545

The Ideal of Virility.   Through *National Geographic*'s eyes, as through the filter of much mass media, the world is mostly male. Nearly two-thirds of all photographs focus chiefly on men, while about one quarter show all or mostly women.[11] While in some cultures there are constraints on the entrance of male photographers into groups of women, it is no doubt also the case that the world of men is seen as of greater interest to readers. The *National Geographic* here follows the androcentric pattern identified in a host of cultural productions, from television serials and school textbooks to movie characters and news accounts. The focus on men, at least in part, emerges from the Western model in which things cultural are masculine and things natural are feminine (Ortner 1974). To search for exotic cultural practices, then, is to search for males. The representation of the tribal person as somewhere between nature and culture makes the issue more complex.

Almost 80 percent of all photographs show all or mostly adults, although pictures of smiling children are a staple of the magazine, with 14 percent of photos focused mainly or exclusively on children. Most commonly, infants are shown in their mother's arms and older children doing chores. Relatively scarce in the *National Geographic* are the elderly, with only 10 percent of the photos including at least one older person and a small fraction of that number foregrounding them.

In many ways, the age structure of the non-Westerners photographed reflects Western cultural attitudes. The invisibility of the elderly in American society, that is, their relative absence from larger households and from media images, accompanies a cultural emphasis on youthful beauty and on productivity defined as the ability to earn wages. The *Geographic*'s treatment of children likewise reflects a cultural set. Its focus on the child alone or in groups of other children is consonant with the sociological reality in which children are not integrated into the adult world of work or leisure and with the cultural belief that the child is a special kind of person rather than a miniature or even protoadult. The romanticizing of childhood is also reflected in their often lyrical photographic treatment, as in the December 1984 shot of two Indonesian girls in the rain, brimming to the edges of both the pages it occupies, with a soft haze of blurred greenery behind them. The girls are huddled warmly

---

11. The figures are 65 percent focused on men, 24 percent focused on women, while the remainder (11 percent) are pictures with an evenly divided gender ratio. We refer here to the gender of adults in the picture. We do not know whether a pattern of male predominance also occurs in photos of children.

National Geographic's romanticizing of childhood is often reflected in the lyrical photographic treatment of children, as in this December 1984 shot of two Javanese girls in monsoon rains. (Photo: Steve McCurry, Magnum Photos)

against each other and against the rain, their eyes huge as they look out from under a flat basket held gracefully by one of them.

Natural Humans without History

National Geographic has typically focused on those whom Eric Wolf (1982) has called the people without history. Wolf's thesis is that Western culture often presents non-Europeans as having timeless societies and personalities. Only now are they seen as responding to the "onslaught" of civilization or modernization; hitherto all dynamism, change, and agency have been ideologically apportioned to the West. This view of the non-Westerner as unchanging and as more primitive than civilized lends itself to the portrayal of the people without history as also the people of nature. Those without history, seated in the natural rather than the cultural realm, have a morphology rather than a trajectory.

Rosaldo (1989) draws a related but more complex picture when he notes that a kind of tripartite scheme has been in use in which the evolutionary ladder has bottom rungs that are precultural (for example, the

Tasaday or Papuans); more thoroughly cultural middle rungs, because some historical dynamism is attributed to their societies (India and Japan); and a top occupied by the Western observer, who is presented as postcultural. This latter perspective on American identity is evident in the melting-pot norm that sees immigrants as gradually shedding, perhaps over generations, their cultural veneers on the way to becoming simply modern people. We might say that Americans see themselves as no longer in possession of a culture but as holding on to history through their scientific advancements and their power to influence the evolutionary advance of other peoples to democracy and market economies. The National Geographic Society headquarters in Washington clearly organizes the visitor's experience around these notions in its opening exhibit—portraits of the Tasaday on the left, a floating American astronaut on the right (time, like English text, reads left to right). The magazine's soft evolutionism contrasts, however, with harder types still in use elsewhere, as in a cartoon in the *New York Times* in 1991 showing the devolutionary process as a descent from Clark Gable to ape to Saddam Hussein as snake.

We can now look in more detail at how naturalization and this evolutionary scenario have been achieved through the images.

The Halo of Green.   One of the most distinctive features of *National Geographic's* coverage of the world is its sharp focus on the people of the fourth world as peoples of nature. This was often explicitly the case in the colonial period, as when an April 1953 article on New Guinea interspersed photos of Papuans in elaborate, sometimes feathered dress, with photos of local birds. In more recent years, local people are sometimes portrayed as conservators, holding a special relationship with nature, rather than directly in and of it. In either mode, the magazine's attempt to cover the earth comprehensively may have lent itself to shoring up some preexisting cultural notions about the naturalness of the non-Westerner, many readers already having an answer to the question of what the following articles in a typical issue have in common: "The Planets," "Koko [the gorilla]'s Kitten," "Yosemite—Forever?" and articles on Jamaica and Baghdad (January 1985). Aside from the effect of juxtaposition, the magazine's self-presentation as a scientific journal has drawn on the equation of science with the study of nature rather than of society, which might suggest why people construed as natural so frequently occupy its pages.

In nearly a third of all photos, the non-Westerner is presented against a background that gives no evidence of social context. This includes pictures in which there is no recognizable background at all, only an aestheticized blur of color produced by a narrow depth of field. It also includes photographs of people against purely natural backgrounds. Such pictures can pass as depictions of the "natural man" of earlier centuries' imaginings about the people beyond Europe and can evoke in readers the nostalgia for an imagined condition of humanity before the industrial revolution and environmental degradation broke the link between humans and nature (MacFarlane 1987).

These pictures of naturalized societies stand in marked contrast to the reverse strategy of anthropomorphism employed in *National Geographic* nature photography. In one series of such pictures, a lioness is described as running a cub "day care center," and a group of chimps is captioned as a "family portrait." Standing more directly at the crossroads of what Haraway (1989) terms the "traffic" between nature and culture is the picture that follows, in which a pair of tawny stallions rear wildly. The caption tells us that the photographer intentionally used the image "to capture the proud spirit of the Spanish men" in his magazine piece on that country (National Geographic Society 1981:334).

National Geographic has focused heavily on people in rural settings (68 percent of the total of sample pictures whose location could be determined). The rural backdrop can serve to tell different kinds of stories, from the jungle fecundity of a sexualized other, to his or her innocence, to the similarity to a Western farmer or frontiersman. Rural photos are more common in certain regions than others, in particular Africa and the Pacific. Regardless of the actual urbanization rate in any world area, these regional differences in pictorial representation are susceptible to characterological interpretations and, even more, to estimates about the degree of civilization of a region.

For the magazine to avert its gaze from the massive urbanization of the planet during the postwar period was standard practice until recently. After 1977, a year marked by the beginnings of change in editorial policy, there is a sudden drop in the number of rural photos presented to just over half of what had been the norm (see figure 4.2). The rural focus had been crucial to erasing a view of class relations within the third world. Increased urban coverage has gone hand in hand with the partial erosion of the picture of a middle-class world painted by the *Geographic*.

There Are Only Two Worlds. Although the magazine focuses on exotic differences, at many points there appear to be only two worlds—

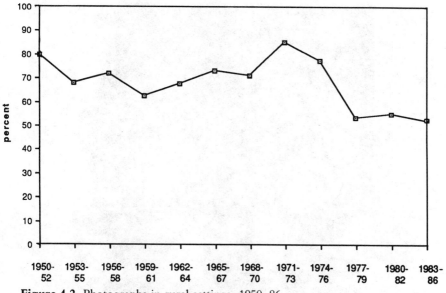

Figure 4.2. Photographs in rural settings, 1950–86

the traditional and the modern; the world before "the West" and its technological and social progress came to "the rest" and the world after. The narrative structure of many images is one of progress or modernization, as demonstrated in the titles of two articles: "Yemen opens the door to progress: American scientists visit this Arabian land at the invitation of its king to improve the health of his people" (1952) and "Progress and Pageantry in Changing Nigeria: Bulldozers and penicillin, science and democracy come to grips with colorful age-old customs in Britain's largest colony" (1956). These celebrations of progress exist side by side with articles suggesting the more nearly equal value of both traditional and modern and holding out a kind of promise of stasis. The caption for a 1965 photo of an Indian woman in nose ring and sari describes her as "Wife of two worlds: Though married in the old tradition, the new Maharani of Rajpipla is a matron of progress. She holds a master's degree in philosophy from Rajasthan University." This framework of balance becomes increasingly common, as when the Apache are said to live, perhaps permanently, in "two worlds" (February 1980).

Why has the *Geographic* focused so relentlessly on photographs and text that set up and explore a contrast between the traditional and the modern, particularly in the post–World War II period? While we will return to this question in more depth later, we can begin here to consider

Photographs contrasting traditional and modern worlds or elements, often showing them coexisting without conflict, were prevalent in the 1960s. (Photo: Jack Fields)

how these pictures play a role in dealing with the changing national identity of the American state in the same period. Increasingly it is correlated with capitalism and contrasted to other economic systems. When *Geographic* photographers and writers talk about their travels as trips through time, the main signpost is often the commodity. When Thomas

Abercrombie describes his decades of work in the Middle East, he writes that

> what makes the Middle East a joy is the time warp. . . . Often I found [people] living out what seemed chapters in the history of mankind. Over dusty tracks or down four-lane expressways, a Land-Rover became my time machine. I drove across the centuries, from Stone Age Bedouin in the sand mountains of Saudi Arabia's Empty Quarter to the old walled cities of Oman; then back to the computerized refineries of Algeria's Sahara, the Rolls Royce traffic of Bahrain's financial district, or the boutiques of war-torn Beirut. (National Geographic Society 1981:143)

The center and the commodity stand for the future, the simple periphery for the past, and the contrast builds an American identification of both itself and its market system with the world's future.

Wolf suggests how contrast pictures might have functioned in the context of cold war conflict between the superpowers. He notes that the distinctions between a traditional, developing, and modern world "became intellectual instruments in the prosecution of the Cold War . . . [with] communism a 'disease of modernization' (Rostow 1960)" (E. Wolf 1982:7). The therapeutic goal could then be to push the third world toward the Western model of modernity, even to the point of saturation bombing of the countryside in Vietnam to advance, according to one political scientist, "urbanization and modernization which rapidly brings the country in question out of the phase in which a rural revolutionary movement can hope to generate sufficient strength to come to power" (Huntington 1968 in Drinnon 1980:373). The contrast between traditional and modern also allows readers to model the melting-pot imperative for immigrants to the United States. The traditional immigrant, these contrast pictures say, is not a threat but simply a stage on the way to full Americanization.

Decolonization brought interesting changes in the structure of contrast pictures, something Pratt drew our attention to with her brilliant analysis of landscape descriptions in Western travel literature (1982). Pratt finds that in both colonial and contemporary postcolonial travel accounts the narrator is often looking down on an exotic scene from mountaintop or hotel balcony. This stance and its related stylistics she calls the-monarch-of-all-I-survey scene, giving its narrator the opportunity to examine and evaluate the whole and to thereby assert dominance over it. Pratt discerns a dramatic change, however, between the colonial and postcolonial travel literature; while both view the landscape from above, the colonial observer glorifies it, seeing a country which is beautiful, rich in resources, and therefore "worth taking." Sir Richard Burton describes his first view of Lake Tanganyika from a hilltop in 1860:

> Nothing, in sooth, could be more picturesque than this first view of the Tanganyika Lake, as it lay in the lap of the mountains, basking in the gorgeous tropical sunshine. Below and beyond a short foreground of rugged and precipitous hillfold, down which the foot-path zigzags painfully, a narrow strip of emerald green, never sere and marvelously fertile, shelves towards a ribbon of glistening yellow sand. (Cited in Pratt 1982:145)

Contrast this with Theroux's 1978 vision of Central America, narrated from his hotel balcony:

> Guatemala City, an extremely horizontal place, is like a city on its back. Its ugliness, which is a threatened look (the low morose houses have earthquake cracks in their facades; the buildings wince at you with bright lines) is ugliest on those streets where, just past the last toppling house, a blue volcano's cone bulges . . . [The volcano's] beauty was undeniable, but it was the beauty of witches. (Cited in Pratt 1982:149)

Rather than the colonial portrait of a cornucopic Eden, here "the task to be accomplished is a negative one of rejection, dissociation, and dismissal" (Pratt 1982:150), the landscape seen as degraded, polluted, used up. Postcolonial writers, who can no longer see themselves as engaged in either civilizing mission or easy appropriation of a country, draw a picture of incongruity, disorder, and ugliness.

A similar, if less dramatic, shift can be observed in *National Geographic* photography. From its inception at the beginning of the colonial era through the 1960s, the editorial commitment to portray the world in a positive light was rarely violated. Decisions to move to a more journalistic and balanced stance occurred in the postcolonial period and have resulted in a new picture of the world which is now both beautiful *and* ugly, ordered *and* disordered.

Two landscapes drawn from the pages of the *Geographic* make Pratt's point. In the first, taken in 1956, a white hiker on the island of Mauritius looks out from a mountaintop over a wide expanse of lush, bright-green forested valley. The sun is out, the landscape looks rich and unspoiled. Come forward to 1982 and a photograph taken from a rooftop in Khartoum, Africa. This is Pratt's postcolonial landscape view, with its muddy, dark colors, its depiction of low urban sprawl, its lack of a focal point. This picture does not celebrate what it sees. In the thirty-year space between the pictures, the white observer, while still at a height, has disappeared, resources have been used up, the sun has gone in.

The Naked Black Woman

Nothing defines the *National Geographic* for most older American readers more than its "naked" women. The widely shared cultural experience of viewing women's bodies in the magazine draws on and acculturates the audience's ideas about race, gender, and sexuality, with the marked subcategory in each case being black, female, and the unrepressed. This volatile trio will be examined in greater detail later. For now, it is enough to point out that the magazine's nudity forms a central part of the image of the non-West that it purveys.[12]

The first inclusion of a bare-breasted woman in the pages of the *Geographic* occurred in 1896, and was accompanied then, as now, by shameless editorial explanation. The pictures, Gilbert Grosvenor said in 1903, were included in the interest of science; to exclude them would have been to give an incomplete or misleading picture of how the people really live. This scientific goal is seen as the sole purpose of the photos, with the National Geographic Society taking, according to one observer, "vehement exception to comments about the sexual attraction or eroticism of the photographs" (Abramson 1986:141). The breast represents both a struggle against "prudery" (Bryan 1987:89) and the pursuit of truth rather than pleasure. The centrality of a race-gender code to decisions about whose breasts to depict cannot be denied, however. With some very recent exceptions (photographed discretely from behind), none of the hundreds of women whose breasts were photographed in the magazine were white-skinned. The struggle against prudery did not lead to documentation of the coming of nude sunbathing to Mediterra-

12. Of the 235 sample photographs containing women, 11 percent showed women in what, to most Western eyes, would be some degree of undress, the great majority showing the breasts. Of the 425 sample photos with men in them, 13 percent showed shirtless men, and less than half of those were also "bottomless" to some degree.

nean beaches, and we recall the case of the photo of a bare-breasted Polynesian woman whose skin tones had been darkened in the production process (Abramson 1985:143). Moreover, genitals are rarely photographed, even where full nudity is customary. In the November 1962 issue a very young Vietnamese girl, bare-bottomed and facing the camera, has had her vulva airbrushed (p. 739).

The imputation of erotic qualities or even sexual license to non-Westerners (particularly women) is one likely result of *National Geographic* presentation of their bodies for close examination. In addition, the nakedness of the *Geographic's* subjects might be seen as continuous with the nude as a perennial theme in Western "fine arts." While some of these women are posed for surveillance and resemble the mug shot more than the oil canvas, many are rendered through pose and lighting so as to suggest artfulness. In Western cultural rhetoric, women are beautiful objects. Their photographs in the magazine can play a central role in allowing the art of photography to exist silently beneath a scientific agenda and thereby increase readership and further legitimate the *Geographic's* project as one of both beauty and truth. All of this elaborate structure of signification, however, is built on a foundation of racial and gender subordination: in this context, one must first be black and female to do this kind of symbolic labor.

Conclusion

We have seen how *National Geographic* presents a special view of the "people out there." This view—a world of happy, classless people outside of history but evolving into it, edged with exoticism and sexuality, but knowable to some degree as individuals—is both distinctive in comparison with other mass media representations and continuous with some prevailing cultural themes. The contrast in the magazine between the other as familiar, one of the family of man, and as exotic is played out in sharper relief when the magazine is compared with those media in which the master figures are Libyan terrorists and Iranian mobs, Ethiopian famine victims and Vietnamese communists. These representations, dripping with evil, threat, and hopeless social and economic disorganization, may be given at least part of their force by the background of unperturbed *National Geographic* images which the viewer of nightly TV news has previously seen. These kinds of broader cultural systematics bear further examination.

The *National Geographic* images are continuous, on the other hand, with a number of themes that have appeared and reappeared over the centuries of contact between West, South, and East. These include themes of the natural man, of societies with no historical dynamism of their own, of the evolutionary ladder of societies with Africa at the bottom rung and Asia at the middle and with all as aspirants for the top—a place equivalent to a modern, Western life style. They are continuous with other long-standing anxieties about the sexuality of the racially different and anxieties that result in a studied looking away from economic exploitation and resulting miseries of poverty and ill health.

This view can be evaluated in a variety of ways—as innocent/kindly/relativistic, as naive/out of touch, as a special kind of neocolonial discourse which ultimately degrades its subjects, or as humanistic/liberal. Ultimately, the evaluation should be based not on the intentions of the magazine's makers but on the consequences of its photographic rhetoric. In what ways do these photos change or reinforce ideas about others held by their readers? How might these photos influence the practices of readers—as voters, neighbors to new immigrants, as white male coworkers with blacks and women, as consumers of products marketed as exotic?

We can now ask how each of these general themes appears when the *Geographic* has looked at any one world area. These regions, which have highly distinctive personalities in American popular culture, each get somewhat distinctive treatment in the magazine's pages.

Five

Fashions in the Ethnic Other

The Tasaday arrive and depart, and others come to take their place, who in turn take their leave and return again. At the end of the anthropological field glasses . . . what appears is the *anthropos du jour*.

(Dumont 1988:273)

In the years from 1950 to 1986, the *National Geographic* has covered almost every nation in the world. It has sought out the kinds of images that other magazines and news organizations ignore, and has emerged with a cornucopia of peoples and places. While the *Geographic* has tended, more than other mass-culture texts, to avoid telegraphing regional stereotypes to its audience, it has addressed the preconceptions of its American readers. In answering questions that they assumed readers at various periods were asking—in striving to be popular—the *Geographic* tells us about shifting American viewpoints on individual countries.

Fashions in Coverage

The magazine has had a long-standing policy of avoiding too frequent coverage of individual areas. A number of regions, however, have received more attention than one would anticipate on the basis of population, and a number have received less. In general, the frequency of coverage of the six traditionally defined world regions in the magazine corresponds to actual population figures for the period. The *level* of correspondence between the population of a region and its magazine coverage, however, varies greatly. Thirty-five percent of all articles from 1950 to 1986 were on Asia, nearly 22 percent on Latin America, 15 percent on the Middle East and North Africa, 12 percent each on Africa and the Pacific Islands, and 6 percent on the Polar regions (see figure 5.1).[1] Latin America and the Middle East have had more than twice the number of articles one would expect on the basis of their population and the Pacific more than fifty times the number. Articles on Africa are found in equal proportion to the region's population figures, while articles on Asia occur at roughly half the rate at which they could be expected.

The underrepresentation of Asia and the overrepresentation of the Pacific are partly accounted for by each region's unusual size and the magazine's frequent use of the nation-state as a unit of coverage. The editorial policy of even coverage then inflates the Pacific numbers and deflates the Asian, given the huge populations of China and India. When these regions are excluded, Africa is underrepresented by a wide margin (see figure 5.2).

There are also differences in the frequencies with which individual nation-states are covered. The countries most frequently covered from 1950 to 1986 are Japan (23 articles), India (21), Mexico (20), Brazil (20), China (17), Taiwan and Hong Kong (14), Indonesia (13), New Guinea (13), Vietnam (11), Egypt (10), Nepal (10), Israel (8), Iran (7), Philippines (7), Micronesia (7), and Korea (6; five cover South Korea, the other covers North). The most strikingly overrepresented countries on the basis of population are Japan, Mexico, and Papua New Guinea.

Both the regional and the national discrepancies in coverage might be explained by referring to one explicit intent of editorial policy at the *National Geographic,* which has been to bring "the remote corners of the earth" into American homes. This may help explain why we find what, despite the proviso above, must still stand as heavy overrepresentation of the Pacific. Traditionally defined as one of the most isolated areas, the magazine reflects commonly held notions when it refers in titles of articles and in picture captions to the "remote Pacific island." The Middle East and Latin America would be considered *more* accessible than any other region, however, and they are also overrepresented. Con-

1. In assigning countries to each region, the "Middle East" includes North Africa, and Asia includes the Philippines. Average population figures for each region for the thirty-seven-year-period were used to compare with representation of articles. Percentages do not total to 100 percent given rounding.

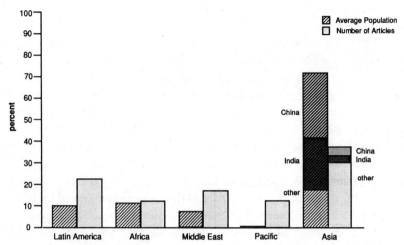

Figure 5.1. Regional population compared to *Geographic* articles published on region, as percentage of total, 1950–86

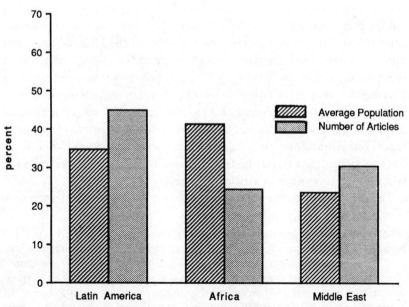

Figure 5.2. Regional population compared to *Geographic* articles published on Latin America, Africa, and the Middle East, as percentage of total, 1950–86

versely, areas of interior China would be considered equally remote, and are underrepresented.

Other implicit criteria must also be at work, and these criteria might be subsumed under the notion that the market for images of particular ethnic groups, countries, or regions varies over time. As we have seen, *National Geographic* editors have marketing information on the popularity of their articles and pictures. More important, they see themselves as sharing cultural attitudes and preferences with their readers, and they follow through on those shared instincts in deciding what to cover and how to cover it. These popular attitudes toward regions do not simply reflect a stable cultural matrix of ideas but are generated and changed in response to world or regional events as the latter are portrayed by television news and newspapers. If *National Geographic* editors see themselves as peeling the onion of spot news, the onion is grown and harvested in these other arenas of popular culture.[2]

Changing patterns of coverage at *National Geographic* reflect, we would argue, what Dumont (1988) describes as fashions in the ethnic other. "Fashion" should not suggest arbitrary fads and fancies; as we will see, there are political and economic foundations to shifts and emphases in the magazine's coverage, which indirectly reflect the prevailing perceived national interest of the United States government as well as public preoccupations.[3] *National Geographic* covers more extensively countries and regions considered friendly toward the United States; and this impression of friendliness is formed in the public's contact with other news media. In keeping with their policy of avoiding negative coverage of an area, *Geographic* editors have ignored countries not in their own or their readers' political favor because they can be defined as unstable, in economic turmoil, or otherwise without positive features to report on. Abramson (1987) finds no articles on the Soviet Union from 1945 to 1959. Conversely, he finds a pro-Anglo-Saxon stance reflected in a very high number of articles on Britain.

The *kind* as well as the amount of coverage given to an area or people

---

2. The very important process by which "the news" itself is generated has been examined by others (Gans 1979; Parenti 1986; Said 1981; Schudson 1978).

3. A time lapse must be taken into account in determining how contemporary events are reflected in the waxing and waning of interest in particular regions or countries. Editorial decisions to produce pieces on an area will follow shifts in national policy as mediated through their attitudes and those of their readers, but will only produce results in published articles more than a year later, sometimes several years.

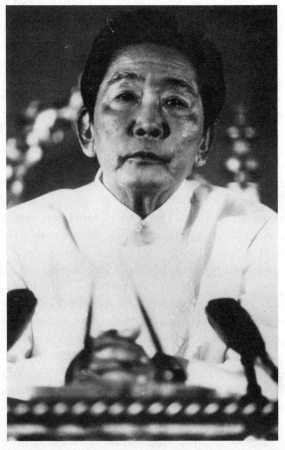

Changing American views of Ferdinand Marcos are reflected in two images, only one of which we have received permission from the photographer to reprint. The absent September 1966 photograph showed Marcos as a family man in front of what the caption identified as "the Philippine White House." That picture appeared during a period when Marcos's regime was being courted by the United States for its anticommunism and willingness to allow American military bases in the Philippines. The photograph reproduced here, from July 1986, shows a less idealized Marcos just before his departure from office. (Photo: Steve McCurry, Magnum Photos)

varies with changing international relations. People or political leaders in favor with the United States receive different kinds of treatment before and after their fall from grace. Take the example of Ferdinand Marcos, whose repressive and corrupt regime was heavily courted by successive U.S. administrations for its anticommunist sentiments and its willingness to allow capital and U.S. military bases relatively free entrance to the country. His portrait in the September 1966 issue shows a smiling family man, with a lovely wife and two happy children. Both the picture's form—which is middle-class, informal family snapshot rather than stiff aristocratic portraiture—and its caption stress how much he is like "us": "President Ferdinand E. Marcos relaxes with his family at Malacanang, the Philippine White House." Two decades later, another portrait of Marcos shows him alone at a microphone announcing his resignation (July 1986). The sharp focus of the shot and its coloration show us facial blemishes and blotchy, oily skin, although this distinctly unattractive face is set above a crisp white shirt and a caption that celebrates him, noting that he "bowed out" of office, "avert[ing] a bloodbath" by his quick departure. The latter picture is less idealized than the first, and shows us not our Asian self but the noble though degenerate savage.

National Geographic responds both to reader interest and to actual constraints in access that may exist for American journalists in particular times and places. These constraints are sometimes explicitly imposed by a government and at other times reflect photographers' perceptions of appropriateness or danger; colonial era photographers, for example, were, Geary tells us, "less attracted to regions that resisted colonial domination" (1988:44). On the other hand, Gilman (1985:35) argues that the tendency to find the peoples of other regions good to think about has other psychological dimensions which work at cross-purposes to these factors in a photographer's choices. In his view, people too distant and too controlled by colonial domination do *not* make good sites for the projection of desire. The *Geographic* may not, then, have always provided its readers with the ideal projective screen by its search for the remote and its tendency to avoid somewhat the too uncontrolled other. The regular news media, in focusing on Nicaragua and Iran in the 1980s, would seem to be more in tune with the economy of desire that Gilman argues is structuring how we look at other peoples.

An equally important criterion guiding coverage is the perceived beauty and value of an area. As we will see, this perception has more to do with racial attitudes and cultural ideas about the nobility of the primitive than it does with foreign policy interests per se.

The special status of the U.S.'s nearest neighbors to the south has been marked since the Monroe Doctrine first enunciated policy. A signal of this status is found in the *Geographic,* where coverage of the Caribbean, Mexico, and the rest of Central America constitutes fully 11 percent of the surveyed articles published in the magazine, and half of those published on Latin America as a whole. Explicit parallels have frequently been drawn between the historical experiences of North and South Americans in both popular and academic writing, and the *Geographic* is no exception. This assumption of commonality leads to the use of similar metaphors and other representations of South America.

Brazil, in particular, is often portrayed in popular culture as a kind of sister state to the United States, complete with the same vast area, wealth of resources, frontier with Indians, and much immigration. The parallels are sharply drawn in a 1977 article titled "Brazil's Wild Frontier: Treasure Chest or Pandora's Box?" The simultaneous identity and nonidentity of the Brazilian experience is expressed in the caption to a photograph of an elderly immigrant of Northern European descent: "Prussian, he came to Brazil when it was still a nation of immigrants and amassed adventures to match his age. Now, as in the United States of generations past, he and his adopted Brazil sense a manifest destiny on the western frontiers." Brazil's experience is identified with that of the United States but then distinguished from it. As with many other countries in the popular imagination, their present is our past.

The image of the Middle East in the United States over the last century has sounded one central theme: the Islamic religion explains *all* cultural, political, and social differences found there (Graham-Brown 1988:6). Until the postwar oil boom, and even since, the region is seen as having a virtually timeless social order, embedded in the invariant Koranic text. The *Geographic* has developed the more general cultural theme that the area is the home of ancient civilizations related in significant ancestral ways to American civilization. Many of its articles on the Middle East focus on the roots of Western religion, with articles titled "Crusader Lands Revisited" (December 1954), "Holy Land, My Country" (December 1964), and "Mount Sinai's Holy Treasures" (January 1964). A book on *National Geographic* photography published by the Society (*Images of the World*) emphasizes the theme of the area's "ancient" roots when it calls a trip to the Middle East "a trip back in time." These religious emphases no doubt contribute to the magazine's popularity and its image as solid, "family" reading matter.

Text and, more rarely, pictures portray the region as enmeshed in turmoil, and, particularly since the "oil shortage" of the mid-1970s, as including countries hostile to the United States. There has also been some focus on the wealth and power of countries in the region from the mid-seventies through the eighties. United States foreign policy has portrayed the Middle East as vital to the national interest. The massive amounts of foreign and military aid that flow to the region, primarily to Israel and Egypt (who together received 32 percent of all U.S. foreign aid in 1987), are an index of its perceived importance. Egypt and Israel's strategic interest and their reputation as "Bible lands" are reflected in significant coverage in the *National Geographic*—they account for more than a quarter of all articles on countries in the Middle East (18 out of 67).

Favorite subjects for the *National Geographic,* as for anthropologists, have been the veiled woman and the romance of the Bedouin.[4] Images of freedom-loving nomads are popular in this and other regions. One prototypical shot is acheived by the photo of a Tuareg man, shot from below as he sits atop his camel, blue sky behind him, and a look of noblesse oblige on his face as he stares thoughtfully off into the distance (April 1974:558).

The image of Asia in the *National Geographic* is more complex. As we have seen,. neither China nor India could be expected to have coverage in proportion to its population. Also crucial, however, is that the People's Republic of China was virtually ignored by the magazine until 1979. The seven articles published on the PRC from 1950 until 1978 contrast markedly with the seventy China-related articles from the pre-Communist, pre-war period, 1900 to 1935 (Bryan 1987). From 1950, relatively frequent coverage of Taiwan corresponded to the United States policy of "recognizing" only one China; six articles on Taiwan appeared before early 1977, and one after that. The sudden surge of interest in the PRC in the *National Geographic* beginning in the late 1970s followed the several Beijing banquets during the Nixon presidency which symbolically marked the official transformation of China from pariah state to friendly giant (see figure 5.3). China was no doubt born again for most Americans by way of the images which began to pour from the magazine; that is, it was both made visible and rehabilitated. Ten articles came forth from the *National Geographic* over the next eight years, none more striking in its message than "Sichuan: China Changes Course" (September 1985). The feature article for the issue includes a cover picture that plays at partially reproducing "American Gothic" with Chinese farmers, husband and wife, smiling broadly into the camera, holding two clean, pink pigs.

4. See Abu-Lughod (1989) for a revealing analysis of the role of regional stereotypes in anthropological writing on the Middle East, and Appadurai (1986) on the same issue in other regions.

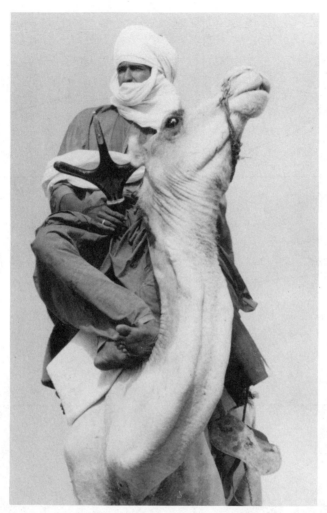

Photograph of a Tuareg noble from the April 1974 issue. The *National Geographic*'s coverage of the Middle East has tended to emphasize the roots of Western religions, nomads, and the veil. (Photo: © Victor Englebert 1993)

This country's military involvement in Asia is chronicled by extensive coverage of Korea and Vietnam. The camera not only covered the American soldiers fighting in those wars; the articles also purport to be about local war efforts and their impact. Detailed coverage of countries at war would seem to be at odds with the *National Geographic* policy, in force until quite recently, to say nothing at all if nothing nice could be said.

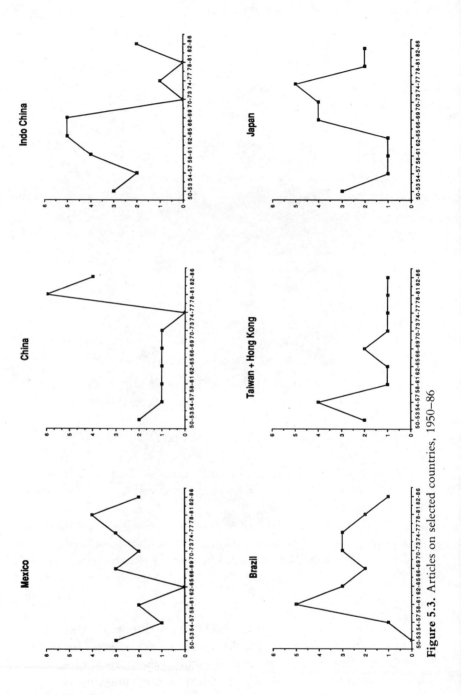

Figure 5.3. Articles on selected countries, 1950–86

And indeed, other wars, not explicitly or openly involving U.S. military personnel, have been assiduously avoided by the journal. Central American countries outside of Mexico are underrepresented in this regard. Moreover, coverage of the Southeast Asian countries most directly involved in the wars sponsored by France and the United States —Vietnam/Indochina, Laos, Cambodia/Kampuchea—follows an interesting pattern (see figure 5.3). Five articles appeared from 1950 to 1955 (roughly the period of the French campaigns), none for the second half of the fifties, and fourteen from 1960 through 1968). For the next thirteen years (1969–81, inclusive), however, only one article on these countries was published. Government support for the war continued until much later, but by 1968 there was no longer a set of purportedly neutral terms acceptable to a politicized reading public. The eye of the *National Geographic* has tended in Southeast Asia, as elsewhere, to follow the interested gaze of Washington, although controversy and conflict within the readership over how to interpret a region seems to have dampened the magazine's enthusiasm for covering it.

At least as striking as the absence of China before 1979 is the profusion of interest in Japan. More articles (twenty-three) have been written on that country than on any other non-Western nation. While Japan's representation was typical for other countries its size during the fifties and early sixties, beginning in 1967, a spate of pieces appeared, totaling fourteen articles in the twelve years from 1967 through 1978, all portraying the country in an extraordinarily positive light (see figure 5.3). The Japanese are more likely than others to be shown smiling, and much attention is paid to the arts, social gatherings, festivals, and home life, all subjects that would valorize and humanize the Japanese for an American audience.

A large number of Japanese images are also reproduced in the National Geographic Society's book *Images of the World* (1981), including many centered on the culture's emphasis on beauty. Coverage of local artists can help build a positive image of a country, given that the artist is seen as contributing objects to the pinnacle of a cultural hierarchy and that his or her creativity can sometimes be portrayed as "rupturing" tradition (Price 1989:46). (Although Japanese art is not presented in that fashion in the magazine, Brazilian and Iraqi art are, in two issues from 1978 and 1985.) The notion of an aesthetic country is illustrated by a two-page layout (June 1976:844–45) of human-made artifacts of beautiful patterning, including one photo of a tea picker, his body in a graceful curve under the burden of his basket amidst evenly spaced, bright green waves of tea bushes.

The themes of industry and success ("success" appears in the titles of two articles) are prominent, drawing on American readers' ideas about what constitutes a sensible and good set of human goals or values. The idea that the Japanese represent a special case of a non-Western people who have achieved the full measure of progress thought to belong to the West is also evident in the treatment of nineteenth-century photographs from Japan in Banta and Hinsley (1986). Reading one photograph of a samurai warrior, they note his "imposing stance" (1986:40) and claim that the Japanese generally maintained their identity in front of the camera "without being shadowed by Western interpretation" (1986:43), this in contrast with many other peoples documented by nineteenth century photography. The Japanese here, as in the pages of *National Geographic,* are portrayed as strong, non-manipulable, and unique.[5]

The Vietnam War may have influenced the efflorescence of Japan in the magazine, for it begins to be covered at the same time (1967) that Vietnam and Southeast Asia suddenly disappear (1968) from the pages of the magazine. Positive images of the Japanese could serve as an antidote to the "bad Asian," whose Vietnamese face was constantly being studied across the American media. In an astute analysis of the rise and fall of interest in the Tasaday people of the Philippines in the early seventies, Dumont (1988) claims that they represented for many Americans the "good savage" as reprimand and reminder of the Vietnamese "violent savage." More generally, Dumont suggests that the duality of Western views of the other, as either good and peaceful or bad and violent, led to the requirement that the savage Vietnamese have their noble counterpart. While his argument that the Tasaday play that role is convincing, it is a role that required ample buttressing. *National Geographic's* treatment of Japan (and presumably that of other media) may

5. This view of the Japanese is also consistent with late nineteenth- and early twentieth-century American views. Rydell's description of the reception of the Japanese exhibit to the Chicago World's Columbian Exposition of 1893 sounds remarkably like both *National Geographic* and the coverage of that country by other contemporary American media. "The astonishing progress of Japan in arts and civilization," reported the *Inter Ocean,* "is one of the wonders of the age." Not only was Japan rapidly progressing, it was doing so without moral decadence. *The Popular Science Monthly* attested to the purity and decency of Japanese life: "Filial piety, connubial affection, parental tenderness, fraternal fondness" (1984:50).

be interpreted as giving the necessary support. The dualism the Japanese help to build is a slightly different one; they stand as the civilized alien as opposed to the savage alien. Is this a more salient distinction for contemporary American readers and makers of *National Geographic* than that between noble and ignoble savage? And does the distinction now, as in previous periods in history, revolve around perceptions of race? As much is suggested when the prominence of Japan is contrasted with the underrepresentation of "darker" areas of the globe.[6]

Africa is, outside of the People's Republic of China, the most under-represented area of the world. In some ways this is puzzling. Africa has many of the attributes that otherwise qualify an area for inclusion in the magazine: it has a great diversity of cultures, a cornucopia of ethnic groups whose material culture is often distinctive and picturesque to Western eyes, and a large hinterland outside of the modern transportation system that retains the lure of the relatively "undiscovered." Africa has the exotic in abundance. What Africa does not have is either the imputed strategic value of other world regions such as Latin America and the Middle East or the imputed beauty and civilization of Asia and the Pacific.

Race is the background text that appears to constrain the roving eye of the camera. Black Africa, the dark continent of the Victorians, re-mains outside the camera's flash for reasons that are perhaps little dif-ferent from those which influenced the nineteenth-century European explorers and home consumers of images of the non-Western world (Hammond and Jablow 1977; Monti 1987). In the scale of evolutionary progress, which was thought to reach its pinnacle in the English, Afri-cans were found at the bottom of the human scale, while Asians fell midway between the two groups (Rydell 1984). The poor standing of Africa in this earlier period persists, as shown by research on school textbooks in which Africa is equated with the tribal and the primitive (Preiswerk and Perrot 1978:81–82). While *National Geographic* has been concerned with "the world and all that is in it," local notions of what is worth knowing nonetheless enter in. Whether it is contemporary state policy that defines the strategically worthwhile or long-standing Western

6. During World War II, by contrast, the Japanese received a heavily racist treatment in political cartoons (Dower 1986). In contrast to the German enemy, who were depicted as big, brutal humans, the Japanese were frequently shown as small, myopic monkeys. A related phenomenon occurred in war photogra-phy, where the mutilated bodies or soldiers dying painfully were almost exclu-sively Japanese rather than German (Moeller 1989:228–34).

cultural views that influence the value the eye wishes to behold, Africa sits at the periphery of the gaze.

The articles on Africa which do appear in *National Geographic's* pages are among the least popular, according to surveys done by the promotions department (see figure 5.4). On a scale of 1 to 942, articles on Africa average a popularity score of 761, while the average for all other regions combined was 522 (still below the mean for articles of all types). A particularly unpopular mix appears to be coverage of social problems in Africa. Articles in the last decade entitled "Encampments of the Dispossessed," "Somalia's Hour of Need," and "Eritrea in Rebellion," fall in the bottom 6% of articles ranked by popularity. There was, in fact, a higher percentage of articles whose titles mention problems on Africa (60 percent) than on any other region. The average for other regions was 34 percent negative, with the Pacific having the lowest coverage of problems (21 percent). As we will see, reader response to African photographs draws on notions of race and social evolutionism generated elsewhere in popular culture.

This is not to say that American readers simply dismiss material on Africa. Some force has been retained by the European tradition which saw Africa as "a land of overwhelming charm because everything is

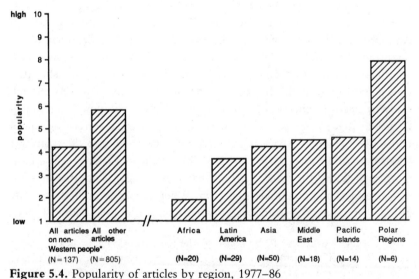

Figure 5.4. Popularity of articles by region, 1977–86
*This average has been computed on the basis of each article's rank-order popularity. Therefore, the means for individual regions do not average to this figure.

excessive, incommensurable, prodigious, incomprehensible, and, in short, inhuman." (Monti 1987:81) There is a long-standing sense that the value of Africa lies in its hold on remnants of free and primordial nature, something reflected in its popularity as a subject of American fiction and art (Torgovnick 1990). For contemporary Americans, the *Geographic*'s focus on African wildlife has helped to secure, along with innumerable television nature shows, Africa's continued reputation as the main site of a fantastic and untamed nature. In both the nineteenth and the later twentieth century, however, the African people have been dwarfed in imagination by their landscapes and animals, as they were in the 1990 *Geographic* article on Botswana, which consisted mainly of animal photographs.

Paradise and the Black Narcissus: The *National Geographic*'s Pacific

A closer analysis of the portrayal of one region can give us a more fine-grained sense of how coverage responds to national interests and preoccupations. Because the Pacific has occupied a privileged place in the pages of *National Geographic* and because one of us has specialized in the ethnography of the area, we examine this region in greater detail. Among the most important factors contributing to its frequent coverage (67 of 592 non-Western area articles from 1950 to 1986) is the romantic image that the region has for Americans, one both tapped and recreated by *National Geographic,* as one of the last unpolluted areas of the world. As Brookfield notes (1989), "The developed world loves the stable Pacific it has created through its own mythology. . . . Brilliant blue lagoons, white beaches, palm trees, and smiling, gaily dressed people twanging sugary music on imported guitars are the key elements of an image loved from Trömso to Dunedin" (14). Pacific area coverage can appeal to the lure of both those characterized as Stone Age people, primarily Papuans, and those in Polynesia and Micronesia portrayed as gentle nobility. A striking evocation of Gauguin's paintings of Tahitians is found in a hazy, attractive, double-page photo of two lounging Micronesian women (October 1986:490–91), their hands and poses gesturing openness, even availability. Titles of articles and captions of pictures have reflected these images by referring to "paradise" and "Eden" and by playing on themes of romance and sensuality: Tahiti, for example, is "every man's vision of delight" (July 1962:1). To maintain its high circulation, the magazine must appeal to preexisting, culturally tutored

An October 1986 photograph of two Ulithian women portrays them in a style reminiscent of Gauguin's Polynesian paintings. (Photo: David Hiser, Photographers/Aspen)

notions about the Pacific, as well as search for a novel, more stimulating image of the area. This dialectic of familiarity and novelty is played out in single articles and across decades.

While photos of the Pacific tell time-tested stories about a world of plenty, sensuality, and orderly social change, they have also told a radically changing story about a Pacific that, like much of the third world, is increasingly degraded and dangerous. We will examine these latter photographic changes as well. But the Pacific has been perceived until very recently as firmly within the American sphere of influence, and its people portrayed as particularly friendly. The history of the representation of the Pacific in the West goes back much further, of course.

In his monumental art history (1985), Bernard Smith demonstrated that Europeans' drawings of the Pacific in the late eighteenth and early nineteenth centuries reveal as much about European ideas of the exotic islander as about Pacific societies themselves. These ideas were varied by period and by promulgator (missionary, scientist, sailor), and the iconography is Smith's key to those differences. In one example, we are

Two English artists' versions (above, from 1784; below, from 1837) of a scene of human sacrifice in Tahiti. The later version, more influenced by missionary purposes, accentuates elements (such as the skulls) that suggest savagery. (1784 version, © British Museum)

shown several versions of a popular woodcut by John Webber depicting human sacrifice in Tahiti. The missionary purpose of one reproduction, the lower one, has led to the accentuation of those features of the original which would suggest the savagery of the Tahitians. The background field of skulls and emotionally provocative drummers are brought forward and the Tahitians rendered as "squat, very swarthy [read racially different], and barbaric" (1985:318).[7]

Photography took over the role of the graphic artist in the twentieth century in representing the Pacific for a Western audience, most prominently through tourism advertising, Hollywood movies, World War II photojournalism (see Lindstrom and White 1990), and the *National Geographic,* which remains one of the major routes by which Americans of the postwar generation have constructed their image of the region.[8]

Although the Pacific photographs in *National Geographic* share many features with those from other regions, they differ in telling ways. Pacific people are shown smiling more often than those in any other region. They are more often seen in leisure activities and sitting or lying passively. Shown in Western-style dress more frequently than anyone but Latin Americans, they are portrayed in the presence of Western technology as often as people elsewhere are. These comparisons will be explored below in connection with the photographic coverage of Micronesia.

Micronesia: Sensual Women and Skillful Sailors, Crossing Centuries. Micronesia has been covered as a region twice in the period we are examining, first in 1967 and again in 1986. Comparison of the photographs in these two articles reveals some dramatic contrasts and even more striking parallels in the narrative content and style of the pictures. These emphasize the "toplessness" of its women, the exoticism of its dancers, the romance of its navigators, and the juxtaposition of things native and things modern or Western, including the artifactual remnants of World War II.

7. Here and elsewhere in the iconography of the period, drawings of the human figure announce their makers' adherence to a variety of ideals, including those of soft primitivism, in which the purported sentimentality, sensuality, and luxury of the primitive world are celebrated, or hard primitivism, in which the natives' value is seen to inhere in their "heroic stoicism," self-discipline, and courage.

8. For many older readers of the magazine, the mainly black-and-white photographs of war in the Pacific must have contrasted sharply with the later colorful images of plenty in the *Geographic*'s Pacific. Moeller (1989:238–39) has pointed out that the effect of photographing in bright tropical sunlight gave the World War II Pacific photojournalism a distinctive feel in comparison with photographs from Europe; she notes that sharp blacks and whites, and a wide range of grey tones gave them a clarity and crisp aesthetic which might also have given a more positive sheen to the region itself in the minds of viewers.

The most important of these four narrative threads is the first: the woman with breasts. The opening two pages of both articles include a full-page shot of a teenage, topless woman in indigenous dress, taken from the knees up, nearly full face to the camera. Both pictures are relatively aestheticized, depicting the women in soft light with blurred backgrounds, emphasizing sensuality. Additional topless women appear in each article, though many more in 1967. While the *National Geographic's* search for the topless woman is by no means limited to region, articles on the Pacific feature far more toplessness than other areas. Fully thirty-two percent of all pictures in our sample that included at least one woman also included toplessness—more than three times the rate for any other region.

The second story told is about the dancing arts of Micronesian women and men, both showing stick dancers in energetic leisure. In this, they follow the pattern of presenting the other engaged in exotic pursuits, including ritual, and of accentuating spectacle. This suggests a continuity with the Western representations of earlier periods in which Oceanic people were seen as living in an earthly Eden where fruit dropped to the ground and people lived lives of easy, if undisciplined, affluence. The Pacific's peasants, taro gardeners, and wage laborers are crowded aside by these dancers and loungers.

If Pacific women are sexual icons, its men (at least in their Micronesian and Polynesian guises) are skillful navigators. While in this respect, the *National Geographic* may reproduce in some simple form a native Pacific view of masculinity as fundamentally a thing of the sea, its take is somewhat different. In both 1967 and 1986, the canoe is made part of a story about people who sail between two worlds. The canoe becomes a route out of a traditional life-style as much as an icon for it. We can see this in the caption of a canoe crew which focuses on the navigator's education in the United States, while others show Puluwat navigators shopping in a store for Western manufactured goods and returning home from their "shopping spree." The romance of the navigator is depicted in another shot of canoes in full sail at sunrise, here paralleling a theme in film and in ethnographic writing on the Pacific.

A final continuous narrative thread in the photographs is the radical juxtaposition of Micronesian and American elements to tell a story about the effects of the coming of modernity to the premodern world of the Pacific. While the story is told in different ways in the sixties and the eighties, as we will see in a moment, the narrative structure is the same. In picture after picture, both pictorial composition and caption tell us to see the march of time, often of progress, in the synchronic elements. The new Western element is tacked onto an old Micronesian pattern, often to improve on, supplement, or substitute for that pattern: the layout of a page in 1967 tells us to see the contrast between rather than within pictures, as when a Micronesian navigator's stick chart is placed just before (and sized a bit smaller than) a United States Navy man's radar screen.

In these pictures, the contrast is presented as an anomaly that has resulted from the Micronesians being out of historical time, out of world space, or out of sync with a more common world developmental cycle. The area has been outside history; the picture of a Peace Corps volunteer teaching children with polio to swim is part of a pattern, the caption says, of "helping Micronesians catch up to a century that almost passed them by." The area is also in a kind of warped space: numerous captions to the contrast photos say that Micronesians "look for a place in the modern world" (1967) and are "about to step onto the world stage" (1986). Occasionally Micronesia is portrayed as a child maturing into the adulthood of Western technological and cultural patterns, even while the retention of traditional elements is portrayed as a strong, beautiful feature of the society, as when the 1986 article is titled "The Birth of Nations" and when the caption to one set of photos of people in indigenous dress tells us that "the innocence of Eden still sets Yapese styles."[9]

These pictures are also often intended to explain the colonial situation. They present it as something which *naturally* evolved from World War II and the Micronesians as having chosen everything that followed, either taking or buying the commodities that stand for modernization. The value of modernization (and implicitly the benefits of colonization) shifts somewhat over the period, but the story is always about the Micronesians' move through this version of the social evolutionary tale prevailing from 1950 forward.

While the picture contrasting modern and traditional is a fundamental building block of many *National Geographic* articles on the non-Western world, the frequency of this type in Pacific articles might explain the popularity of the region for Western audiences. The Pacific pictures in our sample focus on rural areas as much as or more than other regions'

9. There is an interesting reversal in the relationship between the titles of these articles and their themes. The 1967 article is titled "The Americanization of Eden," suggesting an ambivalent view of the process of acculturation even while the pictures and their captions are merely celebratory. The 1986 title more strongly suggests the notion of progress and development, which is denied by its pictures. Thus each era contains the theme of the other in muted form.

pictures, but people in them are shown, more than in any other region, in the presence of Western technology and wearing western-style dress. Here, as in the earlier periods described by Smith, Pacific islanders may be represented as a relative to the American or European, a simpler version of ourselves, or at least a people easily and readily being transformed into moderns (read Westerners).[10]

Decolonization and the Pollution of Micronesia.   Many things have changed in the Pacific communities photographed during the twenty years between these two articles, and the photographs reflect some of them. What has also changed, however, are American and *National Geographic* institutional notions about themselves and their relationship to the rest of the world. The independence of African states and the defeat of American forces in Vietnam stand out as two elements of the decolonization process that disrupted an earlier post–World War II American self-image as an all-powerful, progressive, paternalistic state called to the job of developing the world and protecting it from communism. While these changes have not gone so far as to prevent popular support for the invasion of Panama or the massive bombing of Iraq by the United States, they have meant fundamental changes in how that other, who is less controllable, is conceptualized. As the perceived dynamics of international relations shift from East–West to North–South, the third world becomes seen (in mass media images if not in much popular thought) less as a set of pawns in European chess matches than as a powerful, more agentic and often treacherous set of peoples, less as a place of pleasant possibilities, more as a degraded environment.[11]

Take two pictures with strikingly similar content and composition.

10. These same four themes are foregrounded in a 1952 article on Yap. While the article's narrower scope kept it from inclusion in the analysis here, it too includes a full-page portrait of a topless woman in a grass skirt (p. 813), a picture of a line of dancers (p. 816), two pictures of boats in use or construction (pp. 809, 825), and three pictures contrasting Western progressive elements with traditional Micronesian ones, the latter positioned precisely below the former in the photographic frame.

11. The changes to be described are at both national and institutional (National Geographic Society) levels. The latter include a shift during the 1980s in editorial policy to attempt to move away from the "rose-colored glasses" approach editors at the magazine acknowledged to have existed and toward a more "journalistic" one, more "in touch with reality." These changes, described in previous chapters, can be seen as the result of the international changes described rather than providing competing explanations for changes in photographic style and content.

Both show a Micronesian atoll beachfront. Both are large-format pictures running across two pages, and both show lagoon with small wading figures to the left, beach to the right, and the rusting metal brought by colonial powers in the lower right foreground.

The meaning of the rusted metal and thus of the whole scene is fundamentally different in the two pictures. The airplane carcass, the 1967 caption informs us, is a boon to the Micronesians, for "scrap metal provides the Territory's second most valuable export." The rusted metal on Ebeye in 1986 is "pollution in paradise, junk overwhelm[ing] a beach." Neither the scale of the trash in 1986 nor the captions are needed, however, to send the pictures' intended messages. The lyrical curve of the beach in 1967 gives way to the harsh straight line of the 1986 shoreline, the sense of envelopment and closure of one to the anxiously endless perspective of the other; the bright, sunlit, optimistic colors of the former to the muddy, forbidding tones of the latter; the small parent-child group here to the anomic individuals there. The expansive sky of an earlier period is squashed years later; neither the graceful palm frond nor any touch of greenery remains in 1986.

The later picture stands not just for Ebeye, but for all of Micronesia and the Pacific. This is so for two reasons. A significant proportion of *National Geographic* readers do not look at either captions or text, and so will not know where in Micronesia Ebeye is or how general the problem is. In the 1986 article the only beachfront picture is an aerial photograph. In addition, beaches are the essence of the Pacific for many Westerners, as travel posters attest; the beach should be a scene of pleasure, not of work or unpleasant sights. If the Pacific is paradise, as the caption and countless other cultural images tell us, then our despoiling of it is sacrilege here, merely commonplace elsewhere. Moreover, the 1986 lagoon suggests something not just about the Pacific but about the potential end to the dualism of the civilized and the natural human. The tragedy suggested by the picture and its caption is the end of our ability to define ourselves by way of this long-standing dualism. These pictures replicate, in many ways, the pattern of postcolonial disillusionment with the formerly colonized world described by Pratt (1982) and discussed in the last chapter.

Contrast three other photos which tell of the encounter between traditional and modern in Micronesia. A 1952 photo shows a U.S. official shaking the hand of a Yapese man who has just been elected in an "American style" vote. The man has changed his loincloth for Western clothes only out of respect for the American, the caption informs us.

The shame of tradition, the need for progress, and the long road to modernization are all suggested. In 1967, technology and commodities stand as America's most fundamental contribution to Micronesia. Sunglasses, radios, books, even teen culture are an unalloyed boon, as indicated by a two-page spread of a topless teenage girl photographing a loinclad boy next to his shiny red motor scooter. In another photo, teenagers in native dress of lavalava and loincloth use microscopes and pipettes in their classrooms. The bright lighting and the smiles seen in these pictures suggest that the threshold to modernity has been crossed. Both worlds—the traditional and the modern—are portrayed as valuable.

By 1986, however, the juxtaposition of modern and traditional elements in a series of Micronesian photographs is jarring, absurd, even senseless. Western contributions are often portrayed as negative, as when a full-page shot teems with cases of beer being unloaded in Belau. A young Belauan man, wearing a loincloth and diving goggles sits under water in the rusting cockpit of a sunken World War II Japanese airplane, his face distorted by water pressure, his presence there seeming ludicrous. The beachfront shot on Ebeye shows nothing but mounds of trash alongside a dark lagoon; here there is no traditional world left to contrast with the modern.

American democracy *is* celebrated, however, with pictures showing a happy campaigning candidate and proud, smiling students holding up their new flags. A potential ironic comment on the contrast between flashy flag-symbols and the dilapidated school building behind them, is muted by the captioning: "New flags go on proud display at Truk state's Xavier High School, still scarred by World War II shells."

Similarly, the articles both show slum housing but undermine the visual message in different ways. The 1967 picture shows a woman and child in the doorway of a shack; the caption says this, too, is progress: "Yearning for jobs, schools, movie theaters, and American food and clothing, Micronesians move into such homes to be near district centers and military bases." This picture and caption occurred at the same time that American policymakers were advancing the same kinds of arguments about urban migration and poverty, illustrated by infuential political scientist Samuel P. Huntington's observation that "the urban slum, which seems so horrible to middle-class Americans, often becomes for the poor peasant a gateway to a new and better way of life" (cited in Drinnon 1980:372). The only such picture in 1986 shows "substandard" houses along the road in Ebeye, but it is almost too small to be readable;

A May 1967 photograph of rusting metal on a Micronesian atoll beachfront is captioned "Scrap metal provides the Territory's second most valuable export." Beyond the rusting metal the scene is tranquil and sunlit. (Photo: Jack Fields)

Another photograph showing scrap metal on a Micronesian atoll beachfront, twenty years later (October 1986) into the postcolonial era, emphasizes degradation and lowered horizons. (Photo: Melinda Berge)

it too is captioned on a positive note: "The U.S. is financing an intensive program to improve living conditions on Ebeye." Ebeye is not shown in 1967. When it does make an appearance, layout has been careful to avoid placing pictures of the lush Kwajalein missile base on the same page with those from Ebeye. Here as elsewhere, the *Geographic's* explicit attempt to achieve a balanced account can be construed as its aiming to present both pleasant and unpleasant facts about an area without connecting the two kinds of facts in a historical or sociological analysis.

The American role in Micronesia, no less significant today than in 1967, is nonetheless muted in the 1986 issue. The American presence is foregrounded in 1967, with four pictures showing Americans in helpful roles (a store owner, a missionary, a science teacher, and a Peace Corps volunteer) and an unabashedly celebratory picture of U.S. military power (a large-format, double-exposure shot of a missile taking off from Kwajalein overlaid with a large American flag waving in the foreground, bathed in misty exposure). In 1986, Americans have all but disappeared, and those who remain are shown shopping at a Kwajalein supermarket and providing medical aid. The American military role is almost erased: the 1967 missile and flag photo becomes, by 1986, a small picture of the trails of a rocket targeting Kwajalein's lagoon. The Americans have retreated from direct contact, not in reality (missile testing was as active as ever) but in image, as their relationships with these others becomes more conflicted, difficult, and ambivalent. Between the confident paternalism with which an American teacher stands behind his students working on a laboratory project in 1967, presenting them with the unambivalent good of Western science, and the depiction of people lined up for food programs in 1986 came decolonization. Despite the fact that Micronesia remains firmly under U.S. control, the independence and anti-nuclear movements in Belau and the self-determination movements of other regions make for a photographic response in which it is declared that, should we lose Micronesia, it would not have been worth having.

The photographic representation of Micronesia in *National Geographic* is similar, in broad outlines, to the representation of Polynesia. While the question of American self-identity and its relationship with the third world is brought into sharper relief in Micronesia than elsewhere in the Pacific, similar stories are told about Polynesia: the sexuality and beauty of its women, the vagabond nature of its men, and the same shift from a story of progress in one era to one of pollution in the next. Contrasts between the treatment of these areas and of Melanesia are striking, however, and it is to these pictures we now turn.

The Black Islands, The Savage Narcissus. The *National Geographic* tells several stories about Melanesia, New Guinea particularly, and each is a narrative fundamentally structured by racial attitudes similar in basic outline to those that dictated the naming of Melanesia (the black islands) in contrast to Micronesia (the small islands). They are also resonant with the racial focus of some anthropological writing, as in Douglas Oliver's comment that every white traveler to the Pacific "learned soon to distinguish between the copper-skinned, straight-haired, nearly amphibious canoe-men living in the eastern islands and the brown or black, frizzly-haired savages in the west" (1961:14). Race, both in anthropological writing and in the *Geographic,* can be an organizing substructure to narratives told about the region.

The first story told is one about decorating the male body. Photo after photo shows us a head-and-shoulders shot of men with painted faces, artifacts through their nasal septums, and feathers running up from their headpieces, giving some articles the feel of a gallery of heads. The Melanesian and the Western reader come face to face, not because there is a push toward intimacy, but because male finery and self-display have been the most salient feature for makers of the magazine. This fascination may relate to both the sheer variety and elaborateness of the decorations and the fact that here males rather than females dress in this fashion. Such an interpretation is supported by the fact that many photos depict men holding mirrors, in the process of applying face paint or paraphernalia. These mirrors can be read as a sign of vanity, a reading captions often encourage by references to "primping" (September 1973) and the decorated subject as "proud" (April 1953). Take the caption from July 1969 for a picture showing a heavily decorated man smiling widely into a mirror: "Chuckling with delight, a tribesman admires the result of hours of primping." Captions might direct attention to vanity both to point to the sin of pride (particularly noteworthy for occurring, relatively "unnaturally," in the male sex) and to anticipate and protest such a reading. Such a rhetorical effect can be achieved by raising and rejecting the idea that the photographed New Guinea men are ashamed to be seen so dandified; they are, we are told, culturally different and proud of it.[12]

12. The focus on male exotic dress is paralleled by frequent photographic attention to ritual, ranging from initiation rituals to head-hunting, to mortuary ritual, to land diving (jumping from a tower with one's free fall stopped at the last minute by a rope attached to the ankle) in the New Hebrides (extensively covered in both January 1955 and December 1976). As we have seen, the focus on dress and ritual is a common feature of coverage when and where it has

The focus on decorated men is in striking contrast to the fact that, for most other regions, women alone populate galleries of portraits. The classic gallery, in a July 1962 article on Polynesia, shows a group of women posed very much on the order of classic fashion or makeup photography of the time. This is a gallery, both pose and captions tell us, of beautiful women. The contrast with the Melanesian galleries of males is also found in the focus on the men's dress, and the Polynesian women's faces or bodies. The male gallery is an inspection of cultural elaboration while the female one is a survey of natural beauty. Given white American cultural attitudes about the relationship between race and beauty, the relative absence of the Melanesian woman is not surprising.

The women who are included fall into several types. A number of photographs focus on women holding their babies, but in odd ways, as in a net bag or strapped on the back while gardening. As we will see in the next chapter, the *Geographic*'s rendering of women focuses on their universal motherhood. Cultural variety in motherhood is seldom at issue, but the Melanesian shots of "odd" mothering come close: motherhood, like beauty, is thought to be central to the definition of femininity, and Melanesian women are anomalous on both counts. They are often depicted at work and often in relatively grey and oppressive light. While the Melanesian man is presented as a skilled archer and hunter (April 1969; July 1969) the woman is presented as a laborer, doing work which is a burden rather than a skill and which "makes her a drudge" (April 1953).[13]

Two of the central impressions one gets from a survey of Melanesian articles is that the region is, first, an area of violence, taboo, and danger/adventure, and second, a land out of time, *the* Stone Age area par excellence. The camera dwells on the skulls of the headhunted and the merely deceased, accentuating the Melanesian's nearness to the violence and fearsomeness of death. The magazine has at least twice (May 1962 and March 1972) published photos that show a man asleep with his head on a skull, in this way dramatizing both the sinister quality of this region

---

attempted to render others exotic. What should be noted here, however, is that the ritual is often depicted as somewhat bizarre, not sacred.

13. There are, of course, exceptions, as in the May 1962 issue where a small but brightly lit photo (p. 617) shows decorated women planting crops and notes that "skilled gardeners" like these "produced 50,000 pounds of vegetables a month for U.S. forces" during World War II.

CALABASH MASK and bush of feathers disguise a clansman. His trip to the fair was the first ever made outside his remote neighborhood.

MEDALS on foreheads identify luluais and tul-tuls, village leaders appointed by island officials.
626

CIGARETTE rolled in newsprint relaxes a dancer.

GREEN SCARAB beetles adorn a golden headband.

The decorative practices of Melanesian men have been frequently displayed—here in 1962. For most other world regions, only women are portrayed in this way. (Photo: John Scofield, © National Geographic Society)

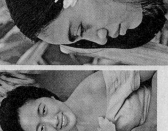

"Their physical beauty and amiable dispositions harmonized completely with the softness of their clime" wrote

Arriving at Tahiti, Wallis's men "swore they never saw handsomer made women in their lives." Generations of navigators and travelers have agreed with them.

Of the girls pictured here, Vairea (opposite), with her swan neck, finely penciled eyebrows, and lustrous eyes, resembles the Egyptian queen Nefertiti.

Tarita (right), a native of Bora Bora, won the leading part in the film *Mutiny on the Bounty*, playing opposite Marlon Brando.

Tetuanui at lower right displays classic Polynesian features. Girl at lower center is pure Chinese. Each (below) wears a crown of *tiare Tahiti*, a species of gardenia.

40

A typical "gallery" of beautiful women—these from Tahiti in 1962. Naming each woman, the caption says that the one on the left "resembles the Egyptian queen Nefertiti," thereby evoking the long-standing Western theme of Polynesian nobility and possible common an-

IMPORTED BEACH HATS

ECUADORIAN PLAID STRAW, along with the other beach styles shown on this page, is now perfectly acceptable for wear in town (Madcaps, $7.95).

CAPRI COOLIE HAT is made of straw braid stitched together in striped effect. A straw cord loops beneath wearer's chin (Capri Import Co., $3.95).

PUERTO RICAN ROLLER has printed bandanna attached which crosses under chin, ties in back and keeps hat and hair in place (Alexanne, $9.95).

CONTINUED ON PAGE 91

Fashion photography, *Life* 1954. The search for female beauty in *National Geographic* has been implicitly guided by white Western standards and sometimes followed commercial photographic conventions of youth and posing. (Photo: Paul Himmel, courtesy Life Picture Sales)

Melanesia has been portrayed both as a region of violence, taboo, danger/adventure and as a land out of time. The caption of this March 1972 photograph says that these headhunters "keep grisly relics of ancestors as well as of victims." (Photo: Malcolm S. Kirk)

and the quotidian, accepting nature of their response to the otherwise frightening cultural environment. Similarly, we several times find photos focusing on bloodletting; the use of blood to attach a drumhead to its base is mentioned in an April 1969 caption and shown in a March 1972 photo. Captions, particularly in the fifties and sixties, run through a panoply of expressions meant to evoke the horror of the savage, referring to sorcery, head-hunting, and taboos while describing a "ghoulish mud man" who will perform a "macabre dance" (March 1972), others as "eating voraciously" (April 1953), speaking a "guttural language" (March 1972), and the entire land as living with the "dark terrors of ignorance" (May 1962). We are told that "New Guinea's primitive tribesmen live with danger," "fighting for survival against neighbors and nature" (April 1969).

Melanesian music plays an interesting role in this regard. Several captions reveal their author's projection of feelings of danger through their reference to "eerie songs" (September 1973) and "haunting songs out of a fevered dream" that accompany "the mad rhythms of a tribal dance" (April 1953). On the other hand, at least three pictures (February 1961 and March 1972) show a white explorer playing back music, tape-recorded locally, to Melanesian listeners, who are depicted as encountering this technology for the first time. This experience, we are told through facial expression and caption, is a delight for those who heretofore did not know themselves in this way. Music thus parallels mirrors in telling a story about the coming of self-awareness to primitives by way of the encounter with the West.

The vision of terror in the jungle is accompanied and increasingly supplanted by a story of progress. The savage terrors of the place are ultimately explained by the standard evolutionary model, as Melanesians are repeatedly referred to as Stone Age men. When New Guinea was first encountered, its people represented "living exhibits in a museum of early man," found "as at the beginning of time."[14] They are, moreover, "lost in time," sometimes not brutal but "as idyllic as a dream" (May 1962). These Stone Age people are increasingly depicted as making a move from their location in time past to time present, as they "leap from the Stone Age to tomorrow" with the "fatherly advice" and help of their Australian colonial masters. Here, as elsewhere around the globe, there is both deep nostalgia for the past and applause for the changes as an old way of life "dies" or "inevitably fades" or "succumbs" to the twentieth century.

Conclusion

One question left open by this account is what fantasies these photographs have actually provoked in the readers of the last three decades. Nor have we addressed their effect on readers' behavior as voters, tourists, or consumers of advertising images (and then of products) which may draw on the sometimes romantic preparation the *National Geographic* has provided. Arguably, the images articulate more with the selling of coconut oil suntan lotion, Ocean Pacific shorts, or Caribbean vacations (in the case of the Micronesian or Polynesian images) and

14. A 1936 article on Micronesia, titled "Mysterious Micronesia," also labels those islands "museums of primitive man." The difference in the dates of the Melanesian and the Micronesian reference is important, however, as is the much more positive tone of the latter, in which notions of primitiveness remain relatively underdeveloped.

National Geographic photographs serve as an acculturating background to the many ads that use Pacific motifs to mark products as sensual and feminine. (Photo courtesy Tanning Research Laboratories, Inc.)

American race relations (in the case of the Melanesian) than they do with actual social relations between Americans and Pacific Islanders. Take the example of advertising. The *Geographic* likely helped direct tourists to the Pacific, and has also served as an acculturating background to the many ads that use Pacific motifs to sell a product as sensual, often as feminine. Modleski (1986) shows that tropical island settings are *often* conflated with femininity and sexuality in advertisements. The naturalism and eroticism of at least some of these islands is a cultural theme already made available through the *National Geographic* images just described and used thereafter to work more on gender identities than on ethnic ones.

Images from this region mediate nature and culture for Westerners in more powerful ways than those from any other part of the world. They offer Westerners ways of thinking about a primordial past either innocent (in the Micronesian version) or savage (in the Melanesian). As such, they provide the elements for powerful stories about the origins and rationality of gender and race distinctions, as well as about the role of colonialism in human progress. We can treat these representations as artifacts that have some social force, shaping people's thinking and behavior. The social pragmatics of the images need investigation, not in order to see whether or not they influence some independent reality but to understand how the photographs are constructed and how they operate in a world in which they are as real as the Pacific. While not ignoring the difference between photographs and people, such an analysis does mean we are more likely to notice that those who control the means of mass representation have the means to create powerful constraints and paradigms for both the photograph's subject and its audience, ethnographers included.

How these pictures and those from other regions have worked in relation to the history of American race and gender relations is the topic of the next chapter.

Six

The Color of Sex: Postwar Photographic Histories of Race and Gender

Again and again, when the negative space of the woman of color meets the Age of Mechanical Reproduction or, worse yet, Baudrillard's "simulations," the resulting effect is . . . a form larger than life, and yet a deformation powerless to speak.

(Wallace 1990:252)

Race is, as Henry Gates has said, "a trope of ultimate, irreducible difference between cultures, linguistic groups, or adherents of specific belief systems which—more often than not—also have fundamentally opposed economic interests" (1985:5). It is a trope that is particularly dangerous because it "pretends to be an objective term of classification." Gates points to the profoundly social nature of racial classification. Social groups engaged in struggle define racial boundaries in the contexts of that struggle; powerful groups then invoke biology in a post-hoc justification of the boundaries they have drawn. Those in power elaborate observable physical differences—no matter how subtle— into explanations, affirmations, and justifications for inequality and oppression. Once this work is done, and the boundaries are intact, racist theory produces full-blown descriptions of culture and personality that juxtapose powerful ego and degraded/dangerous alter, "lending the sanction of God, biology, or the natural order to even presumably unbiased descriptions of cultural tendencies and differences" (Gates 1985:5).

As Gates and others have so eloquently pointed out, racial difference—and its supposed cultural concomitants—is thus not the *source* of the many contemporary conflicts where it is said to be at issue. It is never a simple matter of two groups in contact finding themselves so physically and culturally different that they just cannot get along. Rather, racial and cultural difference become coded ways of talking about other differences that matter, differences in power and in interests.[1] For this reason—however absolute and intransigent they may seem—racial/racist theories must retain flexibility and are frequently ambiguous. As Omi and Winant (1986:x) have said, race is an inherently unstable "complex of social meanings, constantly being transformed by political struggle." To work to uncover the social arrangements that give rise to and reproduce racism is to place its analysis in realms of human agency and to emphasize the specificity of its historical forms.

Tranquil Racial Spaces

Race theories form one of the most powerful and lethal systems in the world for communicating about difference. Zora Neale Hurston wrote, "Race consciousness is a deadly explosive on the tongues of men" (1984:326). It has justified the most heinous of social relations, including slavery, genocide, and apartheid. Yet, dangerous as they are, race theories have infiltrated the commonsense thinking of most people in the United States, profoundly influencing the ways they perceive and account for cultural difference. Like other forms of essentialist reasoning, racist thought has the appeal of simplicity, and it draws authority from invoking biology and nature. The hegemony of a theory of race that insists on two "bounded" human categories has been challenged in the 1970s and 1980s by new waves of immigration from Asia and Latin America, confronting white America with tremendous diversity in physical appearance and widely varying relationships between race and class, education and social standing.

National Geographic magazine is the product of a society deeply permeated with racism as a social practice and with racial understandings as

---

1. This is not to deny that there are complex correspondences between culture and racial categories as socially deployed. Once race has been used to marginalize and isolate social groups, shared experiences of oppression, coping, and resistance may give rise to shared cultural premises. The "culture" or "cultures" that result, however, are at least partly a consequence of the deployment of racial categories and not evidence of the validity of the categories themselves.

ways of viewing the world. It sells itself to a reading public that, while they do not consider themselves racist, turn easily to race as an explanation for culture and for social outcome. The Geographic headquarters itself has had few black employees up to the present, despite the predominantly African-American citizenry of Washington, D.C. It is not surprising, therefore, that while race is rarely addressed directly in the magazine, American racial categories powerfully structure the images contained in its pages.

One of the most powerful and distinctive tenets of racism in the United States is that "blackness" is an all-or-nothing phenomenon. Racial law through the period of the Civil War, and after, held that any "black" ancestry was sufficient to define one as black. As recently as 1983, this type of reasoning was upheld by the State Supreme Court of Louisiana, when it refused to allow a woman descended from an eighteenth-century white planter and a black slave to change the classification on her birth certificate from "colored" to "white" (Omi and Winant 1986:57). The laws in question and the cultural preconceptions upon which they were based insistently denied the reality of interracial sexual relations or of the sexual exploitation that so frequently accompanied the master/slave relation. They insisted on pure and unequivocal categories with which to reason about difference. Such airtight categories were viewed as necessary to guard the privileges of "whites" as absolute and to justify the denial of equality to "blacks" as an impossibility.

Nevertheless, when Euramericans turned their eyes outside the borders of their own country, other forms of reasoning prevailed. Evolutionist thought dominated attempts to understand the human diversity of the non-European world. Such thinking needed a continuum, one that was grounded in nature. Skin color is obviously highly variable, only with some difficulty made to accommodate the simple binary classification "black"/"white" in the United States. A continuum of skin color was thus a perfect biological substratum on which to graft stories of human progress or cultural evolution.

As described in chapter 2, late nineteenth-century fairs and expositions frequently organized the world cultures they presented along an evolutionary scale. These almost always corresponded to a racial continuum, as Rydell (1984) has noted, from the "savagery" of the dark-skinned Dahomeyans, to the Javanese "Brownies," to the "nearly-white" Chinese and Japanese. As evolutionary trajectories were reproduced over the course of the twentieth century, in anthropological theory and in white popular consciousness, they were almost always connected to a scale of skin color, which was then construed, in many cases, as an independent form of verifying their correctness.

As we turned to *National Geographic* photographs, we hypothesized that it was this more differentiated scale—rather than the simple binary opposition called into play for analyzing American culture—that would inform the ways *National Geographic* would portray, and readers would interpret, images of the third world. Distinctions in popular stereotypes of the peoples of Northern and sub-Saharan Africa, or of Melanesia and Polynesia, indicated that Euramericans drew conclusions about others based on the *degree* of darkness of skin color. As we analyzed constructions of race in *National Geographic* photographs, we thus coded them in a way that would allow us to determine whether "bronze" peoples were portrayed differently from those who would be more commonly seen as "black"; to see, in other words, if simple binary constructions informed the images, or if more complex evolutionary schema structured their messages. This determination was based on the same coding procedure described in chapter 4, n. 3. It was based solely on observable skin color (not cultural characteristics). We used a decision rule that deliberately maximized polarization of categories; that is, when it was difficult to decide whether an individual was "bronze" or white, we coded white. When it was difficult to decide between bronze and black, we coded black. We coded only individuals identifiable as native to the region portrayed, eliminating the few Westerners who appeared in the photographs.

The period for which we analyzed photographs—1950–86—encompassed times of great turmoil in racially defined relationships in the United States. The late 1950s and early sixties saw struggles to overturn racial codes that were more intense than any since the Civil War era. Participants in the civil rights movement sought to obtain basic civil liberties for African Americans; they used the egalitarian verbiage of federal law to challenge the restrictive laws and practices of states and municipalities. Such changes did not simply require a change in the legal codes and their implementation, however; they also demanded, as Omi and Winant have argued, "a paradigm shift in established systems of racial meanings and identities" (1986:90).

Nonviolent tactics such as freedom rides, marches, attempts to desegregate key southern school districts and universities, and sit-ins at segregated lunchrooms characterized the period up until the passage of the 1964 Civil Rights Act and the voting rights legislation of 1965. By the mid-sixties, however, many who had worked and hoped for these changes were disillusioned. Changes in legislation had profound symbolic value, and materially benefited a small number of middle-class African Americans. But they did not alter the economic circumstances of the vast majority of blacks living in poverty, and they did not adequately challenge the tremendous and continuing burden of institutional racism. This led to an increasing radicalization of key branches of the civil rights movement and to angry rioting in places like Watts and Newark (Harding 1981; Carson 1981).

The civil rights movement contested white privilege and its counterpart, the institutionalized oppression of black Americans. It also contested the very meaning of race in American culture. As white Americans were deprived of one of the master tropes explaining their privileged position in the world, race became an uncomfortable topic for them. This discomfort was reflected in the pages of *National Geographic*. Clearly the magazine did not cover the turmoil in American cities during the period. At the same time, it sought to ease anxieties in its portrayal of the third world. As late as the early 1950s, the Euramerican reading public could comfortably view Asian and African peoples attending white explorers and photographers—carrying them across rivers, pulling them in rickshaws, carrying their packs and bags. By the late sixties, however, these images were too disturbing, the possibility of rebellion and anger too present. White travelers simply disappeared from the pictures (see figure 2.2), removing the possibility of conflictual relationships.

With this action, third world spaces were cleared for fantasy. Black and bronze peoples of Africa, Asia, and Latin America were shown going about their daily lives—happy, poor but dignified, and attuned to basic human values. The photographs themselves were not much different from those of previous decades; however, in the racially charged context of the fifties and sixties their meaning had changed. The implicit contrast with Watts and Newark, or even with Selma and Montgomery, operated behind the scenes. The third world was constituted as a safe, comfortable space, where race was not an issue and where white people did not have to reevaluate the sources of their privilege.

Apparently, though, in the minds of *National Geographic* editors, too much of even a reassuring fantasy could be disturbing. Until 1961, the numbers of white, black, or bronze people appearing in any given issue of *National Geographic* was variable. In 1952, for example, only about 15 percent of people depicted in articles on the third world were dark-skinned; in 1958, the figure was about 46 percent. Beginning in 1961,

As late as the 1950s, the Euramerican reading public could comfortably view images such as this—of Asian, African, and here New Guinea peoples attending white explorers. Images of Westerners, and so of racially mixed groups, declined sharply in the late 1960s (see figure 2.2). (Photo: E. Thomas Gilliard and Henry Kaltenthaler, © National Geographic Society)

however, a remarkably stable pattern began to appear. For the next twenty-five years the percentage of dark-skinned people in any issue held very constant at about 28 percent. People who could be categorized as bronze formed a fairly regular 60 percent of the total, with the remaining 12% constituted by light- or white-skinned third world peoples. The intense stability of this pattern, and particularly the almost invariant proportion of dark-skinned people represented, suggests that editorial attention may have been focused on the issue.

This is admittedly indirect evidence. We did not find anyone at *National Geographic* who was willing to say that skin color per se was a consideration in putting together issues (although conversations in planning meetings suggest that it may well be). We do know, however, that *National Geographic*'s marketing department gathered significant amounts of data on the popularity of different kinds of articles and that

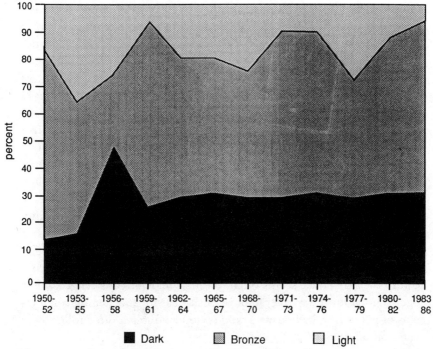

Figure 6.1. Skin color in photographs, 1950–86

Africa was by far the least popular world region. By marketing definitions, African peoples constituted a difficult topic; to the extent that market concerns drive content, one would thus expect some sort of regulation of their coverage.

In photographs where dark-skinned peoples were portrayed, there were interesting regularities—contributing to an overall image of contentment, industriousness, and simplicity. The activity level of individuals portrayed in the photographs, for example, clearly sorted out on an evolutionary scale marked by skin color. Individuals coded as black were most likely to be depicted in high levels of activity—engaged in strenuous work or athletics. People coded white were most likely to be engaged in low-level activity—seated or reclining, perhaps manipulating something with their hands, but rarely exerting themselves. Those coded bronze were most likely to be found engaged in activities that fell somewhere between the two extremes, such as walking or herding animals. In keeping with this pattern, people of color (both black and bronze) were most likely to be portrayed at work in the photographs we examined, while people with white skin were most likely to be found at rest.

The determinants of such a portrayal are complex, and the message it conveys is multifaceted. We cannot rule out the brute empiricist interpretation that what is portrayed is determined to some extent by events in the real world: that photographers found dark-skinned peoples at work more often than lighter-skinned peoples. Yet when we are dealing with sets of published photographs that are chosen out of a universe of tens of thousands that were taken, we are clearly dealing with a problem of representation as well.

Portraying people at work is in keeping with an editorial policy that demands a focus on the positive as construed in the United States, that is, the work ethic. It is possible to imagine that editors sought to counter images of the laziness of non-white peoples (in the Euramerican imagination) by deliberately presenting an alternative view. At the same time, in the contradictory manner characteristic of colonial/neocolonial mentality (see Bhabha 1983), it is also possible that deeply ingrained notions of racial hierarchy made it seem more "natural" for dark-skinned peoples to be at work and engaged in strenuous activity. White ambivalence toward the black male seems often to center on issues of strength: while vigor is good for the worker to have, it also has the threatening connotations of potential rebelliousness, and so some hobbling often follows the rendition of strength.

Few topics have occupied as much space in colonial discourse as the relationship of blacks to labor. As Euramericans sought to build wealth on the backs of colonized peoples and slaves, they sought to continually refine methods of maximizing the labor they were able to extract. Colonial administrators and plantation bosses continually reported on the success and failures of innovations in the process. The double mentality reflected in the reports was plain—while people of color were inherently suited to labor, they never wanted to work hard enough in the fields of their white masters. The image of a tremendous capacity for work, coupled with an unwillingness to actually work, gave rise to contradictory stereotypes. The heritage of these stereotypes and the labor relations that gave rise to them can be traced in the strenuously employed black bodies portrayed in the pages of *National Geographic*.

In equally regular ways, black and bronze peoples were more likely to be portrayed as poor and technologically backward. Individuals coded as white were more likely to be wealthy and less likely to be poor than other categories. Still, only 21 percent of black and 16 percent of bronze people were photographed in contexts of poverty. Fully 70 percent of the former and 72 percent of the latter were shown without any markers of wealth or poverty, and some of each group were portrayed as wealthy. There is clearly a tension at work in the photographs. The greater poverty of darker-skinned individuals may, in part, be empirically determined; it is also in keeping with popular Euramerican stereotypes of the degraded status of dark-skinned peoples. On the other hand, *National Geographic's* policy of focusing on the positive and avoiding advocacy precludes too heavy an emphasis on impoverishment. Dark-skinned peoples have a somewhat greater tendency to be poor—one might construe the statistical weight of the photographs as saying—but in general, they live well.

Individuals coded white were most likely to be depicted with machines of one kind or another; black and bronze individuals were most likely to be shown with simple tools of local manufacture. Not surprisingly, people of color were more often depicted as engaged in ritual. This variable also sorted out along an evolutionary/skin color continuum: the darker the skin color, the more likely to engage in ritual practices. In classic evolutionist terms, superstition (represented by ritual) and science (represented by technology) were counterposed. Similarly, the darker the skin color of an individual, the less likely he or she was to be depicted in western-style clothing. The darker the skin of the people portrayed, the less they were associated with things European, and the more exotic they were rendered.

Given these trends, it was somewhat surprising to find that dark-skinned peoples were not photographed in natural settings (that is, in landscapes or greenery) more often than their lighter-skinned counterparts. They were, however, more likely to appear in settings where surroundings were not clearly discernible. Such portrayals tend to aestheticize the materials on which they focus. In this case, they force attention to the lines, shapes, and colors of the bodies themselves, rather than providing information about the context in which the bodies appear. Because such photos were relatively numerous, dark-skinned people consequently appeared in *social* surroundings less frequently.

People coded black or bronze were more likely to be photographed in large groups than those coded white. They were less likely to be portrayed alone or in small intimate groups. People of color were therefore were less often the subject of individualized photographic accounts, attentive to "biographic" features and life circumstances. They were more often portrayed as part of a mass, perhaps thereby suggesting to readers that they had relatively undifferentiated feelings, hopes, or needs. Individuals coded black and bronze were far more likely to be photographed gazing into the camera than individuals coded white—a stance that, while complex and sometimes ambiguous—frequently suggests availability and compliance.

Despite some Euramerican stereotypes, dark skin was not associated with evidence of aggression in the pages of *National Geographic* through most of the period we have examined. As described in chapter 4, aggression is generally taboo as a topic for *National Geographic* photographs, except in the highly specific case of depicting U.S. military power. Additionally, however, to retain its status as a place where white U.S. readers go to assuage their fears about race and cultural difference, *National Geographic* must studiously avoid photographs that might suggest a potential threat from colonized and formerly colonized peoples. To depict anger, violence, or the presence of weapons is to evoke the fear that they might be turned to retaliation. They serve as an uncomfortable reminder of a world given to struggles for independence, revolutions, and rebellions.

In the marketplace of images, *National Geographic* relies on two intertwined strategies. It relies on recognition—on offering readers what they already know and believe in new and appealing ways. Its reputation and sales also turn on the classic humanism with which it portrays the world. In its depictions of "non-white" peoples, the humanist mission—to portray all humans as basically the same "under the skin"[2]—comes into conflict with Western "commonsense knowledge" about the hierarchy of races.

The organization of photographs into stories about cultural evolution (couched in more "modern" terms of progress and development) provides the partial resolution of this contradiction. These stories tell the Euramerican public that their race prejudice is not so wrong; that at one point people of color *were* poor, dirty, technologically backward, and superstitious—and some still are. But this is not due to intrinsic or insuperable characteristics. With guidance and support from the West, they can in fact overcome these problems, acquire the characteristics of civilized peoples, and take their place alongside them in the world. In the context of this story, the fact that bronze peoples are portrayed as slightly less poor, more technologically adept, serves as proof that progress is possible—and fatalistically links progress to skin color.

At the same time, the "happy-speak" policies of *National Geographic*

2. In part because of its focus on everyday life, *National Geographic* does not trade in the standardized images of black people that have been common in Western art—some of which have been characterized by Honour (1989) as "heroes and martyrs," "the benighted," "the defiant," and "the pacified."

have meant that for people of color—as for others—the overall picture is one of tranquillity and well-being. We are seldom confronted with historical facts of racial or class violence, with hunger as it unequally affects black and white children, or with social movements that question established racial hierarchies. One photographer expressed this discrepancy poignantly, pointing to a photograph of an African family in a 1988 issue on population. "The story is about hunger," he said, "but look at these people. It's a romantic picture."

This is not to say that no one at the National Geographic Society is attentive to these issues. Dedicated photographers and editors worked hard in the 1970s to produce and push into print two deeply disturbing accounts of apartheid. And while this attempt engendered a repressive movement within the Society's Board of Trustees, an article critical of South African black homelands appeared in February 1986.

The same strategies, however, pursued in different epochs, can have different meanings and consequences. The humanist side of *National Geographic* in the 1950s and 1960s denied social problems; it also provided images of people of color living their lives in relatively dignified ways. It gave short shrift to poverty and disharmony, but it permitted a certain amount of identification across racial boundaries. In a period when racial boundaries were highly visible and when African Americans were struggling for equal rights under the law, these images could be read, at least in part, as subtle arguments for social change.

The 1970s have been characterized as a period of "racial quiescence," when social movements waned and conflicts receded (Omi and Winant 1986:2). Racial oppression did not cease, but it was not as openly contested. In turn, the 1980s saw a backlash in undisguised attempts to dismantle legislation protecting civil rights and nondiscriminatory practices. These moves did not require and, in fact, assiduously avoided, an explicitly racial discourse. Busing, originally implemented to desegregate schools, was overturned under banners of "community control" and "parental involvement." Rejections of racially balanced textbooks were couched in terms of battles against "secular humanism" and "political correctness." And in the 1988 presidential campaign, movements of people of color were recast as "special interests" (Omi and Winant 1986:125).

In such a context, classic humanism takes on pernicious overtones. The denial of race as a *social* issue, in a society with a profoundly racist history and where institutional racism still exists, forecloses dialogue on the issues. *National Geographic* has not intentionally contributed to this foreclosure; it goes on producing pictures in much the same way it has for years. And yet the message that we are all alike under the skin takes on new meaning in a social context which denies that discrimination exists or that race has been used to consolidate the privilege of some and oppress others. The racism of the 1980s was not confrontational and defiant; it simply turned its back on the issues. The tranquil racial spaces of *National Geographic* can only contribute to this willed ignorance.

The Women of the World

National Geographic's photographs of the women of the world tell a story about the women of the United States in the post–World War II period. It is to issues of gender in white American readers' lives, such as debates over women's sexuality or whether women doing paid labor can mother their children adequately, that the pictures refer as much as to the lives of third-world women. Seen in this way, the *National Geographic's* women can be placed alongside the other women of American popular culture: the First Lady, the woman draped over an advertisement's red sports car, the Barbie doll, the woman to whom the Hallmark Mother's Day card is addressed. Rather than treating the photos as simply images of women, we can set them in the context of a more complex cultural history of the period, with the sometimes radical changes it brought to the lives of the women who are the readers (or known to the male readers) of the magazine.

Research on the visual representation of women makes clear that female images are abundant in some domains (advertising) and virtually absent in others (photojournalism of political subjects). The invisibility extends much further for women of color. In popular images as well as the dominant white imagination, as Hull, Scott and Smith (1982) have so eloquently told us, "All the women are white, all the blacks are men," and black women are simply invisible. The photographs of *National Geographic* are indispensable because it is one of the very few popular venues trafficking in large numbers of images of black women. While the photographs tell a story about cultural ideals of femininity, the narrative threads of gender and race are tightly bound up with each other. In the world at large, race and gender are clearly not separate systems, as Trinh (1989), Moore (1988), Sacks (1989), and others have reminded us.

For the overwhelmingly white readers of the *Geographic*, the dark-skinned women of distant regions serve as touchstones, giving lessons both positive and negative about what women are and should be (compare Botting 1988). Here as elsewhere, the magazine plays with possibilities of the other as a flexible reflection—even a sort of funhouse mirror—for the self. The women of the world are portrayed in sometimes striking parallel to popular images of American womanhood of the various periods of the magazine's production—for instance, as mothers and as beautiful objects. At certain times, with certain races of women, however, the *Geographic's* other women provide a contrast to stereotypes of white American women—they are presented as hard-working breadwinners in their communities. Primarily, however, the *Geographic's* idealization of the world's people extends to women in egalitarian fashion. To idealize "the other woman" is to present her as like, or aspiring to be like, her American counterpart. The other woman is exotic on the surface (she is dressed in an elaborate sari and has a golden nose ring) but her difference is erased at another, deeper level (she is really just a mother, and like the American woman, interested in making herself beautiful through fashion). The woman's sameness in difference allows us to avoid the sense of threat that confrontation with difference presents and allows us to pursue the illusory goal of wholeness.

As with American women in popular culture, third-world women are portrayed less frequently than men: one quarter of the pictures we looked at focus primarily on women.[3] The situation has traditionally not been much different in the anthropological literature covering the non-Western world, and it may be amplified in both genres where the focus is on cultural differences or exoticism. Given the association between women and the natural world, men and things cultural (Ortner 1974), a magazine that aspires to describe the distinctive achievements of civilizations can be expected to highlight the world of men. But like the people of nature in the fourth world, women have been treated as all the more precious for their nonutilitarian, nonrationalistic qualities. Photographs of women become one of the primary devices by which the magazine depicts "universal human values," and these include the values of family love and the appreciation of female beauty itself.[4] We turn to these issues now, noting that each of them has had a consistent cultural

3. This proportion is based on those photos in which adults of identifiable gender are shown (N = 510). Another 11 percent show women and men together in roughly equal numbers, leaving 65 percent of the photos depicting mainly men.

4. The popularity of this notion in American culture, which *National Geographic* relies on as much as feeds, is also one wellspring for American feminism's focus on universal sisterhood, that is, its insistence, particularly in the 1970s, that Western and non-Western women will easily see each other as similar or sharing similar experiences.

content through the postwar period, during historical changes that give the images different emphases and form through the decades.

The Motherhood of Man.   There is no more romantic set of photographs in the *Geographic* than those depicting the mothers of the world with their children. There is the exuberant picture showing the delight of a Kurd mother holding her infant. Filling much space, as an unusually high percentage of the magazine's mother-child pictures do, the photograph covers two pages despite the relative lack of information in it. Its classical composition and crisp, uncluttered message are similar to those in many such photos. They often suggest the Western tradition of madonna painting and evoke the Mother's Day message: this relationship between mother and child, they say, is a timeless and sacred one, essentially and intensely loving regardless of social and historical context—the

Photographs of women in *National Geographic* emphasize motherhood, as in this 1958 image of a Kurd mother and child. The third-world mother is often backgrounded and iconic, with emphasis placed on the child. (Photo: J. Baylor Roberts, © National Geographic Society)

foundation of human social life rather than cultural difference. The family of man, these pictures might suggest, is first of all a mother-child unit, rather than a brotherhood of solidarity between adults.[5]

For the magazine staff and readers of the 1950s, there must have been even more power in these images than we see in them today. The impact of the photos would have come from the intense cultural and social pressures on middle-class women to see their most valuable role, often their only one, as that of mother (Margolis 1984). The unusually strong pressure of this period is often explained as motivated by desires to place returning World War II veterans (and men in general) in those jobs available and by anxieties about the recent holocaust of the war and the potential for a nuclear conflagration, which made the family seem a safe haven (May 1988). As a new cult of domesticity emerged, women were told—through both science and popular culture—that biology, morality, and the psychological health of the next generation required their commitment to full-time mothering. This ideological pressure persisted through the 1950s despite the rapid rise in female employment through the decade.

The idealization of the mother-child bond is seen in everything from the warm TV relationships of June Cleaver with Wally and the Beaver to the cover of a *Life* magazine issue of 1956 devoted to "The American Woman" showing a glowing portrait of a mother and daughter lovingly absorbed in each other; all of this is ultimately and dramatically reflected in the period's rapidly expanding birth rate. This idealization had its counterpoint in fear of the power women were being given in the domestic domain. In both science and popular culture, the mother was criticized for being smothering, controlling, oversexualized, and, a bit later, overly permissive (Ehrenreich and English 1978; May 1988).

The *National Geographic's* treatment of children can be seen as an extension of these ideologies of motherhood and the family. As the "woman question" came to be asked more angrily in the late 1950s, there was a gradual erosion of faith in the innocence of the mother-infant bond and even in the intrinsic value of children (Ehrenreich and English 1978), centered around fears of juvenile delinquency and the later 1960s identification of a "generation gap." The *National Geographic,* however, continued to print significant numbers of photographs of children, per-

5. The popular Family of Man exhibition also included a substantial section devoted to mothers and infants, unfortunately nicknamed "Tits and Tots" by the staff of photographers who organized it (Meltzer 1978). This exhibit, immensely popular when it toured, became a best-selling book.

The idealization of the mother-child bond, and the cult of domesticity more generally, formed the framework within which *National Geographic* photographs of other women were viewed during the post–World War II period. These photos raised as many questions about the proper role of women in the United States as they did about the lives of the women they portrayed. (Photo: Grey Villet, *Life* magazine, © 1956 Time Warner, Inc.)

haps responding to their increasingly sophisticated marketing information, which indicated that photographs of children and cute animals were among their most popular pictures.

As the magazine has moved into depicting social problems through the seventies and eighties, however, the child has become positioned to tell the most poignant part of the story. In a wrenching photograph that Wilbur Garrett took in Laos, a Hmong family sits on a bench, the mother breast-feeding a baby, the father holding a toddler who appears to be asleep (January 1974:100–101). No one is smiling. The caption lets us know that the older child is dead, the parents grieving. Only then do we comprehend that the mother's hand is touching her child's shroud rather than his blanket and read the parents' faces as mournful rather than simply solemn or strained. While the caption begins lyrically with the magazine's standard infrastructure of balance, "Milk of life, shroud of death," it goes on to give the grim statistics for these people of 50 percent infant mortality rate, 35-year life expectancy.

Throughout the 1950s and 1960s, however, there were few poignant pictures of children, and they remain relatively rare. The more prevalent, pleasant pictures still play a fundamental role in raising the comfort level of those readers for whom articles on nonwhite peoples are the most unpopular type. For them, the loving mother and smiling child are a quick fix. Indeed, the black mother may be the *most* valorized kind of dark-skinned person for magazine readers, as in the culture at large, where one finds the "mammy" figure of film and literature and the stoic, capable single mother on whom documentaries of American life have often focused (Collins 1991:67–90). Why has this woman been such an important figure? In part, it must be because the traditional maternal role is seen as teaching children to be polite, to be good citizens, to reproduce the status quo. If the most valued black person for white Americans will be the least threatening one, then the culturally constructed image of the black mother will fill the bill. The photo of a Bedouin mother and child can suggest, like a number of others, the mother's protectiveness as well as her own vulnerability or fear (December 1972:838–39). We might ask if the perceived danger of things foreign increases the power of the mother to be portrayed as especially protective. Given the kindly intentions in editorial policy, the sympathetic other will often be a mother, protecting both her infant and the reader.

In pictures of mother and child, it often appears that the nonwhite mother is backgrounded, with her gaze and the gaze of the reader focused on the infant. The infant may in fact be an even more important site for dealing with white racial anxieties, by virtue of constituting an acceptable black love object. A good number of pictures in the postwar period have the form of these two: one a Micronesian infant and the other an Iraqi infant, from 1974 and 1976 respectively, each peacefully asleep in a cradle with the mother visible behind. The peacefulness constitutes the antithesis of the potentially threatening differences of interest, dress, or ritual between the photographed adult and the reader.

Women and Their Breasts. The "nude" woman sits, stands, or lounges at the salient center of *National Geographic* photography of the non-Western world. Until the phenomenal growth of mass circulation pornography in the 1960s, the magazine was known as the only mass culture venue where Americans could see women's breasts. Part of the folklore of Euramerican men, stories about secret perusals of the magazine emerged time after time in our conversations with male *National Geographic* readers. People vary in how they portray the personal or cultural meaning, or both, of this nakedness, some noting it was an aid to masturbation, others claiming it failed to have the erotic quality they expected. When white men tell these stories about covertly viewing black women's bodies, they are clearly not recounting a story about a simple encounter with the facts of human anatomy or customs; they are (perhaps unsuspectingly) confessing a highly charged—but socially approved—experience in this dangerous territory of projected, forbidden desire and guilt. Such stories also exist (in a more charged, ironic mode) in the popular culture of African Americans—for example, in Richard Pryor's characterization, in his comedy routines, of *National Geographic* as the black man's *Playboy*.

The racial distribution of female nudity in the magazine conforms, in pernicious ways, to Euramerican myths about black women's sexuality. Lack of modesty in dress places black women closer to nature. Given the pervasive tendency to interpret skin color as a marker of evolutionary progress, it is assumed that white women have acquired modesty along with other characteristics of civilization. Black women remain backward on this scale, not conscious of the embarrassment they should feel at their nakedness (Gilman 1985:114–15, 193). Their very ease unclothed stigmatizes them.

In addition, black women have been portrayed in Western art and science as both exuberant and excessive in their sexuality. While their excess intrigues, it is also read as pathological and dangerous. In the texts produced within white culture, Haraway (1989:154) writes, "Colored women densely code sex, animal, dark, dangerous, fecund, pathological." Thus for the French surrealists of the 1930s, the exotic, unencumbered sexuality of non-Western peoples—and African women in particular—represented an implicit criticism of the repression and constraint of European sexuality. The Africanism of the 1930s, like an earlier Orientalism, evidenced both a longing for—and fear of—the characteristics attributed to non-Western peoples (Clifford 1988:61). The sexuality of black women that so entertained French artists and musicians in cafés and cabarets, however, had fueled earlier popular and scientific preoccupation with the Hottentot Venus and other pathologized renditions of black women's bodies and desires (Gilman 1985).

The *Geographic's* distinctive brand of cultural relativism, however, meant that this aspect of black sexuality would be less written in by the institution than read in by readers, particularly in comparison with other visual venues such as Hollywood movies. Alloula (1986) gives the example of the sexualized early twentieth-century "harem" postcards of North African women. His thesis is that the veil fascinates a Western audience because it is read as a no-trespass message, and it is experienced by outside men as frustrating and attractive for this reason. It became an object of Western quest from a sense of the need to penetrate beyond it through, simultaneously, the light of photography, the reason of enlightened social change, the knowledge of science, and the desire of the flesh (compare Fanon 1965). One can also see the distinctive *Geographic* style in comparison with *Life* photography of non-Western women. We can see the stronger cultural viewpoint on race at work in a 1956 *Life* article on "other women," which ran next to an article on American women of various regions of the country. The two articles read as a kind of beauty pageant, with all the photographs emphasizing the sitter's appearance, sexuality, and passivity. Ultimately, the magazine's editors judged American women the better-looking set (many captions also noted the "natural," "healthy," wholesome—non-perverted?—quality of the American women), but the adjectives they used to caption the non-Western women described their sense of the more passive and sexually explicit stance of the other women. So they are variously praised for their "fragility," "great softness," "grace," "langorous" qualities, and eagerness "to please"; "the sensuous quality often seen in women of the tropics" was found in one Malayan woman. The hypersexual but passive woman here replicates the one found by many Westerners in their imaginary African travels throughout the last century (Hammond and Jablow 1977). In the *Life* article, all of the non-Western women except the one Chinese "working girl" (and many of the American women), touch themselves, their clothes, or fans in the usual pose for characterizing female self-involvement (Goffman 1979).

As in German photography at Bamum in central Africa, those who would communicate the message that non-Western others are enlightened felt the necessity to mute certain kinds of facts. Although King Nioya at Bamum had many wives, there is relatively little evidence of this in European photography of the court, and so, too, the *Geographic* rarely shows female or male sexuality in more explicit forms. Although emphasis on the veil has been strong throughout the *Geographic*'s history, it seems deployed more in a narrative about progress than one about sexuality, as we will see. The magazine and its readers are caught between the desire to play out the cultural fantasy of the oversexed native woman and the social controls of sexual morality, of science, and of cultural relativism.

If *National Geographic* trades on the sexuality of black women, it is less comfortable with that of black men. Men coded black were far more likely than those coded white to appear bare-chested in the pages of the magazine—often in poses that drew attention to musculature and strength. The *National Geographic* has apparently tried to include pictures of "handsome young men" (Abramson 1985:143). For American readers, male muscles take the place analogous to female breasts as signs of gendered sexuality (Canaan 1984). Many pictures visually or through their captions draw attention to the rippling muscles of photographed men. A picture of a man from the Nuba mountains in the Sudan (November 1966:699) fills the page, primarily with his torso rather than face or full body, accentuating his strongly defined musculature. The caption highlights his brawn and implicitly suggests that this physicality is at the expense of intelligence: "Muscles like iron, his leather arm amulet worn as insurance against disaster, a champion wrestler exudes confidence. In his world, a man's strength and agility count for much, and at festivals he earns the plaudits of his peers. But modern civilization—a force beyond his comprehension—threatens his primitive way of life."

The magazine has been extremely skittish, however, about portraying male genitals. As described earlier, a respect for the facts does not inhibit the careful erasure of all evidence of male penises from photographs. In cultures where men do not customarily wear pants, the magazine has relied on lengthening loincloths, drawing in shorts, or simply airbrushing offending body parts to avoid offending the white reading public. The fear of—and desire to erase—black male sexuality has a long tradition in Euramerican culture. It reached its fullest and most heinous development in the paranoid fantasies of organizations such as the Ku Klux Klan and in the castrations and lynchings of southern black men for real or imputed advances toward white women (Carby 1985:307–8). Haraway (1989) and Torgovnick (1990) offer vivid examples and analyses of the evidence of miscegenation and black abduction anxieties in American popular culture materials, such as the Tarzan stories and movies. Masquerading as taste or propriety, however, the underlying anxiety also finds its place in the pages of *National Geographic*.

Like the nude and its role in Western high art painting (Hess and Nochlin 1972; Betterton 1987; Nead 1990), nudity in *Geographic* photographs has had a potential sexual, even pornographic, interpretation. Such interpretations would obviously threaten the magazine's legitimacy and sales, achieved through its self-definition as a serious, relatively highbrow family magazine. Pornography represents just the opposite values: "disposability, trash," the deviant, the unrespectable, the low class (Nead 1990:325). Like fine art, science attempts to frame the nude female body as devoid of pornographic attributes. While art aestheticizes it, science dissects, fragments, and otherwise desexualizes it. The *National Geographic* nude has at times done both of these contradictory things.

The *Geographic* nude is first and foremost, in readers' attention, a set of breasts. This follows the culture at large, where the breast is made a fetish of, obsessed on. And the obsession is not just with any kind of breast. As Young (1990:191) has pointed out, breasts are "normalized," leaving women to feel themselves inadequate for not having the culturally dictated "one perfect shape and proportion for breasts": young, large, round, but not sagging. If the *Geographic* is identified with the female breast, then a cultural history of the *Geographic* must take account of changing attitudes towards women's breasts and bodies over that period.

Unfortunately, significant change has been hard to come by. From the pinup (which still had some currency at the beginning of the period) to the large-breasted model recently heralded by fashion magazines as "back for the nineties," the obsession has continued unabated but for the Twiggy and braless moment of the late sixties and early seventies. If anything, the objectification of the breast has increased; it is now so radical that breast enlargement surgery was undergone by nearly a hundred thousand women in 1986 alone. The *Geographic* may reflect this trend when it increasingly exposed women's breasts in the seventies and eighties, taking them out of the shadows where they were more often found in earlier periods. The now foregrounded breasts are also strikingly more often teenage. A taboo that remains in place throughout this culture is showing old women's sagging or dimpled breasts. The *Geographic* has included these breasts, in the interest of veracity, but bows to cultural pressures by almost invariably printing them in smaller or dimly lit formats.

Two important stylistic changes can be identified in photos of women's bodies in the magazine, one related to changes in commercial photography of women and the other to the growing tolerance of "aesthetic" pictures in the *Geographic* of the eighties. Beginning in the late fifties, certain changes in the way women were photographed in commercials began to be reflected in *National Geographic* images.[6] In early advertisements of the period, women are shown directly involved in the use of a product, as when a woman with a fur stole is shown being helped into her 1955 Chrysler by the doorman of an obviously upscale building. By contrast, a 1966 Chevrolet ad shows a woman lying on the roof of the car putting on lipstick, with a small inset photo that has her sitting on the roof being photographed by a man. The ads of the 1950s show women as domestic royalty; the later ads place them in more straightforwardly sexual roles and postures.

In *National Geographic* documentary images as well, we find a shift, coming some years after that in commercial photography; the naked woman moves from being just an ethnographic fact ("this is the way they dress as they go about living their lives") to being presented as in part an aesthetic and sexual object. After 1970, naked women are less often shown framed with men, less often mothering, more often dancing or lounging.[7] The erotic connotations of the horizontal woman, drawn on by advertisers (Goffman 1975), and of the woman absorbed in dance, combine with more romantic, aesthetic styles to create photos which follow the inflation of sexualized images of women in the culture at large (N. Wolf 1991). Contrast the 1986 highly aesthetic photo of a Micronesian teenager, whose direct gaze invites the reader to make contact and whose hazy green background suggests tropical romanticism, with the more clinical 1970 shot of two women buying herbs at a market in Ethiopia. The breasts of the women are clear and central to the photo's

6. For an example of the connection between *Geographic* and commercial styles, see the similarity between women's fashion photography of the period and the galleries of Polynesian beauties remarked on in chapter 5. One Tahitian woman is posed for a side portrait with her head pushed forward, accentuating a long neck and paralleling the elegance of the model of high-fashion photography of the 1950s.

7. This is based on the twenty photos in our sample of 592 where women are shown without shirts on; half of that number occurred from 1950 to 1969 and the other half from 1970 to 1986 (one would, of course, expect there to be somewhat fewer such photos as urbanization and change in dress styles spread across the globe). Some of the same phenomena noted here have been found in advertising in American family magazines (that is, a decrease in images of married women shown in child care and an increase in those showing them at recreation), although in the latter ads the trends begin earlier, in the later 1940s (Brown 1981).

narrative, but focus is also on the twigs being passed between the seller of herbs and one of the women and on the camels in the near background. The picture's composition and straightforward realism, as well as the informative caption tell us something ethnographic—that is, about something more than women's beauty or women's bodies.

The development of commercial styles elsewhere in the culture amplifies an effect of photographs of women noted by Pollock (1987); the addition of a woman to a photographed scene often succeeds, given cultural ideologies and history, in changing the scene from a still life or object of contemplation to a purchasable commodity. This is because women have traditionally been seen as objects to be possessed, owned, or controlled, and as ornaments to the lives of men. In the case of the *Geographic,* that commodity is a potential tourist destination. Newly glossy images of women led the way in selling the third world to travelers.

A second explanation for changes in rendering the nude woman is found in the increasing tolerance of a more aesthetic rendering of all subjects in the *Geographic.* Aesthetic style, however, has special implications and nuances when the photos are of women. What arises after the fifties in the *Geographic* is not just a more self-consciously aesthetic style but a style whose uses elsewhere in the culture were centered on photography of women, as in fashion and other commercial work.

The cultural debate (however minor in scale and impact) over whether the nudity in the *Geographic* was or is appropriate follows shifting and conflicting definitions of acceptable portrayals of women's bodies (Nead 1990). At issue is not simply whether women's bodies are displayed, but what the cultural context of those images is (Myers 1982; Vance 1990); that context includes the sexualization of the breasts, the objectification of women, the racist understanding of black femininity, and the shame that inheres in American culture to sexuality itself.[8] Nonetheless, the still heavily white male photographic and editorial staff at the *Geographic* appears relatively unaffected by feminist critiques of the use of women's bodies or the critique of colonial looking-relations (Gaines 1988) that prompt both the frequent inclusion and a particular distorted reading by

8. The *Geographic's* breasts should be seen against the broader background of the social changes in the industrial West relating to sexuality. Foucault (1978) has noted that those changes have been mistakenly associated with a "liberation" of sexuality. In fact, he suggests, with the emergence of the modern state and its regulatory needs has come an obsession with talking about and managing sex—through science, state policy, clinical medicine, and now photography.

subscribers of the nude black woman's body. The African-American cabdriver who took one of us to *Geographic* headquarters was less sanguine, even angry, when he noted that the magazine's white women are well covered.

The Kitchen Debates in Africa: Woman's Place in the March of Progress.   In a subtly nuanced analysis of the genre of 1980s Hollywood success movies, Traube (1989) details the influence of the Reagan years and a particular moment of labor demography and consumer capitalism in the construction of the films' plots and styles. These films describe, among other things, the gender-specific dangers and possibilities of the world of managerial work for the middle-class youth who view these movies on their way to corporate work lives. Specifically, they include "warning of the feminizing effects of deference on men and, conversely, the masculinizing effects of ambition on women" (1989:291). The *National Geographic's* women do not provide as easy an identifying anchor for the magazine's readers as do these movies' characters, but their image, too, has responded to changes in the politics and rate of American women's labor force participation. They have also played a role in articulating longstanding cultural notions about the role of women in socioeconomic development overseas. We will now examine problems of the progress of women here and abroad.

Against the indolent native of colonialist discourse, the *Geographic's* industrious native toils in response to an editorial policy which calls for a sympathetic other. The way women's work is portrayed, however, shows some culturally predictable differences from that of men's. As in the wider culture, women's work is sometimes presented as less intellectually demanding, more toilsome. Take the Melanesian man and woman set up on opposite pages (April 1969:574–75). A male archer on the left is labeled "man, the hunter" and, on the right, a photo of a woman with child in a netbag carrying a large load of firewood, "woman, the laborer." The woman smiles under her burden, perhaps thereby evoking images long in circulation in Western culture: these are images that romanticize the hard-working black woman, often ignoring the difference between her enduring and enjoying (much less opposing) oppression (hooks 1981:6). In this latter cultural discourse, the black woman could endure what no lady could and therefore revealed her more natural, even animal nature (81–82). For many readers of the *Geographic,* it may be an easy step from the celebration of the strong working woman to her dehumanization as someone with less than human abilities to withstand those burdens.[9]

Cultural ambivalence toward women working outside the home has been profound during the postwar period, when employment for which women sixteen and older received wages grew from 25 percent in 1940 to 40 percent in 1960. More of this is accounted for by African-American women, half of whom were employed in 1950, with their wage-paying work continuing at high rates in the following decades. The ideological formulation of the meaning of women's work has changed. Working women in the fifties were defined as helpmates to their husbands. Only much later did women's work come to be seen as a means to goals of independence and self-realization (Chafe 1983), although even here, as Traube (1989) points out, messages were widely available that women's success in work was threatening to men. This ambivalence occasionally shows up in the *Geographic* when the laboring woman is presented as a drudge or when her femininity, *despite her working,* is emphasized. An example of the latter is found in a photograph of a Burmese woman shown planting small green shoots in a garden row (June 1974). Retouching has been done both to her line of plants and to the flowers encircling her hair. The sharpening and coloring of these two items lets the picture tell much more clearly a narrative about her femininity and her productivity and about how those two things are not mutually exclusive.

More often, however, the labor of women as well as other aspects of their lives are presented by the *Geographic* as central to the march of progress in their respective countries. Women are constructed as the vanguard of progress in part through the feminizing of the developing nation-state itself (Kabbani 1986; compare Schaffer 1988). How does this work? In the first instance, those foreign states are contrasted, in some Western imaginations, with a deeply masculine American national identity (Krasniewicz 1990, Jeffords 1989), a gendering achieved through the

9. That step may have been taken by white feminism as well, hooks points out: "When the women's movement was at its peak and white women were rejecting the role of breeder, burden bearer, and sex object, black women were celebrated for their unique devotion to the task of mothering; for their 'innate' ability to bear tremendous burdens; and for their ever-increasing availability as sex object. We appeared to have been unanimously elected to take up where white women were leaving off" (1981:6). See Hammond and Jablow (1977) for an analysis of the particular strength of the notion of nonwhite women as beasts of burden in the case of African women; see also Collins (1991).

Photos of working women in the magazine are as ambivalent as their cultural context. Some portray the laboring woman as drudge, while others, like this June 1974 picture of a Burmese woman, emphasize her femininity *despite* her working. The flowers in her hair and the plants she works with have been brought forward by retouching. (Photo: Wilbur E. Garrett, © National Geographic Society)

equation of the West (*in* the West, of course) with strength, civilization, rationality, and freedom, its other with vulnerability, primitivity, superstition, and the constraints of tradition. Once this equation was made, articles can be titled as in the following instance, where progress is masculinized and the traditional nation feminized: "Beneath the Surge of Progress, old Mexico's Charm and Beauty Lie Undisturbed" (October 1961).

From the perspective of the colonial era, the symbolic femininity of the non-Western states would seem to have been solidly established, but this kind of rhetoric may have lost some of its power in the new world of social relations of the 1970s and 1980s. The more salient actors in U.S. media coverage of the third world seem now to be male terrorists in the Middle East and male economic competitors in Japan and Korea. Starving ungendered children have some representational space, but female workers are still not visible. How the Geographic's recent coverage articulates with other media representations of the shifting gender of the foreign remains to be studied.

Fanon (1965:39) pointed out in his analysis of French colonial attitudes and strategies concerning the veil in Algeria that the colonialists' goal, here as elsewhere in the world, was "converting the woman, winning her over to the foreign values, wrenching her free from her status" as a means of "shaking up the [native] man" and gaining control of him. With this and other motives, those outsiders who would "develop" the third world have often seen the advancement of non-Western women as the first goal to be achieved, with their men's progress thought to follow rather than precede it. In the nineteenth century, evolutionary theory claimed that the move upward from savagery to barbarism to civilization was indexed by the treatment of women, in particular by their liberation "from the burdens of overwork, sexual abuse, and male violence" (Tiffany and Adams 1985:8). It "saw women in non-Western societies as oppressed and servile creatures, beasts of burden, chattels who could be bought and sold, eventually to be liberated by 'civilization' or 'progress,' thus attaining the enviable position of women in Western society" (Etienne and Leacock 1980:1), who were then expected to be happy with their place.[10] The Geographic has told a much more upbeat version of this story, mainly by presenting other women's labors positively.

The continuation of these ways of thinking into the present can be seen in how states defined as "progressive" have been rendered by both Western media like the National Geographic and the non-Western state bureaucracies concerned. Graham-Brown (1988) and Schick (1990) describe how photographic and other proof of the progress or modernity of states like Turkey and prerevolutionary Iran has often been found primarily in the lives of their women, particularly in their unveiling.[11]

---

10. Western feminism in the 1970s may have simply transformed rather than fundamentally challenged the terms of this argument as well when it argued that the women of the world were oppressed by men and were to be liberated by feminism as defined in the West (see Amos and Parmar 1984).

11. Although feminist anthropology has analyzed and critiqued these kinds of assumptions, it has nonetheless often continued a basic evolutionary discourse

Indeed, as Schick points out, "a photograph of an unveiled woman was not much different from one of a tractor, an industrial complex, or a new railroad; it merely symbolized yet another one of men's achievements" (1990:369).

Take the example from the *Geographic*'s January 1985 article on Baghdad. Several photographs show veiled women walking through the city streets. One shot shows women in a narrow alley. The dark tones of the photograph are a function of the lack of sunlight reaching down into the alley, but they also reinforce the message of the caption. Playing with the associations between veil and the past that are evoked for most readers, it says, "In the shadows of antiquity, women in long black abayas walk in one of the older sections of the city." A few pages earlier, we learn about the high-rise building boom in the city and the changing roles of women in a two-page layout that shows a female electrical engineer in a hard hat and jeans organizing a building project with a male colleague. The caption introduces her by name and goes on: "Iraqi women, among the most progressive in the Arab world, constitute 25 percent of the country's work force and are guaranteed equality under Baath Party doctrine." On the opposite page, the modern buildings they have erected are captioned, "New York on the Tigris." The equation of the end point (Manhattan) with the unveiled woman is neatly laid out.

The goal of progress through women and of women's progress might have been inferred by many viewers from a 1968 photo from Ecuador (February: 271) showing a family of four in the park, sitting in front of the man's abstract painting. This thoroughly modern nuclear family enjoys the clean and cultivated leisure brought by that progress, with the woman most easily understood as housewife and mother. With the bifurcation of the frame into two halves, one side containing the man's artwork, and the other the mother and her children, the symbolic dualism familiar to Western audiences of women/child/nature and men/independent/art is achieved. This couple has no further to go on the Great March. The photo also shows that the kindly-light policy makes a critique of patriarchy as problematic as a critique of anything else.

This celebration of simultaneous women's liberation and national

---

in the assumption that Ong has identified: "Although a common past may be claimed by feminists, Third World women are often represented as mired in it, ever arriving at modernity when Western feminists are already adrift in postmodernism" (1988:87).

progress is not the whole story, of course. The magazine also communicates—in a more muted way through the fifties and into the sixties—a sense of the value of the natural, Gemeinschaft-based life of the people without progress. Progress can be construed as a socially corrosive process as it was in the late nineteenth century, when non-Western women were seen as superior to their Western counterparts because too much education had weakened the latter, sapping vitality from their reproductive organs (Ehrenreich and English 1978:114). The illiterate woman of the non-Western world still lives with this cultural inheritance, standing for the woman "unruined" by progress.

Another potential factor in the questioning of progress in gender roles is the feminization of natural landscapes. As Schaffer (1988) has shown for Australian culture and Tiffany and Adams (1985) for the Americas, the landscape has been culturally construed as female over the entire period since discovery. The one who comes to exploit and change it is male, and so the undeveloped third world/feminine can be construed as a repository of timeless (not political) wisdom about the values of a simple life, family, and living in harmony with nature.

An example of the contradictory place of progress is found in two photographs that draw attention to housewives. In the first, an Inuit woman wearing a fur-trimmed parka stands in front of a washing machine: "Unfamiliar luxury," the caption says, "a washing machine draws a housewife to the new 'Tuk' laundromat, which also offers hot showers" (July 1968). This picture is deliberately structured around the contrast between the premodern and the modern, with the evaluative balance falling to the luxurious present. It might have still resonated for readers with the image from 1959 of Nixon and Khrushchev arguing over the benefits of capitalism next to a freshly minted washing machine and dryer at the American National Exhibition in Moscow. In those debates, Nixon could argue that the progress of American society under capitalism is found in its ability to provide labor-saving devices to women. "I think that this attitude toward women is universal. What we want is to make easier the life of our housewives," he said. In the gender stories told during the cold war, family life and commodities provided what security was to be found in the post-Hiroshima, post-holocaust world (May 1988). The non-Western woman, too, could be deployed as proof of capitalism's value, of the universal desire for these goods, and of the role of women in the evolution of society.

From January 1971, however, an article entitled "Housewife at the End of the World" documents the adventures of an Ohio woman settling in Tierra del Fuego, and congratulates her on adapting to local norms of self-sufficiency and simplicity. The last photo's caption articulates the theme of the whole article: "Life in this remote land spurs inventiveness. . . . My special interests keep me so busy I have little time to miss the conveniences I once knew." The North American woman chooses to forgo the benefits of progress, in search of an authentically simple place, as her "younger sister" climbs the ladder in the other direction.

In stories of progress and/or decline, Western and non-Western women have often been played off against each other in this way, one used to critique the other in line with different purposes and in the end leaving each feeling inadequate. The masculine writer/image maker/ consumer thereby asserts his own strength, both through his right to evaluate and through his completeness in contrast to women. Although non-Western men cannot be said to fare well in these cultural schemes, they are used less frequently and in other ways (Honour 1989) to either critique or shore up white men's masculinity.

In sum, the women of the non-Western world represent a population aspiring to the full femininity achieved in Western cultures, and, in a more secondary way, they are a repository for the lost femininity of "liberated" Western women. Both an ideal and thus a critique of modern femininity, they are also a measure to tell the Western family how far it has advanced. They are shown working hard and as key to their country's progress toward some version of the Western-consumer family norm. The sometimes contradictory message these pictures can send to middle-class women is consistent with cultural ideologies in the United States that by turns condemn and affirm the woman who would be both mother and wage earner. We can see the women of the *National Geographic* playing a role within a social field where the cold war was being waged and where social changes in kinship structures and gender politics were precipitated by the entrance of white women into the paid labor force in larger and larger numbers.

Conclusion

We have focused here on the rendition of racial and gender difference in the *Geographic*. We can now step back and remind the reader that the color of sex in the magazine emerges first from the photographer's work. The *Geographic* photographer has always been and predominantly remains, both literally and symbolically, a white man. And not just any white man, but the whitest and most masculine version possible: the great hunter/adventurer (Bright 1990:137–38), free to roam the globe in search of visual treasure, flamboyantly virile in his freedom from observation and evaluation, and his bravery in entering the dangerous realms at the ends of the earth, in continents still dark for most of his audience.[12] While the photographs that we find in the magazine are often gentle, beautiful images of people construed as feminine, the image-maker—at least as many viewers imagine—looks out on this exotic world from that Marlboro Country where the jaws are all square with a tough growth of stubble and the Indians are all gone.

We move now to the social positions, viewpoints, and "looks" which constitute the process of making photographic meaning in the magazine.

12. The masculine part of this ethos is found in contemporary anthropology as well, as indicated by Okely (1975). The racially white part is noted by Said (1989).

Seven

The Photograph as an Intersection of Gazes

If photographs are messages, the message is both transparent and mysterious.

(Sontag 1977:111)

All photographs tell stories about looking. In considering the *National Geographic*'s photographs, we have been struck by the variety of looks and looking relations that swirl in and around them. These looks—whether from the photographer, the reader, or the person photographed—are ambiguous, charged with feeling and power, central to the stories (sometimes several and·conflicting) that the photo can be said to tell. By examining the "lines of sight" evident in the *Geographic* photograph of the non-Westerner, we become aware that it is not simply a captured view of the *other*, but rather a dynamic site at which many gazes or viewpoints intersect. This intersection creates a complex, multidimensional object; it allows viewers of the photo to negotiate a number of different identities both for themselves and for those pictured; and it is one route by which the photograph threatens to break frame and reveal its social context. We aim here to explore the significance of "gaze" for intercultural relations in the photograph and to present a typology of seven kinds of gaze that can be found in the photograph and its social context: the photographer's gaze (the actual look through the viewfinder); the institutional magazine gaze, evident in cropping, picture choice, and captioning; the reader's gaze; the non-Western subject's gaze; the explicit looking done by Westerners who may be framed with locals in the picture; the gaze returned or refracted by the mirrors or cameras that are shown in local hands; and our own academic gaze.

The Gaze and Its Significance

The photograph and the non-Western person share two fundamental attributes in the culturally tutored experience of most Americans; they are objects at which we *look*. The photograph has this quality because it is usually intended as a thing of either beauty or documentary interest and surveillance. Non-Westerners draw a look, rather than inattention or interaction, to the extent that their difference or foreignness defines them as noteworthy yet distant. A look is necessary to cross the span created by the perception of difference, a perception which initially, of course, also involves looking. When people from outside the Western world are photographed, the importance of the look is accentuated.[1]

A number of intellectual traditions have dealt with "the gaze," looking or spectating as they occur in photography and art. Often these types of analysis have focused on the formal features of the photograph alone, excluding history and culture. While we are critical of several of the perspectives on gaze that we review below, to view photographs as having a certain structure can be consistent with an emphasis on an active and historical reader. In other words, we will argue that the lines of gaze perceptible in the photograph suggest the multiple forces at work in creating photographic meaning, one of the most important of which is readers' culturally informed interpretive work. One objective of our research has been to test the universal claims of certain of these theories about gaze by looking at actual cases of photographs being taken, edited, and read by individuals in real historical time and cultural space. Nonetheless, the interethnic looking that gets done in *National Geographic* photos can be conceptualized by drawing on a number of the insights of these analyses.

Feminist film theory, beginning with Mulvey (1985), has focused on

1. The same of course can be said for other categories of people who share a marked quality with the non-Westerner, including physical deviants (Diane Arbus's pictures, for example), the criminal (Tagg 1988), and, most commonly, women (Goffman 1979).

the ways in which looking in patriarchal society is, in her words, "split between active/male and passive/female. The controlling male gaze projects its phantasy on to the female figure which is styled accordingly (1985:808). The position of spectator, in this view, belongs to the male and allows for the construction of femininity. John Berger (1972) has treated the gaze as masculine. He points out that contemporary gender ideologies envisage men as active doers and define women as passive presence, men by what they do to others, women by their attitudes toward themselves. This has led to women's focusing on how they appear before others and so to fragmenting themselves into "the surveyor and the surveyed. . . . One might simplify this by saying *men act* and *women appear*. Men look at women. Women watch themselves being looked at . . . [and] the surveyor of woman in herself is male" (1972: 46–47; see also Burgin 1986).

Mulvey and Berger alert us to the ways in which the position of spectator has the potential to enhance or articulate the power of the observer over the observed. Representations produced by the artist, the photographer, and the scientist in their role as spectators have permanent, tangible qualities and are culturally defined as quasi-sacred. Both Mulvey and Berger point out that it is the social context of patriarchy, rather than a universal essential quality of the image, that gives the gaze a masculine character.

Recent critiques of these views take issue with the simple equation of the gaze with the masculine, with the psychoanalytic emphasis of this work and its concomitant tendency to universalize its claims and to ignore social and historical context, as well as its neglect of race and class as key factors determining looking relations (de Lauretis 1987; Gaines 1988; Green 1989; Jameson 1983; Tagg 1988; A. Williams 1987). These critiques make a number of proposals useful in examining *National Geographic* photographs. They suggest, first, that the magazine viewer operates within a racial system in which there are taboos on certain kinds of looking, for example, black men looking at white women. Gaines (1988) forcefully suggests that we need to rethink ideas about looking "along more materialist lines, considering, for instance, how some groups have historically had the license to 'look' openly while other groups have 'looked' illicitly" (1988:24–25). She also argues that those who have used psychoanalytic theory claim to treat looking positions (viewer/viewed) as distinct from actual social groups (male/female) even while they are identified with gender, and in so doing, "keep the levels of the social ensemble [social experience, representational systems, and so on] hopelessly separate."

Work on women as spectators suggests that viewers may have several possible responses to images, moving toward and away from identification with the imaged person and sometimes "disrupt[ing] the authority and closure of dominant representations" (A. Williams 1987:11; compare Burgin 1982). This research suggests that looking need not be equated with controlling; Jameson argues that there may be legitimate pleasures in looking at others that are not predicated on the desire to control, denigrate, or distance oneself from the other. More broadly, we can say that the social whole in which photographers, editors, and a diversity of readers look at the non-Western world allows no simple rendering of the spectator of the magazine, including the spectator's gender.

Much feminist analysis of the power of gaze has drawn on the psychoanalytic theorizing of Lacan (1981). While it carries the dangers of a universalizing focus, Lacan's view of the gaze can be helpful as a model for the *potential* effects of looking. Lacan speaks of gaze as something distinct from the eye of the beholder and from simple vision: it is that "something [which] slips . . . and is always to some degree eluded in it [vision]" (1981:73); it is "the lack." The gaze comes from the other who constitutes the self in that looking, but the gaze the self encounters is "not a seen gaze, but a gaze imagined by me in the field of the Other" (1981:84). Ultimately, however, the look that the self receives is "profoundly unsatisfying" because the other does not look at the self in the way that the self imagines it ought to be looked at. The photograph of the non-Westerner can be seen as at least partially the outcome of a set of psychoculturally informed choices made by photographers, editors, and caption writers who pay attention at some level to their own and the other's gaze. Their choices may be made in such a way as to reduce the likelihood of the kind of disappointment Lacan mentions. What can be done in the photograph is to manipulate, perhaps unconsciously, the gaze of the other (by way of such processes as photo selection) so that it allows us to see ourselves reflected in their eyes in ways that are comfortable, familiar, and pleasurable. Photographs might be seen as functioning in the way Lacan says a painting can, which is by pacifying the viewer. What is pacified is the gaze, or rather the anxiety that accompanies the gap between our ideal identity and the real. This taming of the gaze occurs when we realize that the picture does not change as our gaze changes. In Lacan's view, we are desperate for and because of the gaze, and the power of the pictorial representation is that it can ease that anxiety. Photos of the ethnic other can help relieve the anxiety provoked by the ideal of the other's gaze and estimation of us.[2]

Homi Bhabha (1983), on the other hand, argues that the gaze is not only crucial to colonial regimes, but that a tremendous ambivalence and unsettling effect must accompany colonial looking relations because the mirror which these images of the other hold up to the colonial self is "problematic, for the subject finds or recognizes itself through an image which is simultaneously alienating and hence potentially confrontational (29). There is always the threatened return of the look" (1983:33). In Bhabha's terms, the look at the racial other places the viewer in the uncomfortable position of both recognizing himself or herself in the other and denying that recognition. Denial leaves "always the trace of loss, absence. To put it succinctly, the recognition and disavowal of 'difference' is always disturbed by the question of its re-presentation or construction" (1983:33). From this perspective, which borrows from Lacan and Freud, colonial social relations are enacted largely through a "regime of visibility," in which the look is crucial both for identifying the other and for raising questions of how racist discourse can enclose the mirrored self as well as the other within itself. The photograph and all its intersections of gaze, then, is a site at which this identification and the conflict of maintaining a stereotyped view of difference occurs.[3]

Foucalt's analysis of the rise of surveillance in modern society is also relevant to understanding the photographic gaze, and recent analyses (Green 1984; Tagg 1988) have sharply delineated ways in which photography of the other operates at the nexus of knowledge and power that Foucault identified. Foucault pointed to psychiatry, medicine, and legal institutions as primary sites in which control over populations was achieved. His novel contribution was to see these institutions as exercising power not only by coercive control of the body but by creating knowledge of the body and thereby forcing it "to emit signs" or to conform physically and representationally to the knowledge produced

2. The differences between painting and photography are also important. The gaze cannot be altered at will or completely to taste, and so the looks that are exchanged in *National Geographic* photographs can be seen as more disappointing and less pacifying than are, for example, Gauguin's pictures of Polynesian women.

3. This analysis resembles the less psychoanalytically freighted work of Sider on the stereotype in Indian-white relations. Sider frames the problem as one of "the basic contradiction of this form of domination—*that it cannot both create and incorporate the other as an other*—thus opening a space for continuing resistance and distancing" (1987:22).

by these powerful institutions. The crucial role of photography in the exercise of power lies in its ability to allow for close study of the other and to promote, in Foucault's words, the "normalizing gaze, a surveillance that makes it possible to qualify, to classify and to punish. It establishes over individuals a visibility through which one differentiates them and judges them" (1977:25).

In the second half of the nineteenth century, photography began to be used to identify prisoners, mental patients, and racial or ethnic types. According to Tagg, its efficacy lies not so much in facilitating social control of those photographed but in representing these others to an audience of "non-deviants" who thereby acquire a language for understanding themselves and the limits they must observe to avoid being classed with those on the outside. Foucault's analysis might suggest that the gaze of the *Geographic* is part of the "capillary system" of international power relations allowing for the surveillance, if not the control, of non-Western people. The magazine's gaze at the third world operates to represent it to an American audience in ways that can but do not always shore up a Western cultural identity or sense of self as modern and civilized. The gaze is not, however, as singular or monolithic as Foucault might suggest. In itself, we might say, a look can mean anything, but lines and types of gaze, in social context, tend to open up certain possibilities for interpreting a photograph and to foreclose others. They often center on issues of intimacy, pleasure, scrutiny, confrontation, and power.[4]

A Multitude of Gazes

Many gazes can be found in every photograph in the *National Geographic*. This is true whether the picture shows an empty landscape; a single person looking straight at the camera; a large group of people, each looking in a different direction but none at the camera; or a person in the distance whose eyes are tiny or out of focus. In other words, the gaze is not simply the look given by or to a photographed subject. It includes seven kinds of gaze.[5]

4. Ellsworth's research (e.g., 1975) on gaze in natural and experimental contacts between people (conducted in the United States) has been central in making the argument for a thoroughly contextual view of looking relations in the discipline of psychology.

5. An early typology of the gaze from a colonial and racist perspective is found in Sir Richard Burton's accounts of his African expeditions, during which

The Photographer's Gaze.   This gaze, represented by the camera's eye, leaves its clear mark on the structure and content of the photograph. Independently or constrained by others, the photographer takes a position on a rooftop overlooking Khartoum or inside a Ulithian menstrual hut or in front of a funeral parade in Vietnam. Photo subject matter, composition, vantage point (angle or point of view), sharpness and depth of focus, color balance, framing, and other elements of style are the results of the viewing choices made by the photographer or by the invitations or exclusions of those being photographed (Geary 1988).

Susan Sontag argues that photographers are usually profoundly alienated from the people they photograph, and may "feel compelled to put the camera between themselves and whatever is remarkable that they encounter" (1977:10). *Geographic* photographers, despite an expressed fundamental sympathy with the third world people they meet, confront them across distances of class, race, and sometimes gender. Whether from a fear of these differences or the more primordial (per Lacan) insecurity of the gaze itself, the photographer can often make the choice to insert technique between self and his or her subjects, as can the social scientist (Devereux 1967).

Under most circumstances, the photographer's gaze and the viewer's gaze overlap. The photographer may treat the camera eye as simply a conduit for the reader's look, the "searchlight" (Metz 1985) of his or her vision. Though these two looks can be disentangled, the technology and conventions of photography force the reader to follow that eye and see

---

he felt himself to be the victim of "an ecstasy of curiosity." Wrote Burton: "At last my experience in staring enabled me to categorize the infliction as follows. Firstly is the stare furtive, when the starer would peep and peer under the tent, and its reverse, the open stare. Thirdly is the stare curious or intelligent, which generally was accompanied with irreverent laughter regarding our appearance. Fourthly is the stare stupid, which denoted the hebete incurious savage. The stare discreet is that of Sultans and greatmen; the stare indiscreet at unusual seasons is affected by women and children. Sixthly is the stare flattering—it was exceedingly rare, and equally so was the stare contemptuous. Eighthly is the stare greedy; it was denoted by the eyes restlessly bounding from one object to another, never tired, never satisfied. Ninthly is the stare peremptory and pertinacious, peculiar to crabbed age. The dozen concludes with the stare drunken, the stare fierce or pugnacious, and finally the stare cannibal, which apparently considered us as articles of diet" (Burton in Moorehead 1960:33). One can imagine a similarly hostile categorization of white Westerners staring at exotics over the past centuries.

The gaze of the camera is not always exactly the same as the gaze of the viewer, but in most *Geographic* photographs the former structures the latter in powerful ways. In this August 1976 photograph of a Venezuelan diamond transaction, the viewer is strongly encouraged to share the photographer's interest in the miner rather than in the broker. (Photo: Robert Madden, © National Geographic Society)

the world from its position.[6] The implications of this fact can be illustrated with a photo that shows a Venezuelan miner selling the diamonds he has just prospected to a middleman (August 1976). To take his picture, the photographer has stood inside the broker's place of business, shooting out over his back and shoulder to capture the face and hands

6. Some contemporary photographers are experimenting with these conventions (in point of view or framing) in an effort to undermine this equation. Victor Burgin, for example, intentionally attempts to break this down by making photographs that are " 'occasions for interpretation' rather than . . . 'objects of consumption' " and that thereby require a gaze which more actively produces itself rather than simply accepting the photographer's gaze as its own. While one can question whether any *National Geographic* photograph is ever purely an object of consumption, the distinction alerts us to the possibility that the photographer can encourage or discourage, through technique, the relative independence of the viewer's gaze.

of the miner as he exchanges his diamonds for cash. The viewer is strongly encouraged to share the photographer's interest in the miner, rather than the broker (whose absent gaze may be more available for substitution with the viewer's than is the miner's), and in fact to identify with the broker from whose relative position the shot has been taken and received. The broker, like the North American reader, stands outside the frontier mining world. Alternative readings of this photograph are, of course, possible; the visibility of the miner's gaze may make identification with him and his precarious position more likely. Ultimately what is important is the question of how a diverse set of readers respond to such points of view in a photograph.

The Magazine's Gaze. This is the whole institutional process by which some portion of the photographer's gaze is chosen for use and emphasis, as described in chapters 2 and 3. It includes (1) the editor's decision to commission articles on particular locations or issues; (2) the editor's choice of pictures; and (3) the editor's and layout designer's decisions about cropping the picture, arranging it with other photos on the page to bring out the desired meaning, reproducing it in a certain size format to emphasize or downplay its importance, or even altering the picture. The reader, of course, cannot determine whether decisions relating to the last two choices are made by editor or photographer. The magazine's gaze is more evident and accessible in (4) the caption writer's verbal fixing of a vantage on the picture's meaning. This gaze is also multiple and sometimes controversial, given the diverse perspectives and politics of those who work for the *Geographic*.

The Magazine Readers' Gazes. As Barthes has pointed out, the "photograph is not only perceived, received, it is *read,* connected more or less consciously by the public that consumes it to a traditional stock of signs" (1977:19). Independently of what the photographer or the caption writer may intend as the message of the photo, the reader can imagine something else. This fact, which distinguishes the reader's gaze from that of the magazine, led us to investigate the former directly by asking a number of people to look at and interpret our set of photos. Certain elements of composition or content may make it more likely that the reader will resist the photographic gaze and its ideological messages or potentials. These include whatever indicates that a camera (rather than the reader's eye alone) has been at work—jarring, unnatural colors, off-center angles, and obvious photo retouching.

What *National Geographic* subscribers see is not simply what they get (the physical object, the photograph) but what they imagine the world is about before the magazine arrives, what imagining the picture provokes, and what they remember afterwards of the story they make the picture tell or allow it to tell. The reader's gaze, then, has a history and a future, and it is structured by the mental work of inference and imagination, provoked by the picture's inherent ambiguity (Is that woman smiling or smirking? What are those people in the background doing?) and its tunnel vision (What is going on outside the picture frame? What is it, outside the picture, that she is looking at?). Beyond that, the photo permits fantasy ("Those two are in love, in love like I am with Stuart, but they're bored there on the bench, bored like I have been even in love" or "That child. How beautiful. She should be mine to hold and feed.").

The reader's gaze is structured by a large number of cultural elements or models, many more than those used to reason about racial or cultural difference. Cultural models that we have learned help us interpret gestures such as the thrown-back shoulders of an Argentinean cowboy as indicative of confidence, strength, and bravery. Models of gender lead to a reading of a picture of a mother with a child as a natural scenario, and of the pictured relationship as one of loving, relaxed nurturance; alternatively, the scene might have been read as underlaid with tensions and emotional distance, an interpretation that might be more common in societies with high infant mortality. There is, however, not one reader's gaze; each individual looks with his or her own personal, cultural, and political background or set of interests. It has been possible for people to speak of "the [singular] reader" only so long as "the text" is treated as an entity with a single determinate meaning that is simply consumed (Radway 1984) and only so long as the agency, enculturated nature, and diversity of experience of readers are denied.

The gaze of the *National Geographic* reader is also structured by photography's technological form, including a central paradox. On the one hand, photographs allow participation in the non-Western scene through vicarious viewing. On the other, they may also alienate the reader by way of the fact that they create or require a passive viewer and that they frame out much of what an actual viewer of the scene would see, smell, and hear, thereby atomizing and impoverishing experience (Sontag 1977). From another perspective, the photograph has been said (Metz 1985) to necessarily distance the viewer by changing the person photographed into an object—we know our gaze falls on a two-dimensional object—and promoting fantasy. Still, the presumed consent of the other to be photographed can give the viewer the illusion of having some relationship with him or her.

Finally, this gaze is also structured by the context of reading. How and where does the reader go through the magazine—quickly or carefully, alone or with a child? We begin to answer such questions in the next two chapters. In a less literal sense, the context of reading includes cultural notions about the magazine itself, as high middlebrow, scientific, and pleasurable. Readers' views of what the photograph says about the other must have something to do with the elevated class position they can assume their reading of *National Geographic* indicates. If I the reader am educated and highbrow in contrast to the reader of *People* magazine or the daily newspaper, my gaze may take on the seriousness and appreciative stance a high-class cultural product requires.

The Non-Western Subject's Gaze.   There is perhaps no more significant gaze in the photograph than that of its subject. It is how and where the other looks that most determines the differences in the message a photograph can give about intercultural relations. The gaze of the other found in *National Geographic* can be classified into at least four types; she or he can confront the camera, look at something or someone within the picture frame, look off into the distance, or not look at anything at all.

The gaze confronting camera and reader comprises nearly a quarter of the photos that have at least some non-Western locals in them.[7] What does the look into the camera's eye suggest to readers about the photographic subject? A number of possibilities suggest themselves.

The look into the camera must at least suggest acknowledgment of photographer and reader. Film theorists have disagreed about what this look does, some arguing that it short circuits the voyeurism identified as an important component of most photography: there can be no peeping if the other meets our gaze. The gaze can be confrontational: "I see you looking at me, so you cannot steal that look." Others, however, have argued that this look, while acknowledging the viewer, simply implies more open voyeurism: the return gaze does not contest the right of the viewer to look and may in fact be read as the subject's assent to being watched (Metz 1985:800–801).

7. This figure is based on 438 photographs coded in this way, 24% of which had a subject looking at the camera.

This disagreement hinges on ignoring how the look is returned and on discounting the effects of context inside the frame and in the reader's historically and culturally variable interpretive work. Facial expression is obviously crucial. The local person looks back with a number of different faces, including friendly smiling, hostile glaring, a vacant or indifferent glance, curiosity, or an ambiguous look. Some of these looks, from some kinds of ethnic others, are unsettling, disorienting, and perhaps often avoided. In *National Geographic's* photos, the return look is, however, usually not a confrontational or challenging one. The smile plays an important role in muting the potentially disruptive, confrontational role of this return gaze. If the other looks back at the camera and smiles, the combination can be read by viewers as the subject's assent to being surveyed. In 38 percent of the pictures of locals where facial expressions are visible (N = 436), someone is smiling (although not all who smile are looking into the camera), while a higher 55 percent of all pictures in which someone looks back at the camera include one or more smiling figures.

The camera gaze can also establish at least the illusion of intimacy and communication. To the extent that *National Geographic* presents itself as bringing together the corners of the world, the portrait and camera gaze are important routes to those ends. The other is not distanced, but characterized as approachable; the reader can imagine the other is about to speak to him or her. The photographers commonly view the frontal shot as a device for cutting across language barriers and allowing for intercultural communication. The portrait is, in the words of one early *Geographic* photographer, "a collaboration between subject and photographer" (National Geographic Society 1981:22). In published form, of course, the photographed person is still "subjected to an unreturnable gaze" (Tagg 1988:64), in no position to speak.

The magazine's goal of creating intimacy between subject and reader contradicts to some extent its official goal of presenting an unmanipulated, truthful slice of life from another country. Virtually all the photographers and picture editors we spoke with saw the return gaze as problematic and believed that such pictures ought to be used sparingly because they are clearly not candid, and potentially influenced by the photographer. They might also be "almost faking intimacy," one editor said. Another mentioned that the use of direct gaze is also a question of style, suggesting more commercial and less gritty values. The photographer can achieve both the goals of intimacy and invisibility by taking portraits which are not directly frontal, but in which the gaze angles off to the side of the camera.

To face the camera is to permit close examination of the photographed subject, including scrutiny of the face and eyes, which are in commonsense parlance the seat of soul—feelings, personality, or character. Frontality is a central technique of a documentary rhetoric in photography (Tagg 1988:189); it sets the stage for either critique or celebration, but in either case evaluation, of the other as a person or type. Editors at the magazine talked about their search for the "compelling face" in selecting photos for the magazine.

Racial, age, and gender differences appear in how often and how exactly the gaze is returned and lend substance to each of these perspectives on the camera gaze. To a statistically significant degree, women look into the camera more than men, children and older people look into the camera more often than other adults, those who appear poor more than those who appear wealthy, those whose skin is very dark more than those who are bronze, those who are bronze more than those whose skin is white, those in native dress more than those in Western garb, those without any tools more than those who are using machinery.[8] Those who are culturally defined as weak—women, children, people of color, the poor, the tribal rather than the modern, those without technology—are more likely to face the camera, the more powerful to be represented looking elsewhere. There is also an intriguing (but not statistically significant) trend toward higher rates of looking at the camera in pictures taken in countries that were perceived as friendly towards the United States.[9]

8. These analyses were based on those photos where gaze was visible, and excluded pictures with a Westerner in the photo. The results were, for gender (N = 360) x^2 = 3.835, df = 1, p < .05; for age (N = 501) x^2 = 13.745, df = 4, p < .01; for wealth (N = 507) x^2 = 12.950, df = 2, p < .01; for skin color (N = 417) x^2 = 8.704, df = 3, p < .05; for dress style (N = 452) x^2 = 12.702, df = 1, p < .001; and for technology (N = 287) x^2 = 4.172, df = 1, p < .05. Discussing these findings in the photography department, we were given the pragmatic explanation that children generally are more fearless in approaching photographers, while men often seem more wary of the camera than women, especially when it is wielded by a male photographer.

9. In the sample of pictures from Asia in which gaze is ascertainable (N = 179), "friendly" countries (including the PRC after 1975, Taiwan, Hong Kong, South Korea, Japan, and the Philippines) had higher rates of smiling than "unfriendly" or neutral countries (x^2 = 2.101, df = 1, p = .147). Excluding Japan,

To look out at the viewer, then, would appear to represent not a confrontation between the West and the rest, but the accessibility of the other. This interpretation is supported by the fact that historically the frontal portrait has been associated with the rougher classes, as the Daumier print points out. Tagg (1988), in a social history of photography, argues that this earlier class-based styling was passed on from portraiture to the emerging use of photography for the documentation and surveillance of the criminal and the insane. Camera gaze is often associated with full frontal posture in the *Geographic;* as such, it is also part of frontality's work as a "code of social inferiority" (Tagg 1988:37). The civilized classes, at least since the nineteenth century, have traditionally been depicted in Western art turning away from the camera and so making themselves less available.[10] The higher-status person may thus be characterized as too absorbed in weighty matters to attend to the photographer's agenda. Facing the camera, in Tagg's terms, "signified the bluntness and 'naturalness' of a culturally unsophisticated class [and had a history which predated photography]" (1988:36).

These class-coded styles of approach and gaze before the camera have continued to have force and utility in renderings of the ethnic other. The twist here is that the more civilized quality imparted to the lighter-skinned male in Western dress and to adult exotics who turn away from the camera is only a relative quality. Full civilization still belongs, ideologically, to the Euroamerican.

Whether these categories of people have actually looked at the camera more readily and openly is another matter. If the gaze toward the camera reflected only a lack of familiarity with it, and curiosity, then one would expect rural people to look at the camera more than urban people. This is not the case. One might also expect some change over time, as cameras became more common everywhere, but there is no difference in rate of gaze when the period from 1950 to 1970 is compared with the later period. The heavy editorial hand at the *Geographic* argues that what is

---

which may have had a more ambiguous status in American eyes, the relationship between gaze and "friendliness" reaches significance ($x^2 = 4.14$, df = 1, p < .05).

10. Tagg (1988) notes that the pose was initially the pragmatic outcome of the technique of the Physionotrace, a popular mechanism used to trace a person's profile from shadow onto a copper plate. When photography took the place of the Physionotrace, no longer requiring profiles, the conventions of associating class with non-frontality continued to have force.

CROQUIS PARISIENS

Pose de l'homme de la nature

Pose de l'homme civilisé

A gaze toward the viewer, in *National Geographic*'s photographs, appears to represent the accessibility of the photographic subject. Historically, frontal portraits have been associated with low class status, as suggested by this 1853 Daumier print, "Pose de l'homme de la nature" and "Pose de l'homme civilisé."

at work is a set of unarticulated perceptions about the kinds of non-Westerners who make comfortable and interesting subjects for the magazine. *National Geographic* editors select from a vast array of possible pictures on the basis of some notion about what the social/power relations are between the reader and the particular ethnic subject being photographed. These aesthetic choices are outside explicit politics but encode politics nonetheless. A "good picture" is a picture that makes sense in terms of prevailing ideas about the other, including ideas about accessibility and difference.

In a second form of gaze by the photographed subject, the non-Westerner looks at someone or something evident within the frame. The ideas readers get about who the other is are often read off from this gaze, which is taken as an index of interest, attention, or goals. The Venezuelan prospector who looks at the diamonds as they are being weighed by the buyer is interested in selling, in making money, rather than in the Western viewer or other compatriots. The caption supplies details: "The hard-won money usually flies fast in gambling and merry-making at primitive diamond camps, where riches-to-rags tales abound." The picture of the Marcos family described in chapter 5 shows both Ferdinand and Imelda happily staring at their children, assuring the audience of their family-oriented character.

A potential point of interest in our set of photographs is the presence of a Western traveler. In 10 percent of such pictures, at least one local looks into the camera. Yet in 22 percent of the pictures in which only locals appear, someone looks into the camera. To a statistically signifi-cant degree, then, the Westerner in the frame draws a look away from those Westerners beyond the camera, suggesting both that these two kinds of Westerners might stand in for each other, as well as indexing the interest they are believed to have for locals.

Third, the other's gaze can run off into the distance beyond the frame. This behavior can suggest radically different things about the character of the subject. It might portray either a dreamy, vacant, absent-minded person or a forward-looking, future-oriented, and determined one. Compare the photo of three Argentinean gauchos as they dress for a rodeo (October 1980) with the shot of a group of six Australian aborigi-nes as they stand and sit in a road to block a government survey team (November 1980). Two of the gauchos, looking out the window at a point in the far distance, come across as thoughtful, pensive, and sharply focused on the heroic tasks in front of them. The aboriginal group in-cludes seven gazes, each heading off in a different direction and only one clearly focused on something within the frame, thus giving the group a disconnected and unfocused look. It becomes harder to imagine this group of seven engaged in coordinated or successful action; that coordi-nation would require mutual planning and, as a corollary, at least some mutual gazing during planning discussions. Other elements of the pho-tograph which add to this impression include their more casual posture, three of them leaning on the truck behind them, in contrast with the gaucho picture in which each stands erect. In addition, the gaze of the aborigines is by no means clear, with gaze having to be read off from the direction of the head. The fuzzy gaze is a significant textual device for reading off character, alienation, or availability. Character connotations aside, the out-of-frame look may also have implications for the viewer's identification with the subject, in some sense connecting with the reader outside the frame (Metz 1985:795).

Finally, in many pictures no gaze at all is visible, either because the people in them are tiny figures lost in a landscape or in a sea of others, or because the scene is dark or the person's face covered by a mask or veil. We might read this kind of picture (14 percent of the whole sample) as being about the landscape or activity rather than the people or as communicating a sense of nameless others or group members rather than individuals. While these pictures do not increase in number over the period, there has been a sudden spate of recent covers in which the face or eyes of a non-Western person photographed are partly hidden (November 1979, February 1983, October 1985, August 1987, October 1987, November 1987, July 1988, Feburary 1991, December 1991). Stylistically, *National Geographic* photographers may now have license to experiment with elements of the classical portrait with its full-face view, but the absence of any such shots before 1979 can also be read as a sign of a changing attitude about the possibilities of cross-cultural communication. The covered face can tell a story of a boundary erected, contact broken.

A Direct Western Gaze.   In its articles on the non-Western world, the *National Geographic* has frequently included photographs that show a Western traveler in the local setting covered in the piece. During the postwar period, these Western travelers have included adventurers, mountain climbers, and explorers; anthropologists, geographers, botanists, and archaeologists; United States military personnel; tourists; and government officials or functionaries from the United States and Europe, from Prince Philip and Dwight Eisenhower to members of the Peace Corps. These photographs show the Westerners viewing the local landscape from atop a hill, studying an artifact, showing a local tribal person some wonder of Western technology (a photograph, a mirror, or the camera itself), or interacting with a native in conversation, work, or play. The Westerner may stand alone or with associates, but more often is framed in company with one or more locals.

These pictures can have complex effects on viewers, for they represent more explicitly than most the intercultural relations it is thought or hoped obtain between the West and its global neighbors. They may allow identification with the Westerner in the photo and, through that, more interaction with, or imaginary participation in, the photo. Before exploring these possibilities, however, we will speculate on some of the functions these photographs serve in the magazine.

Most obviously, the pictures of Westerners can serve a validating function by proving that the author was *there,* that the account is a first-hand one, brought from the field rather than from library or photographic archives. In this respect the photography sequences in *National Geographic* resemble traditional ethnographic accounts, which are written predominantly in the third person but often include at least one story in the first person that portrays the anthropologist in the field (Marcus and Cushman 1982). For this purpose, it does not matter whether the Westerner stands alone with locals.

To serve the function of dramatizing intercultural relations, however, it is helpful to have a local person in the frame. When the Westerner and the other are positioned face-to-face, we can read their relationship and their natures from such features as Goffman (1979) has identified in his study of advertising photography's representation of women and men—their relative height, the leading and guying behaviors found more often in pictured males, the greater emotional expressiveness of the women, and the like.[11] What the Westerners and non-Westerners are doing, the relative vantage points from which they are photographed, and their facial expressions give other cues to their moral and social characters.

Whether or not the gaze of the two parties is mutual provides a comment on who has the right and/or the need to look at whom. When the reader looks out at the world through this proxy Westerner, does the other look back? Rich implications can emerge from a photo showing two female travelers looking at an Ituri forest man in central Africa (February 1960). Standing in the upper left-hand corner, the two women smile down at the native figure in the lower right foreground. He looks toward the ground in front of them, an ambiguous expression on his face. The lines of their gaze have crossed but do not meet; because of this lack of reciprocity, the women's smiles appear bemused and patronizing. In its lack of reciprocity, this gaze is distinctly colonial. The Westerners do not seek a relationship but are content, even pleased, to view the other as an ethnic object. The composition of the picture, structured by an oblique line running from the women down to the

11. Goffman (1979) draws on ethological insights into height and dominance relations when he explains why women are almost always represented as shorter than men in print advertisements. He notes that "so thoroughly is it assumed that differences in size will correlate with differences in social weight that relative size can be routinely used as a means of ensuring that the picture's story will be understandable at a glance" (1979:28).

Photographs in which Western travelers are present encode complete messages about intercultural relations. The nonreciprocal gazes in this February 1960 picture encode distinctly colonial social relations. (Photo: Lowell Thomas, Jr., 1954)

man, shows the Westerners standing over the African; the slope itself can suggest, as Maquet (1986) has pointed out for other visual forms, the idea of *descent* or decline from the one (the Western women) to the other.

A related function of this type of photo lies in the way it prompts the viewer to become self-aware, not just in relation to others but as a viewer, as one who looks or surveys. Mulvey (1985) argues that the gaze in cinema takes three forms—in the camera, in the audience, and in the characters as they look at each other or out at the audience. She says that the first two forms have to be invisible or obscured if the film is to follow realist conventions and bestow on itself the qualities of "reality, obviousness and truth" (1985:816). The viewer who becomes aware of his or her own eye or that of the camera will develop a "distancing awareness" rather than an immediate unconscious involvement. Applying this insight to the *Geographic* photograph, Mulvey might say that bringing the Western eye into the frame promotes distancing rather than immersion. Alvarado (1979/80) has also argued that such intrusion can reveal contradictions in the social relations of the West and the rest that are otherwise less visible, undermining the authority of the photographer by showing the photo being produced, showing it to be an artifact rather than an unmediated fact.[12]

Photographs in which Westerners appear differ from others because we can be more aware of ourselves as actors in the world. Whether or not Westerners appear in the picture, we *are* there, but in pictures that include a Westerner, we may see ourselves being viewed by the other, and we become conscious of ourselves and relationships. The act of seeing the self being seen is antithetical to the voyeurism which many art critics have identified as intrinsic to most photography and film (Alloula 1986; Burgin 1982; Metz 1985).

This factor might best account for Westerners retreating from the photographs after 1969 (see figure 2.2). Staffers in the photography department said that pictures including authors of articles came to be regarded as outdated and were discontinued. Photographer and writer were no longer to be the stars of the story, we were told, although text continued to be written in the first person. As more and more readers had traveled to exotic locales, the *Geographic* staff realized that the picture of the intrepid traveler no longer looked so intrepid. While the rise in international tourism may have had this effect, other social changes of the late 1960s contributed as well. In 1968 popular American protest against participation in the Vietnam War reached a critical point. Huge antiwar demonstrations, the police riot at the Democratic convention, and especially the Viet Cong's success in the Tet offensive convinced many that the American role in Vietnam and, by extension, the third world, would have to be radically reconceptualized. The withdrawal or retreat of American forces came to be seen as inevitable, even though there were many more years of conflict over how, when, and why. American power had come into question for the first time since the end of the World War II. Moreover, the assassinations of Malcolm X and Martin Luther King, and the fire of revolt in urban ghettoes, gave many

12. The documentary filmmaker Dennis O'Rourke, whose films *Cannibal Tours* and *Half Life: A Parable for the Nuclear Age* explore third-world settings, develops a related argument for the role of reflexivity for the image maker (Lutkehaus 1989). He consistently includes himself in the scene but distinguishes between simple filmmaker self-revelation and rendering the social relations between him and his subjects, including capturing the subject's gaze in such a way as to show his or her complicity with the filmmaker. O'Rourke appears to view the reader's gaze more deterministically (for instance, as "naturally" seeing the complicity in a subject's gaze) than do the theorists considered above.

white people a sense of changing and more threatening relations with people of color within the boundaries of the United States.

Most of the non-*Geographic* photos now considered iconic representations of the Vietnam War do not include American soldiers or civilians. The girl who, napalmed, runs down a road towards the camera; the Saigon police chief executing a Viet Cong soldier; the Buddhist monk in process of self-immolation—each of these photographs, frequently reproduced, erases American involvement.

The withdrawal of Americans and other Westerners from the photographs of *National Geographic* may involve a historically similar process. The decolonization process accelerated in 1968 and led Americans (including, one must assume, the editors of *National Geographic*) to see the third world as a more dangerous place, a place where they were no longer welcome to walk and survey as they pleased. The decreasing visibility of Westerners signaled a retreat from a third world seen as a less valuable site for Western achievement, more difficult of access and control. The decolonization process was and is received as a threat to an American view of itself. In Lacan's terms, the other's look could threaten an American sense of self-coherence, and so in this historic moment the Westerner, whose presence in the picture makes it possible for us to see ourselves being seen by that other, withdraws to look from a safer distance, behind the camera.

The Refracted Gaze of the Other: To See Themselves as Others See Them.

In a small but nonetheless striking number of *National Geographic* photographs, a native is shown with a camera, a mirror, or mirror equivalent in his or her hands. Take the photograph of two Aivilik men in northern Canada sitting on a rock in animal skin parkas, one smiling and the other pointing a camera out at the landscape (November 1956). Or the picture that shows two Indian women dancing as they watch their image in a large wall mirror. Or the picture of Governor Brown of California on Tonga showing a group of children the Polaroid snapshots he has just taken of them (March 1968).

Mirror and camera are tools of self-reflection and surveillance. Each creates a double of the self, a second figure who can be examined more closely than the original—a double that can also be alienated from the self, taken away, as a photograph can be, to another place. Psychoanalytic theory notes that the infant's look into the mirror is a significant step in ego formation because it permits the child to see itself for the first time as an other. The central role of these two tools in American society—after all, its millions of bathrooms have mirrors as fixtures nearly as important as their toilets—stems at least in part from their self-reflective capacities. For many Americans, self-knowledge is a central life goal; the injunction to "know thyself" is taken seriously.

The mirror most directly suggests the possibility of self-awareness, and Western folktales and literature provide many examples of characters (often animals like Bambi or wild children like Kipling's Mowgli) who come upon the mirrored surface of a lake or stream and for the first time see themselves in a kind of epiphany of newly acquired self-knowledge. Placing the mirror in non-Western hands makes an interesting picture for Western viewers because this theme can interact with the common perception that the non-Western native remains somewhat childlike and cognitively immature. Lack of self-awareness implies a lack of history (E. Wolf 1982); he or she is not without consciousness but is relatively without self-consciousness. The myth is that history and change are primarily characteristic of the West and that self-awareness was brought to the rest of the world by "discovery" and colonization.[13]

In the article "Into the Heart of Africa" (August 1956) a magazine staff member on expedition is shown sitting in his Land-Rover, holding open a *National Geographic* magazine to show a native woman a photograph of a woman of her tribe. Here the magazine serves the role of reflecting glass, as the caption tells us: "Platter-lipped woman peers at her look-alike in the mirror of *National Geographic*." The *Geographic* artist smiles as he watches the woman's face closely for signs of self-recognition; the fascination evident in his gaze is in the response of the woman, perhaps the question of how she "likes" her image, her own self. An early version of this type of photo a quarter of a century earlier shows an explorer in pith helmet who, with a triumphant smile, holds up a mirror to a taller native man. He dips his head down to peer into

13. Compare the pictures of natives looking into a mirror with that of an American woman looking into the shiny surface of the airplane she is riveting in the August 1944 issue. It is captioned, "No time to prink [primp] in the mirror-like tail assembly of a Liberator." The issue raised by this caption is not self-knowledge (Western women have his) but female vanity, or rather its transcendence by a woman who, manlike, works in heavy industry during the male labor shortage of World War II. Many of these mirror pictures evoke a tradition in Western art in which Venus or some other female figure gazes into a mirror in a moment of self-absorption. Like those paintings, this photo may operate "within the convention that justifies male voyeuristic desire by aligning it with female narcissistic self-involvement" (Snow 1989:38).

A surprising number of *Geographic* photographs feature mirrors and cameras, with Westerners offering third-world peoples glimpses of themselves. In this August 1956 picture, a staff artist in what was then French Equatorial Africa shows a woman "her look-alike." (Photo: Volkmar Kurt Wentzel, © National Geographic Society)

it, and we, the viewers, see not his expression but a redundant caption: "His first mirror: Porter's boy seeing himself as others see him." By contrast with the later photo, the explorer's gaze is not at the African but out toward the camera, indicating more interest in the camera's reception of this amusing scene than in searching the man's face for clues to his thinking. It also demonstrates the importance of manipulating relative height between races to communicate dominance. In the same genre, a Westerner in safari clothes holds a mirror up to a baboon (May 1955). Here as well, the *Geographic* plays with boundaries between nature and culture. The baboon, like third-world peoples, occupies that boundary in the popular culture of white Westerners (see Haraway 1989);

This February 1925 photograph is captioned "His first mirror: Porter's boy seeing himself as others see him," suggesting that self-awareness comes with Western contact and technology. (Photo: Felix Shay, © National Geographic Society)

its response to the mirror can only seem humorously inadequate when engaged in the ultimately human and most adult of activities, self-reflection.

The mirror sometimes serves as a device to tell a story about the process of forming national identity. National self-reflection is presumed to accompany development, with the latter term suggesting a process that is both technological and psychosocial. The caption to a 1980 picture of a Tunisian woman looking into a mirror plays with this confusion between individual and nation, between the developing self-awareness of mature adults and historically emergent national identity: "A moment for reflection: Mahbouba Sassi glances in the mirror to tie her head-band. A wife and mother in the village of Takrouna, she wears garb still typical of rural women in the region. Step by step, Tunisia has, by any standards, quietly but steadily brought herself into the front rank of developing nations."

Cameras break into the frame of many *National Geographic* photographs. In some, a Westerner is holding the camera, showing a local group the photograph he has just taken of them. Here the camera, like the mirror, shows the native himself. Frequently the picture is handed to children crowding happily around the Western cameraman. Historically it was first the mirror and then the camera that were thought to prove the superiority of the Westerner who invented and controls them (Adas 1989). In many pictures of natives holding a mirror or camera, the magazine plays with what McGrane (1989) identifies with the nineteenth century European mind, the notion "of a low threshold of the miraculous [in the non-Western native], of a seemingly childish lack of restraint" (1989:50).

In other pictures, the native holds the camera. In one sense, this violates the prerogative of the Western surveyor to control the camera, long seen as a form of power. In an analysis of photographs of Middle Eastern women, Graham-Brown (1988) provides evidence that colonial photographers were motivated to keep local subjects "at the lense-end of the camera" and quotes one who, in 1890, complained, "It was a mistake for the first photographer in the Pathan [Afghanistan] country to allow the natives to look at the ground glass screen of the camera. He forgot that a little learning is a dangerous thing" (1988:61). The camera could be given to native subjects only at the risk of giving away that power.

Pictures in *National Geographic* that place the camera in other hands, however, merely suggest that the native's use of the camera is amusing or quaint. A broad smile graces the face of the Aivilik man above who uses the camera lens to view the landscape with a companion. At least one caption suggests that, although the subject goes behind the camera—in 1952 a young African boy looking through the viewfinder—what he looks out at is the imagined self at whom the Western photographer has been looking moments before: "Young Lemba sees others as the photographer sees him."

Such pictures were more common in the 1950s. We can detect a change, as decolonization proceeded, in the simple terms with which the problem is depicted in an amazing photograph from August 1982. It sits on the right-hand side of the page in an article entitled "Paraguay, Para-

A rare picture from August 1982 draws attention to the presence of the camera by photographing people being photographed for pay. (Photo: O. Louis Mazzatenta, © National Geographic Society)

dox of South America." The frame is nearly filled with three foreground figures—a white female tourist standing between an Amerindian woman and man, both in native dress, both bare-chested. The three stand close together in a line, the tourist smiling with her arm on the shoulder of the sober-faced native woman. The tourist and the man, also unsmiling, face off slightly toward the left where a second camera (besides the one snapping the photo for the magazine) takes their picture. The caption asks us to look at the natives as photographic subjects: "Portraits for pay: A tourist poses with members of the Macá Indian tribe on Colonia Juan Belaieff Island in the Paraguay River near Asunción. The Indians charge 80 cents a person each time they pose in a photograph."

This rare photograph invites us into a contradictory, ambiguous, but, in any case, highly charged scene. It is not a pleasant picture, in contrast with more typical *Geographic* style, because it depicts the act of looking at unwilling subjects, suggesting the voyeurism of the photograph of the exotic, a voyeurism *doubled* by the presence of a second photographer. Further, the picture's ambiguity lies in its suggestion that we are seeing a candid shot of a posed shot, and that we are looking at the other look at us though in fact the Indian gaze is diverted twenty degrees from ours. This unusual structure of gaze draws attention to the commodified nature of the relationship between looker and looked-at. The Indians appear unhappy, even coerced; the tourist satisfied, presumably with her catch. Here too an apparent contradiction—the diverted gaze and its candid appearance suggest that the *National Geographic* photographer took this picture without paying, unlike the tourists; the caption suggests otherwise.

The photograph's potentially disturbing message for *National Geographic* readers is muted when one considers that the camera has not succeeded so much in representing the returned gaze of indigenous peoples as it has in taking the distance between Western viewer and non-Western subject one step farther and in drawing attention to the photographer (and the artifice) between them. A symptom of alienation from the act of looking even while attention is drawn to it, this photo may exemplify a principle that Sontag says operates in all photography: "The photographer is supertourist, an extension of the anthropologist, visiting natives and bringing back news of their exotic doings and strange gear. The photographer is always trying to colonize new experiences or find new ways to look at familiar subjects—to fight against boredom. For boredom is just the reverse side of fascination: both depend on being outside rather than inside a situation, and one leads to the other" (1977:42). Avoiding boredom is crucial to retaining readers' interest and therefore membership.

One could also look at the photograph from a 1990 issue on Botswana showing a French television crew—in full camera-and-sound gear and from a distance of a few feet—filming two Dzu Bushmen in hunting gear and authentic dress. The Frenchmen enthusiastically instruct the hunters in stalking posture, and the caption critiques them, noting that they have dressed up the natives (who otherwise wear Western clothing) for the benefit of European consumers. While this photograph is valuable in letting the reader see how images are constructed rather than found, its postmodern peek behind the scenes may also do what Gitlin notes contemporary journalism has done: engaged in a demystifying look at how image makers control the face political candidates put forward, they encourage viewers to be "cognoscenti of their own bamboozlement" (1990a).

Ultimately the magazine itself is a mirror for the historical, cultural, and political-economic contexts of its production and use. That context is reflected in the magazine's images, but not in a simple, reflective way, as either the objectivist myth of the nature of cameras and mirrors or as the Althusserian notion of a "specular," or mirrorlike ideology (in which the subject simply recognizes him- or herself) would have it. It is perhaps more in the form of a rippled lake whose many intersecting lines present a constantly changing and emergent image.

The Academic Spectator.   In one sense, this gaze is simply a subtype of the reader's gaze. It emerges out of the same American middle-class experiential matrix with its family of other cultural representations, its formal and informal schooling in techniques for interpreting both photograph and cultural difference, and its social relations. We read the *National Geographic* with a sense of astonishment, absorption, and wonder, both as children and, in a way that is different only some of the time, as adults. All of the looks embedded in the pictures are ultimately being filtered for you the reader through this, our own gaze. At times during this project, we have looked at the reader of an American magazine who is looking at a photographer's looking at a Western explorer who is looking at a Polynesian child who is looking at the explorer's photographed snapshot of herself moments earlier. While this framing of the seventh look might suggest that it is simply a more convoluted and distanced voyeurism, it can be distinguished from other kinds of readers' gazes, including the voyeuristic and the hierarchic, by both its distinctive intent and the sociological position (white, middle class, female, academic) from which it comes. Its intent is not aesthetic appreciation or formal description, but critique of the images in spite of, because of, and in terms of their pleasures. We aim to make the pictures tell a different story than they were originally meant to tell, one about their makers and readers rather than their subjects.[14] The critique arises out of a desire "to anthropologize the West," as Rabinow (1986) suggests we might, and to denaturalize the images of difference in the magazine in part because those images and the institution which has produced them have historically articulated too easily with the shifting interests and positions of the state. The strong impact of the magazine on popular attitudes suggests that anthropological teaching or writing purveys images that, even if intended as oppositional (certainly not always the case),

14. Our interviews with readers show that they do not always ignore the frame but also sometimes see the photograph as an object produced by someone in a concrete social context.

may simply be subsumed or bypassed by the *National Geographic* view of the world.

A suspicion of the power of images is inevitable, as they exist in a field more populated with advertising photography than anything else. The image is experienced daily as a sales technique or as a trace of the commodity. That experience is, at least for us and perhaps for other readers, transferred to some degree to the experience of seeing *National Geographic* images.

Our reading of theory has tutored our gaze in distinctive ways, told us how to understand the techniques by which the photographs work, how to find our way to something other than an aesthetic or literal reading, suggesting that we view them as cultural artifacts. It also suggested that we avoid immersion in the many pleasures of the richly colored and exotically peopled photographs, as in Alloula's reading of Algerian colonial period postcards. He notes his analytic need to resist the "aestheticizing temptation" (1986:116) to see beauty in those cards, a position predicated in part on a highly deterministic view of their hegemonic effect. Alternative, more positive views of the political implications of visual pleasure exist, a view which Jameson (1983) and others argue is achieved in part by unlinking a disdain for popular culture products from the issue of pleasure. Validating both seemingly contradictory views, however, would seem to be the fact that the seductiveness of the pictures both captures and instructs us. We are captured by the temptation to view the photographs as more real than the world or at least as a comfortable substitute for it, to imagine at some level a world of basically happy, classless, even noble others in conflict neither with themselves nor with "us." These and other illusions of the images we have found in part through our own vulnerability to them. The pleasures are also instructive, however. They come from being given views, without having to make our own efforts to get them, of a world different, however slightly, from the American middle-class norm. The considerable beauty with which those lives are portrayed can potentially challenge that norm.

Conclusion

The many looking relations represented in all photographs are at the foundation of the kinds of meaning that can be found or made in them. The multiplicity of looks is at the root of a photo's ambiguity, each gaze potentially suggesting a different way of viewing the scene. Moreover, a visual illiteracy leaves most of us with few resources for understanding or integrating the diverse messages these looks can produce. Multiple gaze is the source of many of the photograph's contradictions, highlighting the gaps (as when some gazes are literally interrupted) and multiple perspectives of each person involved in the complex scene. It is the root of much of the photograph's dynamism as a cultural object, and the place where the analyst can perhaps most productively begin to trace its connections to the wider social world of which it is a part. Through attention to the dynamic nature of these intersecting gazes, the photograph becomes less vulnerable to the charge that it masks or stuffs and mounts the world, freezes the life out of a scene, or violently slices into time. While the gaze of the subject of the photograph may be difficult to find in the heavy crisscrossing traffic of the more privileged gazes of producers and consumers, contemporary stories of contestable power are told there nonetheless.

Eight

The Readers' Imagined *Geographic:* An Evolutionary Tale

We are invited to dream in the ideological space
of the photograph.

(Tagg 1988:183)

There would be no *National Geographic* magazine without its nearly forty million monthly readers. Not only does the magazine make its impact and its income through its readers; those readers exert a more subtle effect on the magazine through their opinions on what the magazine ought to cover and how to do it. These views are discerned through market research and letters to the editor, but the reader is also a product of the imagination of staff members who, as we have seen earlier, sometimes pay little attention to market research or reader feedback and intentionally let their own intuitions and ideas about ideal coverage stand for those of their readers. In this sense, then, the reader is created by the institution, made either a willing amateur scholar or a reluctant one, assumed to be conservative in taste and politics, or left as a blank slate in the form of Mr. and Mrs. Normal American from Peoria. The reader and the magazine staff have an imaginary relationship (that is, they usually guess at each other's intentions), but it is both tangible (they exchange money for photographs) and reciprocal in the sense that each helps to constitute the other.

The millions of *Geographic* readers stand, in institutional minds, for a mandate to produce the magazine and give substance to the producers' claim that *National Geographic* is what the American people as a whole want. They can argue that America wants its education entertaining, that readers ought to have their tastes (by definition normative) in regions, topics, and photographic styles satisfied—or perhaps occasionally ought to be guided in those matters. The celebratory coverage of the magazine in other broadcast and print media during the hundredth anniversary year of the National Geographic Society in 1988 was one bit of evidence that some other sectors of American society see the magazine in the same way: as authentically American, a cultural tradition as sacred and long-standing as almost any other, a sturdy boat steadfastly staying on course in the mainstream of American social life, not political because not contested.

We turn to look at reader responses to the magazine for these and other more specific reasons. The first is our initial goal of understanding what ideas a variety of white Americans hold about the third world and the role *National Geographic* photographs may play in molding those ideas. Simply to examine the photographs as analysts does not suffice, for we look from the particular and perhaps peculiar perspective of one kind of social experience. The diverse readers of the magazine have been tutored in other ways, and neither the analytical view of the photographs as genre nor the institutional view of its goals and practices subsumes those subscriber perspectives.

Those working in cultural studies strongly advocate study of how people respond to cultural products such as television shows or novels. Much previous work has either assumed the consciousness-molding effects of the media (for instance, the Frankfurt school) or has posited an ideal reader or readers who could be expected to respond to a genre or media message in one particular way (as early reader response work did in literary studies). Radway's 1984 ethnographic study of the readers of romance novels broke with the tradition of the docile and imagined reader (see also Morley 1980). She found the women she spoke with not "swallowing" a fixed text whole, but actively remaking the meanings of the romances they read. In this way, she portrayed women's reading as an interpretive act and, more than that, as a social, even political, act: the women, who were often wives and mothers working at home, made time to read as a way of announcing to family members their need and right to nurture themselves.

Debates continue over how to characterize the freedom of audiences to construct their own sense from media, independent of the institutions' intended reading. While some analysts stress the power of media institutions to coerce certain kinds of readings, others have gone so far as to claim that media products such as *Geographic* photographs have no intrinsic meaning but rather are "empty vessel[s]" awaiting audiences to pour meaning into them (Carragee 1990; see also Barkin and Gurevitch 1987:18). They argue that the meaning of media artifacts lies not in the *image* but in the cultural discourses that surround the image (Fiske 1986). These discourses relevant to *Geographic* images would be potentially the entire repertoire of culture, but the most central ones are preexisting ideas about race, progress, and evolution that circulate through the *National Geographic* readership. This claim is obviously true in one sense—meaning implies both meaning makers and social communication, and it implies the possibility for historical and contextual shifts in how a single artifact makes sense to its viewers; but it is false in another, for not all media artifacts are equally likely to have the same cultural ideas deployed to make sense of them. The *Geographic*'s Arabs and Hollywood Arabs can obviously be read in diverse ways, but sympathetic and relativistic readings of cultural difference are more likely to come with the *Geographic*.

This "empty vessel" view of media content often coexists with a view of the reader/viewer as resisting all dominant meanings, as what Carragee (1990:93) has derisively called "semiological guerrillas." This resistance to media representations clearly occurs in some contexts in meaningful form, as when research shows Australian aboriginal children reformulating the Westerns they see on TV and supporting the Indians against the cowboys (Hodge and Tripp 1986; see also Liebes and Katz 1990). The concept of resistance is used, however, to mean "all sorts of grumbling, multiple interpretation, semiological inversion, pleasure, rage, friction, numbness," thereby sadly "stamping these not-so-great refusals with a vocabulary derived from life-threatening political work against fascism—as if the same concept should serve for the Chinese student uprising and cable TV grazing" (Gitlin 1990:191).

Surely readers of the *Geographic* do significant interpretive work on its photographs rather than simply receiving them. They select some articles, photographs, and captions to read and ignore others; they decide to renew their subscriptions or not; and they interpret the photos in distinctive ways rather than simply decoding them by cultural formula. But this reading is never pre-cultural or entirely idiosyncratic. We do not see the photographs as neutral slates upon which viewers can write any tale, the power of the reader nowhere matching that of "a centralized storytelling institution" (Carragee 1990:88) like the *National Geographic*. Its cultural authority is formidable, with its producers being both photographic taste setters and ethnographic fact makers.

It is a commonplace in art historical analysis that whoever pays for art helps determine what kinds of art are produced and what kinds of taste become dominant. In the case of the *Geographic*, readers pay part of the tab, with advertising revenues and state exemption from income taxes footing much, if not most, of the bill. But readers are not the only photographic tastemakers.

Investigation of how readers look at these photographs will show whether they see the *National Geographic*'s foreigners as photographers and editors do—and, more generally, as an elite American political culture does. The people we spoke with expressed little skepticism about the photos as objective documents. Media consumers in America are sometimes critical of the claims of documentary or journalistic work, but this may be mainly in relation to depictions of American social life or more politicized issues. Moreover, the *National Geographic* is a powerful and revered social institution that has the means not only to purvey these images but to present itself as on a mission that is educational, scientific, and benign. The *National Geographic* has, in other words, cultural authority, and the average white middle-class reader may find little in his or her everyday social experience to contradict it.

We have already considered some of the social and cultural sources of the magazine's success and have noted that the photographs of the third world have had a changing relationship to that success. The *Geographic* has succeeded in telling "consensus narratives" (Thorburn 1988), that is, pictorial stories that employ a stock of common symbols and that can be understood by most people. As in other countries and with other photographic genres, viewer perspectives have "commercial as well as validating capabilities that [give] rise to certain genres of highly successful images" (Geary 1988:11).[1] To actually know what makes an image

---

1. Geary demonstrates this effect in early twentieth-century German photography of the Kingdom of Bamum in Cameroon. The extreme popularity of one photograph showing the local king on a throne with a servant bowing before him is explained by the resonance of this image with desires to see "the exotic display of wealth and splendor" and preexisting ideas about "royal splendor and etiquette" (1988:50). So too have Alloula (1987) and Monti (1987) shown how popular photography of Africa fits (as well as reinforces) viewers' stereotypes of the region.

Geary also emphasizes the power of the photographic subject to determine

popular in a particular time and place requires conversation with readers. We have already attempted to explain the popularity of *National Geographic* photos from earlier decades through the less than ideal method of inference from the social history of the period. The readers of the 1950s and 1960s looked with a "period eye" (Baxandall 1985) that was, we might speculate, more optimistic, more self-confident, or more enamored of pictures of technological progress and less willing to focus on the spectacular surface of the pictures; other, archival methods would be needed to explore these historical readings. In looking at more recent photographs, however, we can ask people what they see and like, and why.

Who the Readers Are

Market research is readily available on the readers of American magazines (Simmons 1987). From these extensive surveys, we know that *National Geographic* readers currently constitute a sizable portion of Americans, with perhaps as many as 20 percent of all adults seeing each issue. The Magazine Research Institute puts the 1989 audience at 30.2 million, while the Geographic Society estimates that there are 37 million readers worldwide. Subscription numbers are smaller, given that several people read each copy, but those numbers too are huge: 10.6 million in 1989, with 2.5 million subscriptions sold overseas, primarily in Europe. It has been called America's favorite magazine on the basis of the numbers, satisfaction, and loyalty of its readers (Magazine Research Institute 1989).

Fifty-five percent of the in-home readers are male, 96 percent white (versus 86 percent of the general population), and their median age is forty-two. They are wealthier and have had more formal schooling than the average American; 33 percent graduated from college (18 percent is the national figure); 65 percent have household incomes of $30,000 or more (47 percent of American households have incomes of that sort); and 25 percent have professional and managerial positions (versus 16

---

how he or she is presented. While she demonstrates this in the Cameroon case, it seems clear that the subject has much less control here than in earlier periods and other cases. This is due to changing technologies of photography (for example, zoom lenses), changing cultural preferences in photographic consumers, including increasing intolerance for posed shots, and the *Geographic*'s methods of selecting published photos from a huge number of shots.

percent in the population at large). More generally, 30 percent of the readers can be categorized as in the two highest social classes (upper and upper-middle) as against seventeen percent of the general public. The magazine knows, but does not release, the political party affiliations of its members.[2]

While the respectable and scientific aura of the magazine might suggest otherise, *National Geographic* readers are not at the very top of magazine readers in class position. A good number of popular magazines have significantly more upper-income and college-educated readers, including *Gourmet, Psychology Today, New Yorker, Scientific American, Tennis, Travel and Leisure, Natural History,* and *Smithsonian,* as well as the finance-oriented magazines such as *Money, Barron's,* and *Fortune. National Geographic* readership includes a substantial segment of the middle and working classes, with nearly seven million in-home readers from the working and lower classes. In sum, while the magazine is primarily read by a white and upper-middle-class audience, its photographs and texts must appeal to that 43 percent of readers who have not attended college. Its readership therefore includes a significant number of people with aspirations to knowledge and perhaps higher class position. While these readers are presumably of less interest to advertisers, they play an important role in the National Geographic Society's view of itself. The special version of populism that exists at the Society and its commitment to a mission of educating as many people as possible has made these readers' interests, at least as they are imagined by editors, important to those who produce the magazine.

These marketing figures cannot tell us much, however, about the interpretive communities within the magazine's readership.[3] Are a sig-

2. The demographic figures are taken from Simmons 1987 Study of Media and Markets, which involved a sample of 19,124 adults. The latter figures represent the "in-home audience," which excludes those who read the *Geographic* in their doctor's office or library and includes more than the individual subscriber. The social class designations are made by Simmons following Hollingshead's five-tier classification system. These figures are somewhat different from the numbers produced by the National Geographic Society, which does its own demographic research as well. Like many magazines, the *Geographic* guards its demographics to avoid appearing to serve a narrow segment of the American public, or at least emphasizes those demographics that show a broad range of people with expendable income reading their product.

3. The numbers available on most media use patterns are less than fully helpful for a cultural analysis, in part because they are intended to be used in negotiating advertising cost between corporations and the media rather than to give either

nificant segment "animal people" who only subscribe for the nature pictures and who also support animal protection societies? What proportion are liberal Democrats for whom the magazine stands for their vaguely internationalist sympathies? Do large numbers of younger subscribers who are also parents get the magazine as an educational resource for their children rather than themselves? Given the vast number of readers, these interpretive communities will be many, but understanding the popularity and meaning of the magazine requires going beyond demographics to knowledge of these diverse groups of readers and their ideas. We could then ask how *this* genre of photograph, the *National Geographic,* attracts *that* particular audience and what cultural discourses (such as primitivism) are available to and used by them to interpret the pictures (Jensen 1987:28).

The Photographs Viewed

We asked fifty-five people to look at a set of relatively recent photographs from the magazine and to respond to them. They were volunteers who responded to newspaper advertisements, and a few people known to the interviewers beforehand.[4] Selected to represent a range of social experiences, they were made up of two cohorts, one we called a Vietnam cohort (those who first came to social and political maturity during the Vietnam War and were thus between thirty-four and forty-nine years of age when interviewed) and the other a post-Vietnam cohort (a group of eighteen- to twenty-five-year-olds who were young children during the war). An equal number of males and females made up each cohort.

---

group a sense of the cultural lives of their customers. It is the practical separation of these two tasks that gives the National Geographic Society separate marketing and promotions departments, one collecting data on reader preferences for advertisers and for internal use and the other working on signing up new subscribers.

4. The interviews in Binghamton were conducted by the authors, while the Hawaii interviews were conducted by John Kirkpatrick, Dawn Richards, and Amy Howarth. The sample size was gauged to allow for comparison of the subgroups to be described below and was close to the maximum feasible size given our budget and the time required to transcribe and analyze the interviews. The newspaper ad for Binghamton read as follows: "Research participants wanted. Two SUNY professors would like individuals to assist in a study of *National Geographic* magazine. Participation involves a one-time commitment to view and discuss photographs from this magazine (under two hours). We are looking for Binghamton natives who were born 1940–55 or 1963–70. We can pay a $10 stipend. If interested, please call _____."

We also tried to include people in our sample with a range of experience with racially and culturally diverse people, whether acquired from living in certain communities or traveling overseas. To achieve this objective, interviews were held with natives of the Binghamton, New York area and with residents of Oahu, Hawaii; Binghamton is a white and ethnically European community, while Hawaii is racially and culturally heterogeneous, made up of native Hawaiian, Japanese, Filipino, and other people of Pacific Island descent. We included a few people with extensive cross-cultural experience in the New York group and a few people without such experience (new arrivals from homogeneous mainland communities) in the Hawaii group. The interviewees also included people who were current and/or past subscribers, people who had seen the magazine but never had it delivered to their home, and a small number who had had minimal encounter with the *Geographic*.

In the analysis that follows, we have focused on the cultural discourses that came up frequently across these social segments. In several cases, however, the questions we asked were analyzed for differences among these social groups, that is, by gender, cohort, and cross-cultural experience. As will be seen, these social factors had relatively little effect on the responses people made, at least in regard to the limited set of questions we are able to address in the space of the next two chapters.

The one thing all of the people we spoke with had in common was their race. We limited this initial study to white adults for several reasons, foremost among them our sense of the importance of studying white racial attitudes. Nader (1974) years ago called for anthropologists to compensate for their neglect of the more powerful segments of society. White society is such a segment, and its views of race have been powerfully annexed to American political and social debates about the drug problem, for example, and outcomes such as the income differential between white and black Americans. A white sample would also closely reflect the nature of the magazine readership itself.

A group of twenty pictures showing people in non-Western settings was randomly selected from issues between 1977 and 1986 (see Appendix B).[5] These photos, minus their original captions, were presented one by

5. The period 1977–86 was chosen because significant changes in printing technology used by the magazine occurred just before that time. Older photos could look like historical photos to informants, and we wished to have people respond to photographed people whom they could see as their contemporaries. We selected twenty photographs as our sample size because it allowed for a wide range of views/regions/subjects to be presented without going much beyond an

one to each person we spoke to. Those interviewed were encouraged to say what thoughts the photograph prompted, what they saw "going on" in the pictures. They were also asked a set of open-ended questions about their preferences in the set of pictures, their ideas on cultural differences, and their opinion of the magazine itself. The entire discussion was recorded on tape.[6]

We decided to show the photographs without their captions because of the sense we shared with many theorists of how powerfully captions constrain the reading of a photograph. While it would be important in a future study to examine the effect of captions, we were first interested in how the photographic elements themselves affect readers. This would reflect on how the caption works for or against those elements in reader response but also allows insight into the ethnographic reality of that significant proportion of readers who, according to *National Geographic* surveys, often look only at photographs without going to captions. Moreover, we were interested in maximizing the freedom and creativity with which the people we interviewed might interpret the photographs; the authority of the caption would likely have worked against such moves. While ethnographic realism might demand a fully contextual, natural reading of the magazine, there can be conservative implications to a rigid adherence to this injunction if it leads to a finding of what

---

hour's work for each informant. Coded features of the sample of twenty randomly selected photos were systematically compared with those of the larger 600-photo sample. The interview photos differ from the average picture in the magazine in only a few respects: in the former there were somewhat more pictures with a smiling foreground subject, relatively fewer pictures with only men in them, and more photos with subjects whose skin color was not evident.

6. In looking at the photos, each person was asked, "Please describe what could possibly be going on in the photos. I'd like you to respond to each picture with whatever comes to mind or, in other words, to just say what the picture makes you think about." Among other questions were the following: "In your view, why are there differences between people's customs around the world?" (Q3), "Why do you think there are differences in the wealth or poverty of different people around the world?" (Q5), and "Would an ideal world have many cultures, few cultures, or one culture? Why?" (Q6). The entire interview protocol is available on request to the authors.

The interview transcriptions follow several conventions: (1) Virtually all words are included. Certain vocalizations, such as 'er' and 'um', are not. (2) Laughing is parenthetically noted. (3) All interviewer's comments or questions are included where they interrupt the interviewee's discussion. The code following each interview excerpt that discusses a photo includes an identifying number (see Appendix B).

is rather than what might be. Both are obviously desirable kinds of information; we began with the latter.

How people talk about the photographs in other contexts besides the interview could surely be different, as in easy, bantering conversation with a friend, where less sympathetic or rationalistic discourse might occur than in conversations with an anthropological researcher. We have experienced these contextual effects ourselves in discussing the project with people outside the interviews. Going through a magazine with one nonacademic friend, we came upon a photograph showing a dark-skinned man plowing a dry field of dirt. "*He* seems to be beating a dead horse," she said, laughing. Interviewees were rarely unsympathetic in this way. Another person told us that she comes from a family of Midwest farmers that includes several members of or sympathizers with the Ku Klux Klan. They refer to the *National Geographic,* she reports, as "that nigger magazine."

Socially unacceptable ideas, such as openly racist attitudes, will usually be censored or muted in interviews with a stranger, although several people we interviewed made racist remarks which they may have deemed acceptable. The interviews were a special situation, but they nonetheless allowed people to think about the photographs in ways they might when reading the magazine on other occasions. The extremely interesting and elaborate thinking about cultural and racial difference that *are* expressed in the interviews tell us much about the continuing role of social evolutionism and ideas of progress in American thought.

A detailed analysis of the interviews can also reveal much about what kinds of attitudes might have been censored. As Dijk (1987:18) has noted in his studies of racist talk in Dutch and American interviews, the social desirability effects are not so much a methodological conundrum as an opportunity to examine strategies people use for presenting themselves in socially desirable ways while discussing sensitive topics such as race with people who are not intimates.

We can also add that people often speak, even within a single interview, in several voices. They sometimes express two apparently contradictory ideas with equal conviction. Or they express contradictions in more experimental or ambivalent ways; they try out sometimes conflicting ideas, with tentative or self-assured tones, hoping for one thing and settling on another, seeing how things sound. Looking at a picture of Haitians walking back and forth along a dirt road, one older woman from New York said:

Almost looks like an exodus, like people are being forced out of their village for some reason. But it's probably more like one shift of maybe migrant workers going off and one shift coming on. They don't look real happy but they don't look like they're terribly oppressed. . . . No one seems to have a terrible amount of luggage so I don't think they're being forced to move. I'd rather guess that they're getting out of work—whatever they do. And she has to take her baby to work (CL-6 no. 2).

She begins with a first impression of people coerced, doing something they do not want to do. She moves on to a more pleasant alternative and then rules out two hypotheses about the photographed people's mood: they are, she surmises, neither too happy nor too oppressed, but in the process of negating raises both possibilities—that they have satisfying jobs and lives and that they are severely victimized.[7] In the end, she admits that her bent ("I'd rather guess," she says, not "I'd have to guess") is to believe the happier of the two options. The revealing nature of this sequence of voices, as in many other cases, suggests how unfruitful it is to conceptualize people as holding absolutely to a monolithic set of beliefs that can be concealed or revealed and that vary, at most, by context.[8]

Reading the *Geographic*

Media use involves a set of social practices that can be observed in situ, as demonstrated by recent studies of television viewing (Liebes and Katz 1990) which show how absorbed people become in a program, what kinds of conversation occur among a group of viewers during and after shows, and so on. Ethnographic understanding of magazine reading would have the difficulty that it is likely less often mediated by inter-

7. Other responses to this picture sound remarkably similar, as when one older man from Hawaii said "Mexico, in a very, a very poor town . . . the people look like they're somewhat, they're not real poor, they, they don't look skinny although it looks like the type of living that they have isn't very good" (DR-51 no. 2).

8. In a number of recent anthropological analyses of belief and discourse, the important and varied roles of contradiction are explored, and the result is much more complex and truthful accounts of social and cognitive life. See Abu-Lughod (1986); Billig (1989); Ewing (1990); Strauss (1990); and Luhrmann (1989).

household discussion and less predictable or accessible in the times and places in which it occurs. It would involve learning how people store or display the magazine in their homes, how it might facilitate social relations between themselves and others, how they might use it as part of a presentation of self as educated, well-rounded, or as a photo buff. Short of this kind of home observation, marketing research reveals that subscribers spend an average of over two hours with each issue, although some habitually look only at the photographs (81 percent look at all of the photographs), others reading some or all captions in addition (53 percent), and a minority claiming to read all (20 percent) or most (an additional 14 percent) of the stories accompanying the photos.

While neither this information nor our interviews can be taken for the way people actually read the magazine, we interviewed people about their reading practices. Many expressed great enthusiasm for the *Geographic,* although about ten percent of all interviewees did not like it or were indifferent to it. Which aspects of the magazine people preferred varied a good deal. Many took the magazine because they liked photography per se, others favored the nature articles and tolerated the others, and some were primarily interested in the views provided of other parts of the world.

Only one person claimed never to have read or looked at the magazine. Most others who do not subscribe have either picked it up in a dentist's office or scanned it in the homes of other family members, usually just "browsing through," "looking at the pictures and sometimes the caption for an especially interesting one." Past or current subscribers describe a diverse set of approaches to the magazine, some treating it more casually ("I've got too many other things to do, and too many other things to read"), but most delving into an issue for a considerable span of time. People described fairly elaborate standardized reading strategies, like this man's:

> I don't just look at the pictures and put it down, I—when I
> get it, I look at all the topics and say to myself, oh, when I
> get to that month—I'm usually a couple months behind, but
> I read other books and things, but I pick the ones out that
> I'm going to read—eventually I get to them (CL-8).

Several people use *Geographics* as a reference library (for themselves or for their children's school work) rather than or in addition to reading the magazine when it arrives at their door. Others mention using them to enhance travel experiences:

I try to reference them before I go on a trip somewhere. I've even read them after I've gotten back from someplace because I had a lot of questions. And, you know, [they] created a lot more questions. There's a lot of things that I didn't really understand [on the trip], I went back and they [the magazine] seemed to be very thorough (CL-17).

Like all mass media, the *National Geographic* enters people's lives in diverse ways, by choice or by unexpected proximity, casually or more intensely. Unlike some other media, the *Geographic* is often a gift, usually from a family member. As such, it comes to stand for that relationship in many people's minds—for family memories and personal continuity. People become attached to the magazine in this way.

What else does the magazine mean to people? Two issues people raise have to do with its objectivity and, less explicitly, with its relationship to social mobility. People hold diverse views on the question of the magazine's objectivity, although virtually everyone agreed that it is a valuable source of information about the world. The magazine was also often defined by what it is not—judgmental or controversial. It is seen as simply looking at the world, not criticizing or calling for change:

I find it very good in its perspective of presenting things in a fair, logical way. And it doesn't seem to be politicized too much. . . . It's an educational thing. . . . Although, they have had at times also had some, they've had some pretty powerful statements and pictures in there about war-torn countries and famine and things like that, that make you wish you could change it. [Q: But, you don't consider that politicized? You think that those are pretty fair kinds of—] Well, I think the way that they do it, they just say here it is, here's the facts about it. They don't say that—they don't politicize and say the wealthy nations should give up their wealth and send all their money down there and bring, they don't say it's our duty to bring these people up. They just say this is the way they are. This is the way they live. And you draw your own conclusions. I get that feeling from *National Geographic,* whereas some other magazines or something that might bring something like poverty to light or might be religiously oriented, they're saying it's wrong. They're saying that you've got to correct it. They're saying you've got to do something about it. *National Geographic,* I think, tends to take a more neutral stance. They're just reporting on the fact. They might politicize a little bit without knowing it. You know, I mean, to say that an earthquake's a tragedy. But that's about, I think, as far as they—as they tend to go (CL-9).[9]

While several people share this positive sense of the objectivity of the magazine, many others see it as relativistic and for this reason a vehicle promoting antiracism, world peace, and/or cross-cultural understanding. A woman from Binghamton spoke eloquently about the racism she was brought up with and the role of the magazine in that context:

My grandparents are basically uneducated farmers, and I love them dearly, but anyone who is dark-skinned is an A-rab. And I remember as a child, anyone that, that spoke differently or was colored or was from any country, they were all lumped under one subtitle, A-rab. And it didn't set right with me. . . . And to me that's in part of the founding principles of [the magazine] . . . just to bring the world together and to show us how we're dependent on each other and, and the planet itself. And I think it has made me more, more aware (JC-9).

One gave unqualified praise to Geographic's international scope:

I think it's done a huge job in, in exposing [North Americans] to different cultures, with the right attitude about them—to go there and, and not interfere, observe with respect, honor them for their own, their own selves. And, in general, it fostered a, a whole generation to go out in vehicles like the Peace Corps and stuff (DR-153).

9. One person, a young woman from Hawaii, had questions about whether that objectivity ideal was interfered with by the magazine's attempts to sell itself, although she found this a problem with the texts but not the photos: "I don't often read the articles, because . . . I'm not sure how accurate it is all the time. Sometimes I wonder if, you know, they're not doing this to make it interesting so that, I don't know, so that people want to read it. . . . But the photographs are great" (DR-154).
All responses in this section were to the question, "Could you please describe your impression of the National Geographic magazine? In other words, what do you think of it?"

For at least two people, however, the magazine does not go far enough:

> There's not enough stress placed on the value of these, different cultures. That they really are *valuable*. And I get more of the impression that they're—they might be quaint and interesting and folklorish and of interest but not of intrinsic value to us as a human population on the face of the earth. That in fact, they're dispensable. They're cute now, but "c'est la vie" (DR-4).

And an older man from Hawaii raised the question of advocacy:

> It plays an important role in doing what it does. But there's lots that needs to be done that the *National Geographic* doesn't do. [Q. What do you mean?] There's, there are, the *Geographic* does not advocate in situations where I think it would be important to advocate. They tend not to handle situations that are really filthy or ugly, or disquieting or horrible. And this is a, a real part of our world, and my guess is that they have some pretty severe editing that goes on at the *National Geographic* (JK-1).

One of the most fascinating responses to the magazine has to do with its affording a kind of mobility which, for some people, seems to be physical, touristic mobility and for others the mobility of social class to which they aspire or from which they feel shut out. "I think it's real good to have around, you know," a woman in her twenties from Hawaii said, "'Cause then people like me, who don't have any money to go and travel, can just look at that, and like read the articles and then you really get into it, like you're really there, you know?" (AH-8).

"I've never traveled outside the U.S., unfortunately. I'd love to, if I could afford it, but sometimes the *National Geographic* is, is very good for this," agreed another woman from New York, who later suggested that the magazine allows her access to privileges usually reserved for others, "I'm quite sure an ordinary person wouldn't have had access to [this information without the magazine]" (CL-10).

Response to the magazine is filtered through the class system in other ways as well. A number of people remark on the magazine's "tastefulness," a concept that is a proxy for the cultural choices of the wealthy. An older military man from Hawaii said, "I really enjoy all the articles,

every one. I don't think I've ever had a distasteful article in there"
(DR-3). This same person described at some length his first experience
with the magazine, and its exclusivity-evoking requirement that "you
had to be recommended by a member." One younger man offered the
opinion that there were better and worse reasons for taking the magazine: "I think that's why people read it—because they want to learn
about different cultures. Either, either that or they want to throw it on
their coffee table when company comes over, and think they know about
it. . . . I think it says something about the people that read it, too—I
mean other than the people who have it hanging around the coffee table
just for company to see it. It shows that they're cultural people, that are
interested in other cultures, and that's good" (CL-3).

These people who respond positively to the magazine's classiness sit
alongside another group who seem put off by its higher-brow associations and who may feel excluded by it: "It's definitely a good magazine . . . familiarizing people with, with different cultures. I think that
it represents knowledge, and I don't think that it, because of its reputation, I don't think that it gets to many people. I think it's more—not
that it *means* to be geared towards a group of people, but I think because
of its reputation, it's become only a scholarly magazine" (JC-3).

Others dislike the magazine's focus on what they perceive to be
"poor" people. "When I sit down in the dentist's office, and I pick up
my *National Geographic* magazine, I, I don't know, sometimes I, I just
look through it real quick, because the pictures depress me. I don't like
to see people in countries where, you know, there's no money. . . .
Whenever you pick up *National Geographic,* you're in Africa" (CL-1).
"It seems like their main focus is predominantly African or Indian, very
poor people who are not living in a real modern world, or some Asian,
but not a large percentage of Asian. I think it's really helpful more when
you're in like, grade school, and you always use *National Geographics* for
pictures and reports and stuff. That's how I think of *National Geographic*
magazine" (AH-4). For these people, the magazine suggests something
unpleasant about differences in income, differences they would rather
not deal with.

In going on to examine what people said in the interviews in more
detail, we look first at how they explained the cultural differences they
saw. Then we consider the evaluative strategies people use and the contradictions or ideological dilemmas (Billig 1988) they struggle with in
building both a self-presentation in the interview and an explanation for
the phenomenon of cultural difference.

Reasoning about Cultural Differences

When the people we interviewed saw culturally distinctive people and were asked to account for the difference, they proposed a variety of interesting explanations, including ecological models, education, religion, and more general evolutionist models.

Physical Environment. People commonly went first to climate or geography to explain cultural differences. In this, they were often using a kind of ecological adaptation argument, making patterns of dress and other cultural features a virtually necessary outcome of their environment. In some cases, this ecological view is combined with an evolutionist perspective in which different environments are seen as allowing for only a certain amount of cultural, social, or technological development:

> I think that the geography has a lot to do with it as well, and the resulting culture. I think that there's a lot that can be said for, like in African culture around the equator, that didn't have to develop—even low forms of technology to help them survive. Essentially they were in a pretty benign environment, and able to survive. Whereas somebody in a northern climate, or a harsher climate, in order to survive, they had to learn to manipulate their environment that much more (DR-153 Q5).

> And the geography has affected their politics, their religion, their philosophies, their culture. I'd say geography has a lot to do with it, human evolution (AH-1 Q3).

Education and Opportunity. Education was often seen as central in explaining why people had different customs, degrees of civilization, and amounts of wealth. Given how unequivocally valued education is by most Americans, lack of education must also imply a less adequate form of society or culture. Not surprisingly, then, this explanatory strategy was commonly used in conjunction with relatively heavy use of evolutionist and evaluative language. So an older man from Hawaii, looking at a picture of New Guinea Highlands people, said, "Some have—shirts on and are clothed, so obviously there are, it is a, there are civilized people there, among people that are, possibly, uneducated [those "without" clothes, whom he surmises are from a different society than those with clothes]" (DR-3 no. 1).

Cultural and material differences here came off as a kind of unfortunate accident which could and should be rectified by educating people, almost always, it was obvious, in a Western model of appropriate behavior. This strategy of explanation was often accompanied by somewhat pejorative descriptions of non-Western cultural features, but it also often went hand in hand with a legitimation both of the primitive pattern (they were simply not taught to behave otherwise) and of the Western project of educating the world. The following examples are both from older men, the first from Hawaii, the second Binghamton.

> Education, I would say, would be the biggest thing, the reason for differences. People just don't know the—say the uneducated people have been going through life for centuries just the way they are. And they've never been brought into the realm of higher education or modern civilization . . . and, they're encroaching on these little tribes that have never had a chance to get outside. And some governments say, "Well, leave them as they are." But are you denying them education? Are you denying them the rest of the world as we see it or know it? (DR-3 Q3).[10]

> Education. Like you can go to middle Africa and there's no education except for what the witch doctors, or whatever, teach their kids (JC-2 Q5).

Two exceptions stand out by contrast to these common ways of explaining difference in terms of education. One is the musing of a younger man from Hawaii about the meaning of the photo from South America which shows topless women dancing with men dressed in pants and shirts. He found the mixed patterns of dress "strange" and said:

> It kind of makes me think of—like maybe they're [the men] bringing these people [the women] in as slaves, or servants or something . . . it seems kind of negative. Kind of like the people in the, in the modern clothes are, are controlling the other people. Maybe they have more of an education and so they can—hound over them, or dictate over them (AH-3 no. 14).

10. Note also the degree to which he treats so-called primitive people as the prime example of the culturally different and the passivity with which he portrays them.

Similarly, an older woman from Binghamton saw education as a resource that is often misused: "It's still a situation of where the rich, because of their education, because of their desire perhaps to get what they want at any cost, rule the poor" (JC-9 Q5).

The geographic and educational explanations sometimes came together in a focus on the role of isolation in creating cultural difference. As one woman said, "Isolation has caused these people, these different cultures, to develop rather than all one culture" (AH-2 Q3), while one man from Hawaii pointed to "the rain forest, where they don't know any better or any different. That is their only world and they have no other outside contact" (DR-3 Q3). The inference often seemed to be that people will develop different lifeways if left alone, but will imitate other systems as soon as they come in contact with them. This interpretive scheme often included the assumption that the non-Western societies (especially those termed primitive) would take on Western patterns rather than vice versa when no longer isolated. The statement of a Binghamton man who first voiced and then questioned this position is fairly typical:

> A few will come over and transplant themselves and become educated and then come back and bring some of this knowledge to their area. And gradually it spreads and they, they build up and evolve. Unless, maybe, it's just the way of life they, they really like—their way of life and they're perfectly happy with. They don't want to know any other way of life. It's just hard to say (CL-9 Q3).

Another individual responded:

> As the world evolved—to the point where cultures mixed more and more and more, the cultures that—did mix and learned more about other people, and kept up with the times. . . . I think those cultures got more of an education than the ones that were secluded [and they] became the ones that are richer. Because they were better able to relate, they were able to do better business with, they were able to become more efficient, because they took. . . . the ideas of a larger group of people (AH-3 Q5).

Religious Difference. A significant number of people from Binghamton, but few from Hawaii, saw religious belief as the central reason for differences in culture. Religion could take this role as it was seen as dictating people's behavior. In a few cases, it was portrayed as a negative force, as when, in one person's view, "Their religion says they have to have lots of kids so they can't use birth control [and so are poorer]" (CL-5 Q6) or religious conflicts keep a people from developing economically. Western religious beliefs also led, in one woman's view, to intolerant missionary activity in Africa and elsewhere. More than education, religion can be ambivalently related to cultural difference and evolution. In contrast to education, moreover, religion as a motor for difference and change is originally located outside the West as much as inside it.

The fourth and most significant explanatory frame people used was that of social evolutionism.

Evolution's Motor: Primitive Desire for Modern Goods

Central to people's discussions was a thinking through of the links between what they construed as a traditional or primitive world and a modern world. As we have seen, the photos themselves have often drawn attention to contrasts between tradition and modernity. While readers could ignore, downplay, or interpret these juxtapositions in a number of different ways, they in fact often spontaneously assumed the photos demonstrated social evolution at work. The categories of primitive or traditional, civilized or modern, were assumed by virtually everyone we talked to in the interviews.[11]

Several photographs that people looked at in our study had this structure, as in one large-format photo of a scene in Nigeria. The two fields of this photo include a big, new bridge in the background, while, below and up front, a boy poles a dugout canoe filled with people and a woman in bright African dress washes dishes in the muddy water at the river's edge. People frequently saw modernization as the photo's central theme, as did a younger Binghamton woman:

> It just looks like such an old style boat, and then there's this modern-looking motorcycle in there and there's a bridge, a

11. The concept of primitivity is more often associated with Africa in the discourse of the interviewees than it is with any other region. The deeper historical roots of these ideas in white Western traditions has been extensively considered (Monti 1987; Price 1989; Stocking 1968) as has, to a much lesser degree, their contemporary sources in cultural products such as textbooks (Preiswerk and Perrot 1978).

Many *National Geographic* photographs juxtapose traditional and modern elements, and viewers often interpret the resulting images as making statements
about social evolution. Readers tended to see modernization as this picture's
central theme. (Photo: Bruno Barbey, Magnum Photos)

nearly modern-looking bridge. These people are maybe going to go across this, this river or lake or whatever it is, using this boat instead of driving a, you know, walking over the bridge, or driving a car or something. It doesn't make that much sense somehow. . . . It looks like a place where some people are trying to stick to traditional values, and then other people are moving in building bridges and things like that (CL-5 no. 8).

More striking were cases where people found the same issue raised by a photo in which this was clearly *not* the narrative intended by the photographer or magazine. One of our sample of photos shows a ritual storytelling scene in a Papua New Guinea house. Listeners are gathered around a central figure, who is drawing back his bow in a large gesture. Many viewers saw signs of evolution in a small yellow plastic bag deep in the background and in the shorts worn by some of the watching crowd.

They have a bag, I don't know, it says something on it. And it looks like a, like a Great American [local supermarket] bag, something like that. I mean it looks plastic. . . . It looks like, maybe, a backward country, but with modernization somewhere along the line (CL-3 no. 1).

Ideologies of social evolutionism are not always clearly *in* the picture, but are read in. Changing political economic relations between the United States and the traditional world since 1945 have no doubt meant differing interpretations of such pictures in the past. Ideas of progress might have been articulated with more assurance in the era of greatest American international power in the fifties and sixties, while the focus on commodities as the mark of progress might have intensified with the continued development of consumer capitalism. The politics of these readings of desire for the modern shifts, not only in response to global processes such as decolonization but in relation to changing popular views of the state, of the authority of such cultural-scientific institutions as the National Geographic Society, and of the truth status of photography. Such politics can also be seen as a complex process of the sort that Gramsci described for the ideological terrain more generally. In the Gramscian view, the subordinate classes do not passively receive dominant ideas and values, but negotiate and amend them in line with

Even when traces of the Western world are hard to find, readers may pull them forward to create a story about social evolution. Deep in the background of this photograph, several readers saw a small, yellow plastic bag, which formed the basis for their speculations about the coming of "modern" life to this village in New Guinea. (Photo: David Gillison)

their experience and interests.[12] Hegemonic ideas, however, transform and partially disable developing dissident ideas. These ideas can be used to understand the role of the *National Geographic* in promulgating the concept of social evolution.

Social evolutionism entails a law of progress that allows us to know our past through the present of others, to know the present of others

12. This process is not portrayed by Gramsci as wholly self-conscious or intentional. The reinterpretation of dominant ideas can be seen as an outcome of the divergent social experience of the class which is doing the "reading."

through our own past, and to know their future through our own present. As a concept it has a long history in the West and has taken a variety of forms, although the location and shapes of the concept have been poorly documented for the recent past.[13] These views share a common basic structure: stages of human social organization are passed on the way to a specific goal—a goal synonymous with the contemporary Western social system. Names of the stages have varied, but the most popular contemporary versions include some two-stage sets (primitive/civilized; traditional/modern) and some three (primitive/developing/Western; hunting-gathering/agricultural/industrial). Stages can be passed through slowly or quickly, but only rarely is one skipped or the sequence reversed. These ideas are hegemonic—in Western textbooks (Preiswerk and Perrot 1978), in American official political discourse, and in the *National Geographic*.

Diverse views about the motor of evolution and its inevitability were expressed in the interviews, with some people seeing it as inexorable and others less sure. Doubts often stemmed from a sense that this progress depends on desire or will and that the desire for progress is sometimes absent. Differences between primitive and civilized people were often explained as an inevitable outcome of different geographic locations or through a kind of ecological determinism. In some cases, primitives were seen as being unable to "develop" until their physical isolation from modern society was broken, at which point they could choose whether or not to evolve. By contrast, modernization is sometimes viewed as analogous to transmitting disease—as a kind of physical, determinate process outside human intentionality. This view is evident where people talk about primitive cultures being exposed to civilization: "Our imposition of our culture on other cultures, it started with part of a religious idea. And it's, they've already been exposed to it, so there's not much we can do now, it's been going on for so long" (CL-6 Q4).

In many, perhaps most, cases, however, cultural difference is explained by individual preference and desire, these determining whether individuals or groups of non-Westerners hold on to their own culture or decide to go modern. Choice may be seen as constricted, but the idea of choosing (rather than moral character or genetic disposition) is nonetheless at the center of these discussions. This was expressed by two New Yorkers in the following ways:

13. On earlier notions, including the biologically-racially rooted version of evolutionism, see Hofstadter 1944; Rydell 1984; and Stocking 1968.

People are proud of their traditions now, and customs, and so they don't want to change [to become modern] . . . maybe everybody is happy with what they are (CL-5 Q3).

Some people prefer to remain primitive, don't prefer to improve. I can remember being in a desert in South Israel taking a picture of a shepherd and trying to offer him money and he wouldn't take it. He was insulted. He just preferred what he was doing (CL-17 Q5).

In this last case and many others, becoming modern is associated with valuing money and Western commodities, and accumulating goods. What is most often at issue, in many readers' views, is a choice between a simple life without commodities or a modern one with manufactured amenities. Many people echoed the following sentiments in very similar terms:

Some people don't hold material stuff in all that high regard. You know, Madonna said we're living in a material world, well, that's this part of the world, we're the Americans, we're materialistic. But I think other people, even if they do have a choice, they don't want it. But it's not necessarily bad to be poor. Some people are happy (CL-11 Q5).

Well, [some] people don't have as much wealth . . . so they're not used to having, you know, radios and whatever materialistic things that people in wealthy, economically wealthy countries have. Maybe they don't expect to have the wealth (CL-5 Q5).

People often tried to reason in such fashion about evolution and cultural difference, asking "What do primitives want?" and, more specifically, "Do they want our commodities and if not, why not?"

American conservative culture often portrayed economic activity as "a field for the development and encouragement of personal character" (Hofstadter 1944:10). In the popular imagination, the idea of such links between self and economy has become commonplace, but the implicit assumption is often that consumer rather than productive activity reveals character. While evaluations of the materialistic personality in our interviews vary, most are rooted in a relatively antisociological notion of choice. The standard social evolutionist line is, then, disrupted by use of the psychological discourse of choice, as well as some interviewees' implication that people may sensibly reject "progress."

Evaluating the Other while Balancing on a Contradiction

People, then, do not simply explain cultural differences by appealing to social evolution; they also evaluate them, particularly in terms of the notion of progress embedded in evolutionist discourse. The rhetoric of choice allows for moral judgment of the other because to have choice is to have responsibility. Where sociological language is used, the problem is more often described as one of victimization. In any case, the diverse evaluative strategies that our interviewees use are similar to those that Preiswerk and Perrot (1978:51–57) found used by the authors of European history textbooks in their value-laden descriptions of non-Europeans. They describe eight prototypical strategies that give an underlying coherence to each author's writing about the non-Western world. Preiswerk and Perrot's typology aptly characterizes much of what is said in people's conversations about the *National Geographic.*

Generally speaking, the strategies may be divided into two broad categories. The first set (the first four below) tends to value the European world positively and justify its actions in relation to the non-European. The second set (the second four) can be characterized as making at least some criticism of those actions or as valorizing the non-European world.

Preiswerk and Perrot's eight interpretative strategies are as follows: (1) self-defense, or focus on the value of the Euramerican way of life and its civilizing mission in the world; (2) legitimation, which is similar to self-defense but focuses more on the defects of non-Western cultures that justify their domination by the West; (3) proselytizing, or a focus on the religious benefits of Christianity and the need to spread it through the non-Christian world; and (4) operationality, or the use of utilitarian concepts to portray the role of the West positively—as bringing progress to the rest of the world. The focus in the latter case is on development, efficiency, and wealth, and the local cultural obstacles to such, which would include superstition, lack of motivation, and so forth.

The second, more critical set of strategies includes (5) class antagonism, or attention to the role of power and the concepts of exploitation or structural dependence of the non-West upon the West; (6) balance, or the tendency to see both positive and negative aspects to both sectors, West and non-West, lamenting the loss of traditional worlds while speaking of change as progress; (7) radical relativism, the attempt to suspend comparison between the two groups in question and to use putatively non-Western concepts in describing the latter settings; and (8) xeno-defense, or the obverse of (1), in which the non-Western society in question is seen as having an illustrious cultural heritage that has been interrupted or disrupted by Western contact and Western designs.

These eight strategies are obviously not equally represented in either the textbooks examined by Preiswerk and Perrot or in our interview conversations with magazine readers. In the textbooks, (1) and (2) are most common, (7) and (8) almost absent, while only Soviet textbooks made much use of (5) and ecclesiastical texts much use of (3). What stands out in the interviews is the frequency of (4) and (6). The focus on (4) would seem to be both a reflection of the transformation that has occurred in the American postwar period from a colonial rhetoric of overall cultural progress to a neocolonial rhetoric in which it is purely economic progress that is sought. The people we spoke with have been schooled in both institutional and popular culture arenas to treat progress as primarily a matter of increased access to consumer goods.

At least as interesting is the number of people who express both praise and blame for the non-Western world depicted. This balanced view (6) is associated in most people's minds with being objective (see also Parenti 1986). If one looks dispassionately at the world, this cultural reasoning goes, one will look from a moderate or centrist position which acknowledges the partial truths of more radical left or right positions (associated in this case with either self-defense or xeno-defense). American journalism, in particular, tutors people in this view when it demonstrates its objectivity by presenting itself as neither liberal nor conservative, but centrist.

The *National Geographic* staff embrace the concept of balance in this way. It can also be seen in the technique practiced on the McNeil-Lehrer News Hour of having a conservative and a liberal comment on the day's events, with critical questioning from the centrist newsperson to demonstrate skepticism of either extreme (but not of the center). This version of objectivity is joined with the explicit value Americans place on fairness to further solidify its power as a value. The fact that the American center is a culturally and historically specific place rather than a universal objective viewpoint (or even than a worldwide center position) is not considered.

The balanced viewpoint expressed by the people we spoke with thus replicates the stance of *National Geographic* and other journalists toward the world: the truth lies somewhere between the two, between the bad news and the good news, the poverty and the happy children. In the narrative of progress as told by *National Geographic,* the truth is one in which a traditional world has things of beauty and value in the same way that a modern world of education and material wealth does.[14] The cognitive stance is objectivity, the mood both nostalgic and forward-looking.

As the following example shows, the balanced position for our readers is actually not a stable, intentional paradigm, but involves a kind of waffling back and forth between two or more positions.

> They couldn't possibly, in my point of view, be happy living in poverty, maybe they are, I don't know. Other people have a materialistic drive. Maybe they're better educated or at the right place at the right time. . . . On the other hand, you got the people that don't want to get out of there [poverty]. They're satisfied with staying in poverty, because they don't have the, there's the stress, responsibility. . . . Maybe I shouldn't say this on tape, but instead of giving them . . . oatmeal and a bed, give them condoms, and teach them, education. Maybe that might bring it into control. And teach them farming methods and, it's got to be tough over there. It's not a place I would want to live in. . . . Poverty is going to be there forever. Because without poverty, you don't have anything to, to measure wealth with. Some people just have more drive to get out of it and some people've got the drive and can't get out of it. You know, how do you get those people out of poverty? (CL-14 Q5).

This speaker tries out a number of ideas including, first, the possibility that people don't want to be wealthy; second, that they do but need only education to become wealthy; or, third, that the whole system of inequality is inevitable with the natural symbolic order requiring poverty to define and "measure wealth with."

While the notion of objectivity leads to the expression of both positive and negative views of the non-Western world, the concept of contradiction or ideological dilemma will help us understand more fully how the discourse in our interviews is generated. New views of both culture and ideology have been developed which allow us to see ideological aspects of everyday life, including mass media, as more complex, contradictory,

14. This is a theme found in the photo captions as well. For example, an October 1982 photo of saffron-robed Thai monks standing with their bowls in front of a young couple dressed Western style and offering food to the monks is captioned in part "Thailand honors tradition while striving to prosper."

and emergent than in the past. This is in contrast to the view that cultural ideologies are belief structures with clear, determinant outlines to which individual people either do or do not subscribe. It is also in contrast to the idea that people simply absorb or resist ideas forcefully presented to them by dominant institutions like schools, other state institutions, or the mass media. Ideas about the non-Western world, like other ideologies, are reproduced or retain some cultural continuity and distinctiveness *not* "as a closed system for talking about the world . . . [but rather] as an incomplete set of contrary themes, which continually give rise to discussion, argumentation and dilemmas" (Billig 1988:6).

These interviews, then, involve a subtle and complex dialogue carried on both with the interviewer and between the variety of positions the interviewee has entertained over a period of time. This is evident again and again through the transcripts, as people deploy seemingly contradictory ideas to make sense of the pictures or of our more general questions. They can be arguing two positions at once in order to deplore the inadequacies of each viewpoint, to both decry and utilize prejudicial feelings, or for a number of other reasons. Neither of two seemingly contradictory voices can be treated as less real than the other.

Some of the basic dilemmas people must deal with in looking at the non-Western world are set up by ideas of liberalism. These include the problems of universal tolerance versus particularistic nationalism, with both notions having been ascendant in the twentieth century. This can also be described as the conflict between the values of pluralism and the belief in unilineal progress. American public ideals stress that the many cultural traditions from which the nation has been constructed are all good. The great majority of people answered our question about the value of cultural diversity in the affirmative: it is good, they said, that the world is made up of many different cultures. A belief in social evolution articulated by many people can, as we have just seen, create obvious dilemmas for the notion of pluralism.

The wide public endorsement of both values is evidenced, on the individual level in some cases, in their simultaneous expression.[15]

15. Anthropology as a discipline deals with this same dilemma, particularly as it intersects with the contradiction between expertise and equality. The anthropologist is charged both to appear as the scientific expert and to subscribe to the view that all people (and at least some of their ideas) are theoretically equal. The National Geographic Society has had a more partial investment in the view of itself as expert, having distinguished itself from the sciences in its ability to speak to the public on a kind of equal narrative plane.

National Geographic photographs prevent neither interpretation and in some cases can be seen to actively encourage both. In the photos, people are found doing things familiar to many readers (like the "disco" dancers of one photograph we looked at) and hence tolerable. At the same time, attention is drawn to the boundary between the traditional and modern, as in the topless and Levi jeans style of clothing worn by the dancers, without explaining that difference. Drawing attention to difference among people who are putatively similar to white Westerners appears to stimulate more ethnocentric or nationalistic discourse from the people we interviewed.

The ambivalent response to such pictures follows a long-standing ambivalence to modernity in American history (Lears 1985) and does not entail an equality of sentiment. People place the values of tolerance and the absolute preference for modernity in a hierarchy. They do this in a variety of ways—expressing one value and adding a "but"; leaving the dominant theme unmarked or unremarked upon; speaking at enthusiastic length about one option and in a more muted or anxious way about the other. The ambivalence is seen not only in a slipping back and forth between explanatory propositions but also between sentiments of sympathy and distance.

This vacillation is further determined by what Rosaldo (1989) calls imperialist nostalgia and characterizes as the emotional product of the West's observation of the changes wrought by colonization. This sadness, palpable in many of the readings given these photographs, refers to the loss felt at the changes in the cultural life of people portrayed as noble in their simplicity. The primitive, whether actually vanishing or not, is perceived as being transformed by the encounter with civilization. The value placed on progress and the belief in social evolutionism that accompanies it combine to give these changes the feel of inevitability. The concept of the primitive has been constructed, dualistically, to define the civilized Western self; this means then that "when the so-called civilizing process destabilizes forms of life, the agents of change experience transformations of other cultures as if they were personal losses" (1989:70). This stance, which Rosaldo sharply characterizes as "worshipping what we kill," coexists in contradictory fashion with a disdainful attitude towards the primitive in which "we kill what we despise." So, too, in these interviews we find people for whom the photos of jungle primitives evoke feelings of both attraction and repulsion. This was particularly evident when a man from Hawaii guessed that a photo of a person in a carved and painted mask was an African engaged in a ritual, and then went on:

> A lot of time and attention's been made to make up this person. I don't know if it's meant to scare or attract. As far as I'm concerned it's not attractive (DR-153 no. 12).

In many cases, however, worship and hatred are terms too strong to describe people's reactions; rather, indifference or simple dismissal occurred commonly enough. This would include a small number of responses as extreme as those of one woman who said, looking at the photo of a ritual in Nepal, "Some kind of festivities, probably a traditional dance of some sort. I don't really know. . . . It don't do a thing for me" (JC-10 no. 10).

Laughter, Clothes, and the Incongruous: Primitive and Modern Together

Viewing a photograph of a foreign world sends readers on a trip back and forth between their chairs and the new place they see. Individuals relish the traffic in different degrees. Many people we interviewed responded creatively to the juxtaposition, imagining similarities in the two worlds, or finding humor, irony, or incongruity in their juxtaposition. As we have seen, that juxtaposition is sometimes already made obvious by the *Geographic* photographers, as when they frame together a new bridge and a hand-poled river ferry. The ways people have of thinking about the dualism of traditional and modern are often dramatized by laughter, a signal of the variety of their emotional responses to that cultural gulf and to the idea of progress or social evolution.

Laughter often appears to be a reaction to elements of the photo or scene which seem not to go together and is therefore an assessment of what is normal either here or "over there." It often centers on seeing things categorized as Western in non-Western hands. Clothes, for example, make the man. A significant number of people remarked on the style of clothing being worn in the photograph. Clothes identified as Western seemed often to them not to belong on these people, to be a sign of cultural degradation, while non-Western clothing was taken as a sign of authenticity.

> The dress of the natives in the foreground looks real authentic. Very colorful, but a very plain landscape. And a flag, it

looks like a makeshift flag, that I never seen before. . . . And the village people are just out watching, and the ceremony, but they're too far away, really, to see in much detail, except that they look authentically dressed, like it's really who they are (JC-9 no. 10).

That's an interesting picture, because some of the kids look like they're in authentic, native dress, and some of the other ones look like they're contemporary and modern (JK-1 no. 14).

It looks like they're civilized people, imitating an old historical dance. Because the clothes are bright, they're not dirty or faded . . . their stuff, the, the costumes they have on look, look too, I don't know, too put together, too costume-ish, you know, to be real (AH-4 no. 17).

Another person seemed to suggest that the loss of traditional clothing styles goes along with the loss of cultural traditions which make the primitive "special":

They're dancing, I mean, it's not any special kind of dance, they're just, like, having a party. [Interviewer: What makes you think it's not a special dance?] Well, they would probably be more dressed in, you know—whatever native thing that they wear . . . you know, more the native wear that, you know, and they would be dancing with all makeup on and stuff like that (AH-8 no. 14).

The young people were then doing "just" a dance, which is to say the unmarked, unremarkable Western style of dancing rather than a "special dance," presumably a more ritualized, non-Western, cultural dance. Here, 'non-Western' clothing, as with all other markers of the exotic, stands for culture while the Western version of these things, the modern, stands outside of culture, representing the natural standard.

People often focused on the style of Western dress being worn and found it either funny or unpleasant to see people in styles they identify as out of date. Others found problems with people dressed in an inappropriately mixed style, as when one person noted that the photographed people were wearing "haphazard American dress again" (AH-1 no. 19). The humor this latter person found in the phenomenon led to the following comment:

> I always find it fascinating that some of these . . . non-Western cultures, when they wear Western clothes—this is just a naive comment—but it always seems so mismatched. And as, as the years progress, they become more and more matched . . . I saw this episode of David Letterman once, and he made a joke that he could look back in his video tapes, and tell the year before he even, you know, heard mention of what year it was by the broadness of his slacks. So in the same respect I would guess this picture to be maybe in the mid-seventies (AH-1 no. 8).

A few, who perhaps held more strictly to the ideal of progress, simply stated that the persons depicted needed to be wearing either more or better clothes:

> And it's definitely a poor place, there's really nothing. No plants really, just a lot of cows—and dirt, and dead trees. And they, they desperately need more clothes [laughs]. It's got holes everywhere in his shirt. And they obviously do not have money. They probably still trade, trade off some animals or something, or clothes, since they, you know, don't have any. That's all (AH-8 no. 18).

Even here, ambivalence showed, as when this same young woman from Hawaii seemed not to be able to say whether the bare-breasted women in one photo ought to have been clothed differently: "I don't understand why the ladies are topless and the guys are clothed [laughs]. They should just be both clothed" (AH-8 no. 14).

The centrality of clothing to defining the traditional and the modern is due not just to the visibility of the latter but also to the fact that in American consumer culture, perhaps even more than in most other societies, clothing is a "social skin" (Turner 1980) that represents us to ourselves and others. For many Americans, the answer to the question of who or where I am in time and space is found in one's clothing: the use of acrylic fabrics locating one in the lower classes, the width and color of a man's tie placing him in the corporate hierarchy, the amount of black in a woman's clothes identifying her politics, her skirt length announcing a year.

The native who would go modern presents two problems to the Western viewer. First, he or she no longer allows the Western self to stand, in a unique dress sign, at the head of civilization's march forward. The trousered native also finds, as does the modern, that the stylistic present, the most modern moment, is always slipping into the past. The native dressed in the style of the seventies can then look, to Western eyes, as both a usurper and as a slightly ridiculous figure, "uppity" or a "nerd." This style gaffe can reinforce the conflation in many minds, including the anthropological (Fabian 1983), between ancient time and other places. The basic contradiction can be summed up by saying that people want to dress the native in the raiment of progress but also and simultaneously to keep him or her in the native dress that preserves cultural authenticity and cultural hierarchy (and is in fact the only clothing he or she knows how to wear stylishly or correctly).[16] The primitive desire for modern goods, represented by dress, may make readers nervous for a number of reasons, some self-critical, but it also seems to both validate and threaten the white middle-class viewer's sense of position on the evolutionary scale.

While clothing was the artifact that most frequently stood, in the interviews, for the contradictions of social evolutionism, other things did as well. Several people found a photo of a politician in India odd. A man stands speaking before a crowd (whom we do not see), with a group of people visible behind him and a table to the side with a number of objects on it. Respondents were quick to point out incongruities:

> He might be someone with some kind of title, by the, his cloak looks like he might be, and the belt might be significant. But other than that it looks interesting for the technology of the equipment of the microphone, and in such a foreign place it seems a little bit out. And then ice, a pitcher of ice water on a table. That makes me think that's kind of funny. I think that's kind of funny (DR-4 no. 20).

The clothing plus the industrial artifacts plus the speechmaking behavior didn't add up for a man from Hawaii:

> It's real funny to see them wearing the robes and everything, though. I don't think of people as getting up and addressing

16. To take one further example of this on the individual level, notice the comments of the person (AH-8) who suggests that one photographed group ought to have better, that is, Western clothes while elsewhere suggesting that they ought to be dressed more traditionally. See also Monti (1987) for related observations on the role of native dress in Italian colonial-era photographs of Africa.

Many readers called attention to the combination of
traditional dress and Western artifacts in this picture.
Photographs where non-
Western peoples used Western commodities in unor-
thodox or "dated" ways
aroused both laughter and
anxiety in readers. (Photo:
Thomas J. Abercrombie,
© National Geographic
Society)

a crowd just dressed in like a robe or attire like this, like these
people. . . . But the table here with the roses and the water,
just keep standing out to me. It looks out of place in the
picture. It doesn't look like it should be there (AH-3 no. 20).

A similar but even more pervasive sense of contradiction reappears in
responses to a striking, large-format portrait of a Mexican in a mask
topped with a big pink rose. Many people remarked on the oddness of
the rose, often seeing it as something that did not belong, or as posing
some contradiction:

The rose throws me off, I don't think it goes with this costume. . . . The mask might be totally out of context from
wherever it's from. It doesn't look like, you know, an authentic picture, like, if this mask was on someone who looked
either Polynesian, or, or African, you know, with local cos-

Sometimes the same picture elicits sentiments of both attraction and repulsion. This photograph of a Mexican mask (frequently interpreted by readers as African) was praised for its elaborateness but was generally seen as unattractive. Many readers were disturbed by the juxtaposition of traditional design features and the plastic rose. (Photo: David Hiser, Photographers/Aspen)

tumes and religious hairdo to match, then I could [laughs] you know, feel it was more authentic, but I don't feel that way. Especially with the rose up here (AH-1 no. 12).

This could be either African or Oceania, I think, or the islands in, Oceania. I don't know where they have roses like that in Africa, except some place where the British got to. But that's just speculation (DR-153 no. 12).

For one person, the contradiction was between the mask and the seamed clothing that could be seen on the shoulders below the mask:

He definitely looks—dangerous—and he looks like he's probably going to have some, take part in like a cannibal activity, because it's just a typical looking kind of mask for a ritual, and that just reminds me of, like cannibalism, even though the rest of the picture doesn't really go along with that, because—he or she is also wearing clothing, and so it's not like a, not usually, like a cannibalistic islander. They usually wouldn't be wearing some kind of clothing that has seams on it. And then he's got a big rose on the top of his head, which looks fake to me, but you can't really tell (DR-152 no. 12).

What might most set the rose or the seamed clothing apart from the mask for these people is its Western manufacture and presumably modern origins in contrast to the quintessentially primitive nature of the mask with its popular culture ties to the spiritual, the hidden, and even the sinister (Price 1989; Torgovnick 1990). Insofar as Africa appears to commonly stand for the primitive, it is not surprising that many people placed the mask in an African setting. As one person said, "When I think of masks [and presumably only those masks commonly identified as primitive], I think of African masks." A great many of the other photo juxtapositions that readers commented on had the basic underlying dimension of commodity and its lack, but the rose and the mask pull together what appears to many readers as the core of the cultural difference between the West and the rest—that is, the technological marvel and personal satisfaction of the commodity and the technically simple but exotic and dangerous irrationality/spirituality of the other. This whole system of signification appears to be built around unstated, submerged notions of race, and it is to this question that we now turn.

Race: Its Erasure and the Return of the Repressed[17]

If people look at *National Geographic* photographs of the darker-skinned people of the world and think in terms of what they already know about race relations in America, they exemplify what Strathern has argued in another context: "Culture . . . consists in the way analogies are drawn between things, in the way certain thoughts are used to think others" (1990:3). The powerful issue of race must be a central analogical motor for the meaning readers make of the magazine. Racial categories, though denied, are crucial to people's experience of the photos, as can be seen in the answers to four questions we asked in looking at the transcripts of these interviews.

The first is what was said about race. In fact, very few people explicitly discussed it, and those who did mention skin color often quickly drew away from the topic, the retreat sometimes marked by laughter. Race is apparently a taboo topic here, as elsewhere in white middle-class culture.[18] Many people said, however, that they associate the magazine with Africa, with the place name standing both for the race and for a stereotypical primitivity, the man holding a spear, awash in body paint. Black people from New Guinea were seen as African, light-skinned people from Africa were not.

Second, and despite this reticence, people sometimes spoke at length about the motives, feelings, or typical behaviors of people photographed. More than a third of the photo descriptions we examined made

---

17. The title here borrows from Postone and Traube's (1985) rich ideological and psychodynamic analysis of the popular movie "Raiders of the Lost Ark." They argue that conflicts over female sexuality get played out in part by being transposed into a sense of the depravity of the Indian elite, who are figured as evil oppressors of a noble peasantry. The repression of attraction to the feminine is then also used in service to the legitimization of the dominance of both the masculine and the colonial powers. In the readers' responses to be examined here, it is the repression of the recognition of racial difference and racial oppression which is most at issue. As Postone and Traube conclude, however, "What is repressed then reappears in projected form and seems all the more threatening. The inherent instability of such a resolution presages a future return of the repressed which in turn would have to be denied and rejected all the more strongly" (1985:14).

18. One piece of evidence for this is found in textbooks. Preiswerk and Perrot found that only Nigerian textbooks focused at all on race of the group of otherwise all European books they examined (1978:253).

one or more such attributional statements.[19] The most common psychological elements mentioned are feelings, and these are usually positive
ones such as happiness or pride, as in the following:

> That looks like a grandpa, taking care of his granddaughter
> someplace up in Tibet. And that little girl's face is really
> vivid. She looks, her eyes are so bright, and she looks really
> happy (CL-4 no. 11).

> It's a man with a microphone, expounding on something.
> Appears to be fairly happy, the people seem to be fairly, you
> know, very intent, listening (CL-17 no. 20).

> It's a child, it appears to be overjoyed, either Chinese or
> Japanese, I'd guess. . . . I don't know why a child would get
> so happy about it. Maybe they understand the coming re-
> forms that are going on (CL-16 no. 5).

The question raised was whether the race of the photographed person
made people more or less likely to use such psychological categories.
Such categories are hegemonic in American society, placing a person's
mental and emotional processes and distinctiveness or personality at the
core of being (Carbaugh 1988). American individualism foregrounds and
values personality over roles or ethnic affiliation and one's own intentions and choices over either one's present situation or the goals of others
for the self. For this reason, the *National Geographic's* kindly-light policy
would seem to require presenting racial others as persons with a recognizable, elaborate, and upbeat psychological life. The producers of the
magazine know that people would rather *not* be made uncomfortable by
misery, and many photographs are published specifically because they

---

19. These were a sample of 441 responses from 53 people, of which 164 had
clear intentional attributions, almost all emotional in emphasis. Talk of intentional states in the photographed person was more common in the women we
interviewed and in the younger people. In addition, those two groups were more
likely to use personal than impersonal pronouns in statements describing the
people in the photo. Although the differences are not, of course, absolute, they
are statistically significant and may indicate a greater prevalence of psychological
discourse in those groups in general and/or a different perspective on the non-
Westerner in those groups. Our findings on race suggest that the amount of
attribution someone engages in can be related to the degree of negative feeling
s/he projects onto the other.

present others as happy, affectionate with each other, and so on. The frequency of smiles in the photos nearly demands a comment from readers on the happiness of the subject, with the inclusion of portraits in each article opening the way to characterological interpretation. Working out explanations or justifications for their own status and comfort, or rationales for their government's actions in those areas, first-world readers can imagine others who are neither hostile nor miserable: "They are happy even though they are poor." Positive psychological attribution can serve both commercial and political ends, that is, both sell magazines and advance a view of the status quo as relatively desirable.

This neat picture of planned pleasant attribution is disrupted by the fact that our consultants tended to prefer pictures which were about neither simple, smiling subjects nor overtly unpleasant ones. Pleasant but aesthetically complex or "interesting" pictures were preferred, presumably those for which more diverse attributions are possible. The picture editors we spoke with at *National Geographic* also strove for this response in readers, selecting pictures that would make people stop and ask what was going on in them. A good picture, in other words, would be somewhat ambiguous, making for more variable attributions as a result.

If, however, foreigners or people of other races are seen as different kinds of people, or even as less than fully human, the tendency to attribute inner states to them might be lessened. We were curious whether at least this group of white Americans sees the non-Westerners encountered in *National Geographic* and elsewhere as real people with whom they can identify, whose inner life they can imagine and whose outer life makes sense. In fact, people with dark (black) skin were significantly *less* often described in terms of personality, emotion, or typical behavior.

The third question we asked was whether race makes a difference in what *kinds* of feelings are attributed to the person photographed. When dark-skinned people were attributed feelings, they were more often seen in negative ways—as frightened, angry, cannibalistic, or depressed—than were those with lighter skin. (Forty-three percent of the attributional responses to pictures of people perceived as "African" were negative compared to only twelve percent of those made to lighter-skinned people.) So one person said, in looking at the New Guinea storytelling picture seen earlier: "This looks like some kind of a tribe, headed for a war, or battle or something. It looks like some of the people in the background are, I don't know if they're shivering away or, like I mean, drawing away from him. I mean, looking at the expression on their face" (CL-11 no. 1). A picture of Haitians walking along a road was read by one younger man as follows: "Well, they look like slaves, that are, that are on their way to work. They don't look very happy so, I'd say they're probably poor" (CL-12 no. 2). And the picture of the Nigerian river scene: "I think the people in the boat, they don't have a heck of a lot of, perhaps they don't have a lot of confidence in the twentieth-century means to cross, what I'll call a river" (CL-13 no. 8). In a rare mention of race, a young Binghamton man reasoned that in one picture it "seems like everyone is looking away slightly, or some of them even seem to be scowling. Perhaps it's their darker skin and eyebrows that make them look angry or disgusted" (CL-16 no. 20).

Some of these differences in how people interpreted the pictures of darker- and lighter-skinned people may be accounted for by the differing contents of these two sets of pictures in our sample of twenty, with the latter including more shots of children or of pairs of people in close and presumably affectionate contact.[20] Excluding those pictures of affection, however, leaves a statistically significant difference in how many more of the emotional attributions to darker-skinned people were negative.

When asked which pictures of the interview set they liked most, people were much less likely to prefer the photos with dark-skinned people than those with bronze-skinned people, although they never mentioned race as a criterion in those decisions.[21] When asked about their interest in travel to particular world regions, they consistently put Africa at the bottom of their rankings (Europe was at the top, followed by the Pacific, and, much lower on the list, Asia, South America, and then Africa). Asked which kinds of articles they preferred to read, several subscribers mentioned avoiding articles on Africa: "Now, I found that [article on the Titanic] a lot more interesting than something, than articles on African natives. I just happen to have no interest in that kind of thing. . . . I don't find—Should I say this?—I don't find pictures of natives, you know, in ceremonial dress, that kind of stuff, are not my

20. The larger group of approximately 600 pictures that we looked at were also, as in our interview pictures, more likely to show white- or light-brown-skinned people in small interacting groups of two or three and tended, though not significantly, to show them smiling more often. These photo features might be expected to encourage more positive emotional or other attributions.

21. Those we interviewed much more often liked those pictures in which people were dressed in a native style and those in which one to three individuals were depicted, rather than large groups. Like race, however, these were rarely explicit criteria that people used when justifying their preferences.

favorite. I mean there's other things to look at that are, that evoke much pleasanter than this, you know, for me" (CL-7). One younger man said, "[I] just look at articles that, parts of the world I'm interested in like the Orient or maybe India or Mexico. Usually things about Africa, I don't get too much from" (CL-12). All of this suggests that for many of our white interviewees and likely for many of the magazine's white readers, people with darker skin are seen as a problem race, as poor and unhappy, and, for this reason among others, a source of discomfort to look at.

Competing views of American national identity are explicitly at issue in many mass-media contexts and at least implicitly here in the *Geographic* as well. The self-image of the white middle- and working-class American—who is often portrayed as the prototypical American—is that he or she chooses modernity and its commodities and possesses an inner life of ideas, feelings, and motives, including the pursuit of happiness. Those people more like this prototypical American, in race or modernity, might be seen as characterizable in similar ways. In the fantasy social relations of the mass-media photograph, race and social evolutionism continue to have much to do with what is found in others' hearts and minds. The *National Geographic,* like anthropology, is hypothetically about the business of describing ethnic difference. The traffic between the magazine and its cultural milieu, however, is coded not first in terms of ethnicity but in the concepts of race and, as we saw earlier, gender.

Nine

The Pleasures
and Possibilities
of Reading

What is needed is an understanding of how any picture
could miraculously transform painful information into coherent
social action.

(Jussim 1984:112)

I n this final chapter, we ask two related questions about
readers' responses to the magazine. What exactly are the
pleasures that people find in these photos of the foreign,
and what kinds of progressive political possibilities are
there in the confrontation between readers and photographs? What kinds of questions, in other words, do
these photos encourage contemporary white, middle-class
Americans to ask, and what kinds of questions and critique
might they foreclose? Ultimately, we are brought back to
the question of how an American institution—the Geographic together with its readers—has constructed a world
of racial and cultural difference and what this says about
American society and dominant American politics.

Pleasure

The pleasures of the high-quality photographs in National
Geographic are central to the popularity of the magazine.
These include the pleasures of sight itself—colors, surprising shapes, and varieties of light; the pleasures of living—
happiness in family love, challenges overcome and
achieved, the joy of the new, including reading and learning. The Geographic's pleasures are also those of the familiar, a feature of much mass media. Like other popular

media with long continuity, the magazine has become part of many Americans' personal history, even more "part of the existential fabric of our own lives, so that what we [see in each issue] is ourselves, our own previous [viewings of the magazine]" (Jameson 1979:138).

Other pleasures are reflected in the magazine's facilitation of imagining other, even better, worlds. One person we spoke to about the magazine fervently expressed her enjoyment of its pictures by gesturing toward the Manhattan street we were standing on and saying, "I like knowing that there is something different from all of this, something more natural and peaceful."[1] Unlike some readers who imagine only the justification for their own place at the end of a funnel of the earth's resources, she looks to the magazine to find other possibilities, even utopian ones, for living, imagining a world where people live without a millstone of commodities around their necks, using earth's materials in a sustainable way. Such utopian readings of the *Geographic*—which may be relatively frequent—nonetheless, as Willis notes, should not be confused with "the transformation of daily life. . . . The real struggle is to use the recognition of utopia as impetus for fundamental social change" (1991:181).

People are also drawn to the magazine for the tensions which the pictures can arouse and sometimes quell, a form of stimulation that cannot always be called pleasant but which nonetheless beckons readers. In going to the magazine, the woman just mentioned may find a more complex and stimulating message than the one she claims to receive— she sees that the people of nature are "modernizing," that they are occasionally hungry or at war. In the course of her daily life, she might also wonder if the magazine is a hallucination—TV evening news suggests that those natural people are nowhere to be found; and a constant round of advertising images, supermarkets, and shopping malls suggests that her future will and should be one of more commodities, not fewer. These contradictions give the magazine more, rather than less, value in the lives of its subscribers.

Many people who looked at the photos with us during the interviews voiced their enjoyment, sometimes explicitly ("This is a great picture!"

---

1. In the interviews, people expressed pleasure in the expanded thought world that the magazine makes possible. As one young man said, "A lot of times it makes me think about things outside of my own little life, I mean, even if things are going good or bad, you know, you get still caught up in your own world. And, just being exposed to that stuff, you know, makes me think of what other people have, you know, or what they don't have. So, it just makes me think more. So, that's why I like it" (CL-11 Q7).

or "Her dress is gorgeous") and other times in an inarticulate but expressive way ("Wow!" "Ooh." "Oh my gosh!"). Some people were obviously more enthusiastic about the project and the pictures than others, and some individual photos were more popular than others. People's emotional involvement with the photos can speak to questions raised in the beginning of this book, questions about how mass media photographs of this sort might affect their cultural audience and how *National Geographic* photo selection criteria might mesh with the readers' preferences. Two central issues that emerged from our conversations with people were the pleasures they took in judging the content and aesthetics of the pictures and those some of them found in identifying with the people or scene photographed.

Preferences: Towards Colorful Good Feelings and Peace. People evaluated the photographs both spontaneously and on request. The great majority of pictures were appreciated by the great majority of people interviewed. This *is* a popular magazine. Each person was asked which picture they liked most and which least and why. The best-liked photos were an affectionate grandfather-granddaughter scene in India, a highly aestheticized Japanese street scene including schoolchildren, and a smiling Japanese girl in portrait. Many other pictures received significant numbers of votes. In these three most popular pictures, children were the central figures. This confirms what *Geographic* knows: pictures of children and animals head the list of requests, and the promotions department features them prominently in its mailing.

When, however, people were asked why they liked the pictures they did, the criteria they mentioned most often included the fact that the selected photo showed people feeling good in some way, whether peaceful, happy, or compassionate. Over half said that good feelings, either shown in or produced by the photo, were the reason for their choice. The second most common criterion was the aesthetic quality of the picture, including its colors and composition.

One woman, using both of these criteria, said that she liked best the picture of Japanese schoolchildren walking home because of the "kind of mysterious colors" in it and because "everything in the picture was kind of somber, because it had just rained, and the little kids looked so happy and bright. So it was, it was nice contrast" (CL-4 no. 1). Color contrast is seen as similar to emotional contrast in the photo; we might even speculate that the contrast enjoyed is also that between the moder-

Thoughts?

Of our sample of twenty randomly selected photographs of non-Westerners from *National Geographic,* this picture of a grandfather and his granddaughter was the one readers liked best. One said, "It just showed human values are basically the same around the world." (Photo: Doranne Jacobson, © National Geographic Society)

nity of the children's colorful umbrellas and the traditional world of the almost black-and-white era, the somber Japanese-style buildings.[2]

2. In research on amateur camera clubs, Schwartz and Griffin (1987) find that their members judge photographs by "pictorialist" standards, valuing beauty above all else. They also prefer pictures which follow classic design rules, such as the use of strong diagonals, and those which can be easily understood or have an immediate impact. They conclude that there is a "homogenization of photo-aesthetic codes outside the art world" (1987:215) in the ways just described. While these camera club members might provide a faithful group of *Geographic* subscribers, traditionally finding their codes represented in the magazine, for the readers we spoke with it was a secondary consideration.

A third reason given for liking certain pictures was that one could relate the scene to one's own life or to universal human values.[3] An upstate New Yorker liked the picture of an Indian man holding his granddaughter because "it just showed [that] human values are basically the same around the world and that even when there's desolation and, perhaps a war, hunger, that the spirit is still there, despite all those adversities and that the bond of love is important to young people and old people as a necessary part of life, and is available even during difficult times" (JC-9 no. 1). In sum, people liked pictures showing others feeling good, aesthetically pleasing pictures, and pictures which help them draw links between themselves and those in the frame.

Only one person mentioned a picture's informativeness as the reason for liking it, although the knowledge gained from the pictures is clearly central to people's evaluation of the magazine. The rarity of this response suggests that Jussim, Sontag, and others are correct in seeing the photograph as providing little very elaborate knowledge in and of itself. What can be concluded is that the pleasure of the National Geographic does not consist only or even mainly of its educational input, although most people communicate a sense that one *ought* to read the magazine.

The least popular pictures in our set were overwhelmingly the two that showed military scenes—one, a young Israeli woman sitting alone quietly cleaning her gun, and the other a helicopter landing in a nondescript dirt area with few clues as to the location (although the caption tells us it is the Thai king visiting one of his provinces on a development mission). The reasons given were the expected ones: these pictures were associated with (although neither showed) conflict, destruction, turmoil, or war. The gun-cleaning picture, for example, was disliked because it evokes "the thought that [the] young have to be in situations where they have to be faced with choices of killing or being killed . . . that is devastating or sad." More neutrally, others thought the scene didn't look "like someplace I'd want to be" or complained that "I'm not interested in any of that kind of [military] stuff." Readers' reactions to these photos underscore the point made by National Geographic editors—that viewing pictures ranging from the merely unpleasant to those depicting brutalized human beings might repel viewers.

A second reason people gave for disliking a photo was that it was uninformative or difficult to decipher.[4] On the other hand, people rarely

3. The percentage of our informants who used these criteria were 52 percent (good feelings), 17 percent (aesthetic), and 9 percent (could relate to own life).

4. Forty-one percent of the respondents used the first criterion (conflict or violence suggested), 32 percent the second (inability to decipher), while eight

This picture of an Israeli woman cleaning her gun was the least favored by the readers we interviewed, due to its evocation of conflict and violence and "the thought that [the] young have to be in situations where they have to be faced with choices of killing or being killed." While unpopular, the image provoked many readers to imagine how this young woman might feel. (Photo: Nathan Benn)

said the informational content of a picture made it likable. A picture had to tell a sensible story to be liked, but since most photos were realistic enough to satisfy this criteria, others (like the good feelings criteria) could come forward. Drab pictures lacking color were also disliked. A few people made the distinction between pictures whose content disturbed them and those which they saw as poor pictures in general; unpleasant pictures, they realized, could nonetheless be powerful or useful pictures to publish.

Readers' expressed preferences are not identical with those pictures which might have the most impact on their thinking about the third world. Few people pointed to the one photo with bare-breasted women dancing in tropical South America as one they particularly liked or dis-

---

percent mentioned bad feelings produced by a picture as the main reason for disliking it.

liked. Given the number of people who mention nudity with a giggle when they talk about the magazine, it is likely that this picture makes a significant impression on some people. If pictures like this one raise anxieties and deal with them effectively, they may attract readers but leave them less able to notice or say why.

Identification: Connecting Two Worlds in Imagination.   One of the chief pleasures for some was to draw parallels between their own experience and the content of a photograph. People were reminded of Hollywood movies, familiar artifacts like their "father's gym bag," and their own life situations. The pleasure of making these connections seemed to lie in finding a way to make the strange familiar, in drawing on earlier life experiences where some sense had already been made of the kinds of things in the photograph. The playfulness with which people made these imaginary connections between their world and the *Geographic* world was striking, suggesting that for some readers, the photographs are approached not as documentary objects but as fantastic objects which allow for symbolic play. This does not mean that those two stances are contradictory; rather, they can be alternate moments in reading photographs. The method we used of showing only photos could obviously lead in this direction, but a caption surely does not preclude such imaginative work in viewers.

What exactly did this identification consist of? The most direct approach was through some kind of frame breaking, in which viewers imaginatively enter the picture and speculate about what they would do if actually at the photographic spot:

> I felt like, I'm not much older than her [the Israeli cleaning her gun], and I don't want to go out and kill anyone, you know [laughs]. I felt bad that she was in a place where she had to. I felt almost like I wanted to protect her and stop that from happening, but of course I know it's happening in a lot of parts of the world [laughs] (AH-9 Q2).

> Which one did I like the least? I guess . . . it was the girl with the gun, cleaning the barrel of the semi-automatic rifle and doing it as if she was hanging up the laundry. . . . I guess you think, perhaps of women being the keepers of tradition and sanity and, and that's perhaps just an, an American viewpoint. If America was assaulted on the home front, you might

see American women, and I might be one of them out there cleaning an automatic rifle (JC-9 Q2).

Sometimes this imagining is pleasurable as people see themselves in new, expanded roles or relive pleasant experiences. Of an Alpine scene with tiny figures visible on the mountainside, one person speculated:

This could be one of those hiking expeditions that you read about, like a, you know, to the top of the Himalayas. . . . Or it could be a search expedition. It's very inviting, you know. When you read about things like that you think, Oh, I'd never do that, but then you look at a picture like this—it looks inviting. I think the little lights make it look so. I think whoever took it was brave because they were there. . . . That's a neat picture. It, you're really attracted to the little lights here. It makes you curious as to what's exactly going on (CL-6 no. 4).

I mean she [a smiling Japanese girl in another photo] looks like she's very happy about something, or [laughs] I don't know, she looks like me when I found I got into Columbia. She looks very happy [laughs] (AH-2 no. 5).

As in the first of these two examples, readers' moves into the third world can involve the kind of imaginary tourism that Guimond (1988) suggests is common to many American magazine renderings of the third world, as when one older Binghamton man viewing a Singapore beach scene said it is "someplace I wouldn't mind being right now" (CL-9 no. 19).

For some people, the pleasure that comes from identifying is more negative, entailing relief that their lives do not include some of the pictured elements. This happened fairly frequently in response to the photo of the Israeli woman cleaning a gun. An older man from Binghamton commented that "It's unfortunate to have that kind of, to have all that unrest over there. . . . We're fortunate not to have that here" (CL-14 no. 3). Remarking on a soft-focus photograph of several bicyclists in a rainy Chinese street scene, a young woman from Hawaii expressed similar feelings:

Yeah, I wouldn't want to be out in that [the rain], especially riding a bicycle. . . . I think of the Orient because of the rickshaw and the hat. . . . And the sky is really gray, I would think it's going to rain a very long time. And I have no idea why these people venture out in it [laughs] (AH-9 no. 16).

In other cases, readers simply drew parallels between something in their lives and something in the photo. The first case provided below is tinged with critique, while the second is phrased in more neutral terms, apparently suspending judgment about cultural difference.

This guy looks like some politician [laughs] or something, getting up on a shoe box and dictating to the crowd. Reminds me a lot of our own culture. . . . I don't think of people as getting up and addressing a crowd just dressed in like a robe or attire like this, like these people. It's funny that, to kind of see a relation between our society, but then see a big difference in the way they, they're acting, and the way they're dressed (AH-3 no. 20).

It sort of reminds me of, you know, like those stories that you read when you're kids, about kids growing up on the farm. And, you know, it's something that's really different from my own experience. It makes me wonder if, you know, what sort of work these kids have to do. And, you know, whether he's actually involved in herding the sheep, or if he's just playing with them or what (AH-2 no. 13).

The photographs sometimes provoked the kind of evolutionary comparison discussed in the last chapter, thoughts about "why we are so lucky here in this country."

When we asked people, independently of any one photo, to talk about the value of cultural differences, many people focused on the added interest those differences give to life because of their availability for reflection and comparison. As one person said, "I think there's a lot of richness when people of different backgrounds can talk about that or experience each other's culture, because it makes you think more about your own, gives you more, something to contrast with your experience, and thereby to help you define what's ideal and what's not" (AH-6 no. 6). On a more negative note, another man from Binghamton commented, "God, when I went to Mexico and looked I . . . just realized how, that, you know different places, people live differently in other places. And it's not so bad here, I guess" (CL-12 no. 4).

In several cases, the familiarity of a scene was traced to a mass media product. "This reminds me of a movie I saw . . . called 'The Emerald Forest' " (CL-5 no. 1), said one younger woman with significant travel experience. The television show MASH was evoked for another by the helicopter picture from Thailand.

Some viewers interpreted a foreign country as the historical past. One New Yorker, seeing a photo of some Gambian people subduing a cow to inoculate it, said it was almost like "early American days when the fellows went out to lasso and brand steer" (JC-9 no. 18). In several intriguing cases, the past evoked by the *Geographic* photo was itself mediated by way of media fiction. "Alice's Restaurant" revealed an earlier set of styles to one younger person and was paralleled, for her, by the bare feet and dress style of one photo's teenaged Singapore couple, who evoked "the seventies" for several other readers as well. Another Binghamton woman made a related parallel in looking at a photo of a populated Haitian country road in which a woman walks away from the camera with her dress unzipped down the back:

> This reminds me of . . . a book I just read. If she had been carrying that on her head it would have reminded me more. I just read *Tess of the D'Urbervilles* and it reminds me of the scene . . . where one of the women she was walking with was carrying molasses on her head and it had a leak and it dripped down her back and she ended up taking her, the top of her shirt off. It really, really reminds me of it. She looks tired too. That's what also reminds me of it (CL-1 no. 2).

"Little House on the Prairie" provided the historical lesson on itinerant preachers that was evoked by one viewer who saw a North Indian man giving a public speech.

> My first impression was the way he's dressed reminded me of, like Saint Francis. . . . Looks like something you'd see in a church. Maybe not, maybe not a church. Maybe a, like out of "Little House on the Prairie" when like the preacher used to be on the circuit and they'd come to town and they'd preach under a big tent (CL-1 no. 20).

There were also cases where readers went beyond a visual criterion in interpreting the picture and spoke of smells, sounds, or feelings that the scene behind the photograph must have. One older woman looking at a picture of a young boy picking up a sheep said, "It's got a lot of sound to it—the picture, for some reason, too. You kinda almost hear that herd of sheep digging up the dirt and making the noises" (CL-6 no. 13). Another, responding to the scene with the helicopters landing, explained that "just that hazy, it just gives me a feeling with the, with all the dust coming up and, kind of uncomfortable, you know, that something bad is going to happen" (CL-18 no. 6).

In their study of viewers' responses to the television show *Dallas,* Liebes and Katz (1990) find a variety of reading strategies being used. The viewers, who watched episodes of the show and were subsequently interviewed, came from a variety of cultural backgrounds in Israel, the United States, and Japan. Liebes and Katz categorize their responses as ludic (playful), aesthetic (focused on the show's artfulness or genre faithfulness), moral (passing judgment on characters' behavior), and ideological (concerned with latent, manipulative messages inserted by the show's producers). They discuss the "vulnerabilities" of each of these four strategies: the moral reading gives the cultural object standing by construing it as worthy of argument; the ideological reading tends to an automatic transformation in which the opposite of the message becomes the truth; the aesthetic allows the ideological messages to slip by; and the ludic simply does not force one from the fantastic back "to the ground." They explain their respondents' differing responses by way of their social positions, cultural traditions (especially of critical thought connected to oral or written texts), educational level, and previous experience with the genre of soap opera. Their observations suggest some important questions about the reading of the *National Geographic* photograph.

The Americans interviewed in our study used primarily the first three of Liebes and Katz's strategies in their readings of the photos. In the last chapter, we saw that evolutionist paradigms were frequently evoked by the photos and a moral discourse of progress or noble simplicity pursued within this framework. In the readers' preferences and identifications just discussed, play and aesthetics are paramount.[5] Notably lacking in our informants' interpretations is the ideological reading, a fact that may be related to the cultural construction of the genre of documentary photography or to more general tendencies, in the white middle class at least, to accept authoritative discourse at some level.

Americans are not schooled in the skills of critical photographic reading. Rather, the photograph is most commonly treated as an objective document. Although they are seen as having propagandistic uses (witness the controversies over the Willie Horton photograph in George Bush's 1988 campaign and the wartime photographs of Iraqi-captured American Air Force pilots), photos in a scientific journal are not likely to lead readers to ask about their producers' intentions or their ideological

5. The discussion of readers' preferences focuses on people's responses to our direct questions about which photos they liked and disliked, but in their reactions to the pictures as we went through them one by one they also discussed their beauty, the compositional form, and other such aesthetic issues.

resonances. Familiarity with other types of documentary photography gives most readers at least one platform from which to attempt criticial readings, although most photographic experience comes in the form of commercial photography. Distrust of commercial images may give *National Geographic* images further immunity from ideological readings as they become a refuge from the former. Televised and other magazine images of stronger, more realistic, or more sensationalized subjects could suggest to many readers that the magazine's images take a particular slant on the world, a concern shared by the *Geographic* staff. In our conversations however, this difference between *National Geographic* and other kinds of documentary images does not seem to have led to loss of faith in the magazine's objectivity, nor has it raised the question of photographic epistemology.

Nonetheless, readings that involve identification can be seen as a positive process. People are actively engaged with the photographs, and they are relating their lives to the lives of people in the third world. Most of this work is simply analogical (how my life is or is not like theirs), but this might be a first step to a focus on how those two sets of lives are actually and directly related to each other.

Possibilities

The photographs produced and sold by the National Geographic Society possess a consistent—some would say *in*sistent—style. The twin features of this style are its humanism and its realism. What readers have learned to expect, and what they generally get, from the pages of the *Geographic* are clear, well-focused photographs of good people.

These elements of style have been codified into the doctrines governing production at the *Geographic*. "The first principle is absolute accuracy," its editorial policy states. "Nothing must be printed which is not strictly according to fact." The insistently realist style of photographs, their "readability" to Western middle-class audiences, the captions that draw attention to aspects of their content, all foster the impression that these are clear, unmediated records of a knowable world. The photographs are bathed in a heavy wash of objectivity and authenticity. Not only have they been commissioned and approved by a world-famous "scientific and educational" organization, but their "capture" by the photographer has required travel, adventure, and personal knowledge. The pictures fascinate by their claim to documentary status—someone has actually been "out there" and has drawn close to the people and events they have photographed. They have had the kind of direct personal contact that American popular culture tells us is a particularly reliable basis for knowledge.

Like realism, a certain humanism is mandated by editorial policy at the *Geographic*. "Only what is of a kindly nature is printed about any country or people, everything unpleasant or unduly critical being avoided." While unpleasantness has entered the pages of the magazine increasingly since the 1970s, there is still an assiduous avoidance of criticism. Hunger, poverty, and inequality, to the extent that they are depicted, have been presented as problems that right-thinking people can band together to solve, not as conflicts of interest. Like mainstream news organizations, the *Geographic* adheres to a notion of balance, which assumes truth to lie between the two sides of a conflict. Unlike the news media, it has not seen its job as presenting the two sides, along with a mediating "center" view, but as erasing conflict altogether. Soldiers have been portrayed in acts of kindness; deposed dictators mark "the passing of an era." The cameras of the *Geographic* are trained on the vibrant, ebullient, sometimes long-suffering, but always noble human spirit.

Such a photographic style is coded, within the cuture of the West, as neutral or apolitical. It is read as being above politics, dignified both by virtue of its connections to science and its claims to represent enduring and universal human values. Yet the photographic conventions on which such a position is based are fraught with implicit meanings. They are full of unspoken yet powerful messages about who non-Western peoples are and what their relationships are to white Western readers.

"Political" photography, as traditionally practiced in the West, usually operates in one of two ways. What one might call the didactic tradition attempts to make clear statements about the world that are meant to educate and to motivate a desire for change. From Dorothea Lange's photographs of hungry sharecroppers to Sebastião Salgado's images of famine in East Africa, there exists a tradition of concerned photography that seeks to expose human suffering through the medium of photography; to discover and make real for middle-class Western audiences the pain that goes on outside of their own circles. These photographs shock; they horrify; they move to tears. They often operate by encouraging an empathetic involvement with the photographed subject—a desire to intervene directly within the frame of the photograph in order to ease the depicted pain or comfort a hungry child. At their most effective, these pictures lead us to ask how such a thing can happen—and how it can be kept from happening again.

Images cannot answer that question for us. As Jussim has noted, "A photograph cannot simultaneously contain both an image of the problem and its solution" (1984:112). The interpretation remains with the viewer who, confronted with a disturbing frame, draws on familiar politics and cultural models for explanation. Thus, for diverse viewers, the image of a starving African family may implicate American overconsumption, greedy multinational corporations, corrupt local governments, or the lack of industry of dark-skinned peoples. It may, ironically, confirm Biblical statements such as "the poor will always be with you." As John Berger has warned, "The photograph accuses nobody and everybody" (1980:40). It cannot provide the social analysis that would allow its viewers to act on their unease. The most we can ask of an image is that it leave us with questions, with an aroused interest in the subject, a desire to know more fully the conditions surrounding the representation.

Political photography that seeks to instruct has encountered a profound crisis in the post-Vietnam period. It faced a nation in which many people, weary of images of suffering and death, were bored with attempts to arouse their sense of responsibility. One renowned documentary photographer has expressed her frustration at the sense that she cannot penetrate such defenses: "It's difficult now to feel that I can't make an image to bring the devastation of the war with the contras home, even though I feel a tremendous urgency to do so" (Meiselas in Ritchin 1989:438). For Susan Meiselas, the problem is that what constitutes an "image" worth publishing has been redefined "in Washington, and in the press, by the powers that be." For others, the difficulty of producing effective didactic imagery is a product of the passing of the certainties of the modern era and the advent of a postmodern culture. In that postmodernity, images of disaster proliferate and become mere spectacle, there is widespread disbelief in the facility of significant social change, and images that "appeal to a sense of empathy and concern" are shunned by editors and readers as sentimental and naive (Ritchin 1989:438).

A second tradition in Western political photography does not attempt to instruct about social problems but to disrupt traditional ways of understanding. Through the use of surrealist (or more generally modernist) techniques such as juxtaposition and dislocation, this type of photographic practice raises questions about hegemonic definitions of what is good, normal, and valuable. In these photographs, the camera lens is more frequently turned back on the society that holds the camera. Erich Hartmann's image of a New York City woman looking profoundly uncomfortable in an overstuffed armchair—her body crisscrossed with reflections of pulsing neon lights; Cartier-Bresson's photograph of a terrified monkey hooked up to machinery in a Berkeley lab; Stuart Franklin's eerie renditions of gas masks during nuclear exercises at a military academy; Cindy Sherman's images of herself as famous "personalities" or as corpses—all do this. These photographs seek to make the familiar strange, to inspire self-reflection, and to raise questions about the exercise of power in unexamined arenas.

These images are also profoundly ambiguous. In a culture so dominated by realist conventions, they are seen as inaccessible by much of the public. Viewers who have not been schooled in other traditions of representation often shy away from them as though they are hearing a language they do not speak—although when pressed to spend time with such a photo, they may read it in profound ways. For this reason, however, the public at large is not drawn to such images, and mainstream media generally avoid them.

Such images tend to exercise a critical rather than a tutorial function, and perhaps for this reason may be more pointed than didactic photographs. They are often clearly directed at a particular cultural practice— the inhumane treatment of animals, say, or cultural acceptance of nuclear weapons. The practice—tourism, for example—may be one in which the viewer is implicated. Additionally, the message of such photographs is less often transparent. Not always appealing to the intellect, they use disturbing incongruities in form and content, unexpected aestheticization, and sometimes humor to achieve their ends. For this reason, the questions raised may linger; they may be less easily dismissed because they are less easily put into language—and certainly not into familiar liberal discourse.

National Geographic photos rarely fall into either of these two genres of political photography. There are exceptions, of course. Jim Blair's photographs of South Africa and Nachtwey's images of Guatemala were printed by editors despite their exposure of poverty and oppression. An April 1990 set of photographs of animals, depicting them in highly anthropomorphized ways, possessed distinct surrealist affinities. (Publication of these latter photographs, we were told, was one of the most heatedly contested editorial decisions of the decade.)[6] In general, how-

6. The controversy over the animal photographs (in which various large endangered mammals were set in chairs, draped in gauze, and so on) was also due to the fear of readers being offended by the photographer's treatment of the animals, however mild.

ever, editorial policies demanding readability and balance are effective in screening for political photographs of both types described above.

There are senses, however, in which *National Geographic* photographs can be perceived as making a political statement, although one that—as we shall see—is fraught with contradictions. In its search for the photogenic in the far corners of the world, the magazine consistently beautifies and dignifies (at the same time that it exoticizes and objectifies) people and places that are not ordinarily perceived as beautiful in Western culture. It renders the interior of a mud hut tranquil and homey; it catches the pride on the face of a recently scarified adolescent. In so doing, it obviously authorizes itself to make such judgments, thus preserving the power and privilege of aesthetic and scientific evaluation. We will trace the implications of this evaluative stance more fully below. But the valuation itself is the source of much of the overt meaning of the photographs for Western audiences. It is what fuels the imaginative games in which readers play with the idea of what it would be like to live in another culture in another part of the world.

Our interviews revealed the salience of this response. "Those beautiful houses that are all kind of pushed together, but they still have a lot of space inside . . . I would like to go inside them." "It looks like that's apparently the way you get around. . . . I'd like to live someplace where you just use bikes to get around." Or, rejecting the *Geographic's* aestheticization of a riverside dishwashing scene: "I'd hate to have to eat out of those dishes—it looks like she's cleaning them in the water. It's probably dirty water." Readers actively play with the idea of alternative worlds. For many, this adventure simply validates their own way of life as more comfortable, or more enlightened, than the other scenarios they visit through the images. Yet for large numbers of readers the pictures open up new imaginative spaces. "Fairly modest surroundings, but a lot of human emotion" commented one reader as she examined a photograph of an old man and his granddaughter. She described in detail the rough-hewn logs of the doorway, the gold bracelets against the young child's skin, the smoke from the man's cigarette, the affection of their embrace—clearly imagining what it would feel like to be in a setting that was so foreign, yet where others seemed happy. Readers reserve the right to reject *National Geographic's* portrayal of a scene as interesting or beautiful—"It don't do nothing for me." They seem to understand the *Geographic's* major purpose or goal, however, as this work of validation.

The contradictions of such a photographic practice, as in other acts of collection and presentation, are apparent. As Clifford has said:

Something similar occurs whenever marginal peoples come into a historical or ethnographic space that has been defined by the Western imagination. "Entering the modern world," their distinct histories quickly vanish. Swept up in a destiny dominated by the capitalist West and by various technologically advanced socialisms, these suddenly "backward" peoples no longer invent local futures. What is different about them remains tied to traditional pasts, inherited structures that either resist or yield to the new but cannot produce it (1988:5).

Any conversation, in Trinh's words, "of 'us' with 'us' about 'them' is a conversation in which 'them' is silenced. As in much anthropological writing, 'them' always stands on the other side of the hill, naked and speechless, barely present in its absence" (1989:67; compare Sekula 1975). However sympathetic the presentation, whatever validation is attempted, such objectification is inevitable in the pages of *National Geographic*. Autonomous self-representations are not what the magazine is about.

It is not simply that a Western presentation of non-Western others to fellow Westerners (by way of anthropology or *Geographic* photography) entails objectification. This is the basic power relation within which the conversation takes place, but features of *National Geographic* photos have given that objectification a specific character. One of the most important of these is the anonymous, iconic character of most of the individuals depicted. With the exception of the wealthy and powerful (and of some "common people" in issues of recent years), most of the people who have been photographed through the last hundred years remain unnamed. They are rendered as "typical" rather than as named subjects; they are depicted as involved in the daily or yearly round of activities rather than participating in a specific event. It is in part through this anonymity that they are denied real historical pasts and that they lose the perceived ability, as Clifford points out, to invent their own "local futures." Their story ceases to be about their own autonomous concerns; individuals become signs in a story the West is telling about its relationship to the non-Western world.

An emphasis on the "exotic" qualities of the photographed subject also give a special quality to the objectification that occurs in *National Geographic*. As we described in chapter 4, the rendering of cultural difference as exotic accomplishes a number of things. It rivets attention; it marks a difference between the "normal" self represented by the reader and the other, who is represented in the photo; and it creates distance by treating those photographed as spectacle. The latter two strategies both have complex effects which can enter in divergent ways into readings of the photographs.

The marking of difference is always highly charged. Both structuralist and post-structuralist theory have argued that contrasts usually imply hierarchy. In contrast sets, one term is generally dominant and prior, the other secondary and defined antithetically to the first.[7] Thus, however beautiful and interesting National Geographic renders a ritual act, the marking of exotic difference brings ranking into play. Exotic practices are implicitly contrasted with Western practices, and, in the imagination of most readers, found wanting. This is a paradox that confounded even surrealist photography at its high point. The surrealists often use primitive imagery (drawn largely from Africa) to challenge Western standards of beauty and normalcy. While they relied on a range of complex strategies that sought to establish the "primitive" as the dominant term in the contrast set, they could not guarantee that their images would actually be read in that way. Once turned loose in the world, the photographs could often be read in the same evaluative ways as National Geographic photos are—as marking a lack in the cultures represented. Interesting and beautiful as they may be, right as they may be for East Africans or Polynesians, they do not represent the direction history is taking.

The emphasis on spectacle in the Geographic's photography has tended to flatten out what is presented. The attention to rich surfaces and imagery may work against deeper understanding or involvement (Polan 1986b:63). Particularly because so many rituals, festivals, and gatherings have been presented as prototypical, rather than as unique historical events, they have been read as markers of ethnic identity more than understood as meaningful social interactions. Thus, through the depiction of spectacle as well—which at one level is designed to reveal the beauty of cultural difference—photographs may carry hidden messages that tend to devalue and objectify those they portray. To argue that the photographs in National Geographic possess dual or hidden meanings is by no means to imply that there is a secret agenda at work or that the overt project of valuing other cultures serves only as a cover for objecti-

7. This negative evaluation of difference finds a place in pervasive cultural understandings, in the United States at least, that equate equality and sameness, leaving difference to suggest inequality.

fied and reified presentations. We are not dealing with surface meanings and real meanings, but with highly ambiguous messages.

A second way in which *National Geographic* photographs are arguably political photographs is in the "humanism" they support, as described above. The *Geographic*'s humanism, like that of many other liberal institutions, affirms the idea of a universal underlying human nature. Projects confirming this universal essence have been popular with the Western media since World War II. In 1948, photojournalists from the agency Magnum collaborated on the project "People are People the World Over" for *Ladies' Home Journal*. Each month for a year, the magazine published photographs showing the similar ways in which people around the world shopped, washed their clothes, cooked, and raised children. Some have argued that this project was the inspiration for Edward Steichen's more ambitious "Family of Man" exhibit, which is still "the most widely seen and influential photography exhibit ever made" (Ritchin 1989:431). Projects of this type present the argument that under the superficial veneer of cultural difference human beings are fundamentally the same. To resolve conflict becomes a matter of getting past superficialities and recognizing common interests.

National Geographic photographs are humanist in intent. They do not caricature or denigrate the non-Western world in the ways that other popular cultural forms often do—Indiana Jones films, evening news' rendition of Arab terrorism, or cartoon cannibals, for instance. Neither do they portray people as powerless victims. Their tone is respectful. Yet this humanism cannot find in the third world anything more than a pale reflection of American values. For others to be equal, they must be more or less the same. Their rituals are strikingly beautiful, but they do not suggest a *radically* different religious philosophy. Under the veneer of the exotic, they conceal the same reverence for a higher power that we know in the West. Mothers in Africa may carry babies on their back or in strange baskets. But this does not suggest a radical difference in how mothering is constructed; under the surface it reveals the universality of the mother-child bond. And so on and on—differences that could tell us something important about history, differences that could be turned critically on practices in our own society become construed as superficial, even if attractive, flourishes that can be pulled back to reveal confirmation of important Western values.

To anyone writing in the early 1990s, when new forms of racism and intolerance are reasserting themselves, criticizing even a conservative brand of humanism seems self-defeating. Images are always read in their historical context, and in eras of racial and cultural tension, images of shared underlying values may be understood as direct contradictions of racist ideology. Yet in the end such images may not contribute to social change in the ways that we would hope a political photography would do. They contribute to an erasure of the forms of difference which impel social struggle, at the same time that they conserve notions of ethnic and other identities as stable enclosures that preclude real forms of empathy and communication. Writing of current efforts to contest racism and discrimination, Trinh has contrasted conservative humanist projects from more radical endeavors. She contrasts "projects which contribute to the improvement or enlargement of the identity enclosure, but do not, in any way, attempt to remove its fence, and those which dismantle the very notion of core identity" (1989:94). By arguing that people are basically the same under the veneer of culture, National Geographic photography both denies fundamental differences and reifies the cultural boundary that it depicts.

If there is a single distinctive characteristic of political photography, it is the fact that the images produced leave us with such questions as How could this be? Why did this happen? to What is wrong here? Why does this familiar scene disturb me? The questions generated by such photographs are not easily resolved. The images return to haunt us long after their first viewing. When these images have been broadcast through the mass media, they become points of reference for the culture at large. The most gripping photographic images from the Vietnam War became a national shorthand for sets of questions, rather than for any single attitude, analysis, or understanding. Two decades later, they still recall the painful uncertainties and dilemmas of the war. While such images may generate committed political actions, they do not prescribe them. They work by arousing curiosity, interest, and a desire for change.

It is the hallmark of National Geographic's postwar photographs that they have not often left the reader with fundamental questions.[8] They may frequently pique curiosity through a slightly ambiguous image (Why is this boy smiling/grimacing? What is that woman holding?) or through odd juxtapositions of traditional and modern dress on a single

---

8. Several of the editorial staff we consulted hope to have their pictures generate questions, but it appeared they felt that those questions should be primarily simple information-gathering queries rather than emotionally or politically charged ones. The primary goal seemed to be to get the reader to want to know more about a country or other subject rather than to generate dismay or the desire for change.

individual. They inevitably resolve that ambiguity, however, through the use of captions telling the curious reader exactly what is going on. They may provide isolated images of poverty or of social unrest, but these are always embedded in larger sets of photos designed to balance their impact. "Life goes on" is the larger message. "Families still love each other—the social fabric has not torn." The gradually increasing number of photographs of degraded environments, poverty, and violence since the mid-1970s actually intensifies this message. In a world where newspapers and television carry such disturbing images every day, National Geographic is saying, "We're not denying that such things go on, but look at the larger context." The magazine thus preserves the sense that it has a grip on reality, while retaining its message that all is fundamentally right with the world.

This is, as Jameson has said, the fundamental role of mass media. Its institutions frequently operate by arousing and giving expression to the profound anxieties that people experience in a particular historical period. But they do so in contexts where those anxieties can be given an easy resolution. "You are right to worry about this, but everything will be okay," they seem to say. National Geographic photographs have done this constantly, insistently, resolutely—sometimes in the context of a single photo. A disturbing image of a South African mine worker whose body is being exposed to extreme heat in order to see what temperatures it can withstand was captioned with calming words about how the results will make for better conditions in the mines. Conversely, as one photographer pointed out to us, the text of a 1988 article about population and hunger was illustrated with relatively healthy people clustered in family groups and working. Other times, the cathartic work has been accomplished in the context of a larger article, as when a 1961 article calls Indonesia "young and troubled" in title and text, but whose photos show only smiling tea pickers and elaborate rituals. Trouble has been a minor theme in an overall magazine context of happy, healthy people, of cultural vitality and progress.

National Geographic photographs are highly ambiguous. In part the ambiguities are those endemic to liberal humanism—the paternalism and objectification that necessarily attend the benevolent stances of the powerful. In part they derive from the fact that production at National Geographic is indeed a complicated process; while the editorial hand is heavy, autonomous voices occasionally make their way into the magazine. Editors may envision and map out pieces that make a powerful personal or political statement, and photographers may see the occasional strong picture published. In part, the ambiguity represents a conscious and highly refined editorial strategy designed to appeal to a wide range of tastes and to appear relevant without raising difficult questions. The *Geographic*'s marketing success turns on its acceptability to individuals across the political spectrum. It is also crucial to the organization's carefully constructed image of itself as a scientific and educational association, as it plays into notions of balance and political neutrality.

This ambiguity means that some readers in some historical periods will find their understanding of the non-Western world enriched by viewing *National Geographic* photographs. For well-intentioned, curious readers, the images may help to build certain kinds of cross-cultural understanding; they may raise questions and impel the viewer to seek a deeper knowledge through reading or personal experience. Spending time with the photographs may allow such readers to develop an imagined empathy with the people depicted, although it must be remembered that such empathy is not based on any genuine encounter.

The photographs more generally, however, have exercised a conservative force within the culture. They have rarely cried out for change, raised painful, unresolvable questions, embarrassed, or caused discomfort. In general, they have existed as a beautiful, somewhat compelling body of evidence that the third world is a safe place, that it is made up of people basically like us, that the people who are hungry and oppressed have meaningful lives, and that the conflicts and flare-ups we hear of in the news occur in a broader context of enduring values and everyday activities. These images obscure the American relationships with the third world that have structured life there in profound ways; they deny real social connections even as they evoke empathy. One can imagine these photographs doing otherwise, however—through critical rereading, through changes in photographic practice at the Geographic, but more fundamentally as a consequence of shifts in American international power, in class relations and understandings of them, or in the place of science and photography in their social context. Rather than simply confirming complacent or self-congratulatory American identities, they might question the power we have had to control the lives of others and to leave our own unexamined.

Epilogue

The invasion of Grenada was a central prompt to this project, as we noted at the outset. A little over seven years after that invasion, as the book neared completion, we were confronted with the same questions raised for us earlier, on an even larger scale. On January 16, 1991, the United States began to bombard Iraq in response to its invasion of Kuwait several months earlier. There was much public support, and some protest. "America is still the kindest, gentlest nation on earth," Bush told the public in his address on the state of the union, "and what we are fighting here is nothing less than evil itself." Turning the public's attention away from the complexities of the situation, he reduced the deep-rooted conflicts that have tormented the Middle East to the narrow terms of a moral crusade. For much of the public, watching the parade of new military equipment and reports of successful air attacks that characterized the early media coverage, questions remained, however. Who was Saddam Hussein, and—to paraphrase Freud—what did he want? Rather than examining the complex forms of Arab nationalism, the news media characterized the Iraqi leader as a madman. If his actions were simply the product of individual dementia, however, where did the angry crowds occasionally filmed in Jordan, Iran, and Iraq come from? If the United States were indeed the kindest, gentlest nation on earth, why did these people hate it with such a passion?

In 1991, we brought to these questions some of what we had learned through our examination of the portrayal of distant nations in *National Geographic* magazine. At the most general level, we were able to see more clearly than in 1983 the contradictions and weaknesses of the "classic humanism" (Barthes 1972) with which Americans are taught to see the world. Churches, schools, and popular media have confronted racism, xenophobia, and ethnocentrism with an assertion of universal human nature. The opposite of believing others are bad and inferior, we are told, is believing that they are like us in fundamental ways. Such a framework falls apart in situations of conflict. It cannot accommodate differences of interest or account for incidents of injustice—it cannot, as Barthes has said, bear the weight of history.

Writing of the responses of American children to the Gulf War, Anna Quindlen (1991) recounted the following story. In a television news segment, a psychologist worked with elementary school children to help them overcome their fears related to the war.

> "I was thinking about the kids in Iraq," said one somber little girl. The professional was fast on his feet. "I know it is frightening," he replied. "But it is all happening very far away."

The assumption was that children would be "mainly concerned about themselves, about their personal safety, about assurances that there is no carpet bombing likely in their part of the world." Quindlen demurs:

> The children I've heard are better than that. "Are there kids in Iraq?" my second-grader asked me, a question that implied self-interest—"If it could happen to them, it could happen to me"—but contained a larger empathy as well. Remember all those social studies lessons about children in other parts of the world, about how we are all members of the family of man? They've come home to roost.

This incident, and Quindlen's recounting of it, is remarkable in two important ways. The first is the existence of such empathy in children, and its rejection by adults. The psychologist's words encouraged the child to circumscribe a sphere of interest—my family, my neighborhood—versus the "far away" places where children were dying. The story also illustrates how classic forms of humanism collapse when confronted with real-world events. "Ask the family of Emmett Till, the young Negro assassinated by the Whites," Barthes writes, "what *they* think of *The Great Family of Man*" (1972:101). Barthes emphasizes the need to probe the history of social arrangements. Rather than scratching human history to reach the solid rock of a universal human nature, he argues, a progressive humanism must scour nature to discover history, and finally to establish Nature itself as historical. If the basis for cooperation and peace is a shared human *nature,* then a president who wants to wage war must vilify his opponents as subhuman or demented, outside the pale of normal human relations. We are unable to perceive or address the historical actions, the differences of culture, or the economic pressures that structure politics and public discourse. It is the superficial "humanizing" of others, rather than the empathetic probing of different lifeways, experiences, and interests that creates the crises of understanding that break open at times of war.

Appendix A
Photograph Codes

World location
Unit of article organization (region, nation-state, ethnic group, other)
Number of photos including Westerners in an article
Smiling in photograph
Gender of adults depicted
Age of those depicted
Aggressive activity or military personnel or weapons shown
Activity level of main foreground figures
Activity type of main foreground figures
Camera gaze of person photographed
Surroundings of people photographed
Ritual focus
Group size
Westerners in photo
Urban versus rural setting
Wealth indicators in photo
Skin color
Dress style ("western" or local)
Male nudity
Female nudity
Technological type present (simple handmade tools, machinery)
Vantage (point from which camera perceives main figures)

Appendix B

Photographs
Discussed in
Interviews

1. August 1983: 167, New Guinea ritual storytelling scene
2. March 1985: 401, Haiti, people traveling on road
3. February 1978: 236, Israel, young woman cleans rifle
4. July 1982: 62, Peru, mountainside with tiny figures ascending
5. April 1977: 557, Japan, nearly complete figure of smiling girl
6. October 1982: 492, Thailand, crowd views helicopter landing
7. June 1984: 758, Japan, school children walking along road
8. March 1979: 420, Nigeria, bridge and ferry on river
9. December 1979: 778, Korea, woman in academic regalia trims cap tassel
10. June 1982: 708, Nepal, festival with costumed figure
11. August 1977: 286, India, grandfather holds smiling granddaughter
12. May 1978: 660, Mexico, portrait of person in carved mask
13. June 1982: 776, Namibia, small blond boy holds sheep near herd
14. January 1983: 72, South America, teenagers dance
15. July 1983: 64, China, construction worker looks at camera
16. October 1979: 563, China, bicycle and handcart traffic move through rainy road
17. January 1978: 46, Swaziland, Zulu princess dances with column of women
18. December 1986: 827, Gambia, people wrestle cow to inoculate it
19. April 1981: 561, Singapore, young couple hold hands on park bench
20. March 1978: 337, India, political speechmaker

References

Abramson, Howard S. 1987. *National Geographic: Behind America's Lens on the World*. New York: Crown.

Abu-Lughod, Lila. 1986. *Veiled Sentiments: Honor and Poetry in a Bedouin Society*. Berkeley and Los Angeles: University of California Press.

Adas, Michael. 1989. *Machines as the Measure of Men*. Ithaca: Cornell University Press.

Adorno, T. W., E. Frenkel-Brunswik, D. J. Levinson, and R. Nevitt Sanford. 1950. *The Authoritarian Personality: Studies in Prejudice*. New York: Harper and Row.

Alloula, Malek. 1986. *The Colonial Harem*. Minneapolis: University of Minnesota Press.

Alvarado, Manuel. 1979/80. Photographs and narrativity. *Screen Education* (Autumn/Winter): 5–17.

Amin, Samir. 1989. *Eurocentrism*. New York: Monthly Review Press.

Amos, V., and Prathiba Parmar. 1984. Challenging imperial feminism. *Feminist Review* 17: 3–20.

Appadurai, Arjun. 1986. Theory in anthropology: Center and periphery. *Comparative Studies in Society and History* 28:356–61.

Bailey, Cameron. 1988. Nigger/lover: The thin sheen of race in "Something Wild." *Screen* 29, no. 4: 28–40.

Banta, Melissa, and Curtis M. Hinsley. 1986. *From Site to Sight: Anthropology, Photography, and the Power of the Imagery*. Cambridge, Mass.: Peabody Museum Press.

Barkin, Steve, and Michael Gurevitch. 1987. Out of work and on the air: Television news of unemployment. *Critical Studies in Mass Communication* 4:1–20.

Barthes, Roland. 1972. *Mythologies*, trans. A. Lavers. New York: Hill and Wang.

References

———. 1977. The photographic message. In *Image-Music-Text*, trans. S. Heath. Glasgow: Fontana.

———. 1981. *Camera Lucida: Reflections on Photography*, trans. R. Howard. New York: Hill and Wang.

Baudrillard, Jean. 1968. *Le Système des Objets*. Paris: Gallimard.

Baxandall, Michael. 1985. *Pattern of Intention: On the Historical Explanation of Pictures*. New Haven: Yale University Press.

Becker, Howard. 1978. Do photographs tell the truth? *Afterimage* 5, no. 8: 9–13.

———. 1982. *Art Worlds*. Berkeley and Los Angeles: University of California Press.

Benjamin, Walter. 1985. The work of art in the age of mechanical reproduction. In *Film Theory and Criticism*, 3d ed. G. Mast and M. Cohen, 675–94. New York: Oxford University Press.

Berger, John. 1972. *Ways of Seeing*. London: British Broadcasting Corporation and Penguin Books.

———. 1980. *About Looking*. New York: Pantheon Books.

Betterton, Rosemary, ed. 1987. *Looking On: Images of Femininity in the Visual Arts and Media*. London: Pandora.

Bhabha, Homi K. 1983. The other question—Homi K. Bhabha reconsiders the stereotype and colonial discourse. *Screen* 24, no. 6: 18–36.

Billig, Michael, Susan Condor, Derek Edwards, Mike Gane, David Middleton, and Alan Radley. 1988. *Ideological Dilemmas: A Social Psychology of Everyday Thinking*. London: Sage.

Bolton, Richard. 1990. In the American East: Richard Avedon Incorporated. In *The Contest of Meaning: Critical Histories of Photography*, ed. R. Bolton, 261–83. Cambridge, Mass.: MIT Press.

Botting, Wendy. 1988. Posing for power/posing for pleasure: Photographies and the social construction of femininity. Binghamton, N.Y.: University Art Gallery.

Bourdieu, Pierre, ed. 1965. *Un Art Moyen: Essai sur les Usages Sociaux de la Photographie*. Paris: Les Editions de Minuit.

———. 1984. *Distinction: A Social Critique of the Judgment of Taste*. Cambridge, Mass.: Harvard University Press.

Bright, Deborah. 1990. Of Mother Nature and Marlboro Men: An inquiry into the cultural meanings of landscape photography. In *The Contest of Meaning*, ed. R. Bolton, 125–42.

Brookfield, Harold. 1989. Global change and the Pacific: Problems for the coming half-century. *The Contemporary Pacific* 1:1–18.

Brown, Bruce W. 1981. *Images of Family Life in Magazine Advertising: 1920–1978*. New York: Praeger.

Bryan, C. D. B. 1987. *The National Geographic Society: 100 Years of Adventure and Discovery*. Washington, D.C.: National Geographic Society.

Bucher, Bernadette. 1981. *Icon and Conquest: A Structural Analysis of the Illustrations of deBry's Great Voyages*, trans. B. M. Gulati. Chicago: University of Chicago Press.

Buckley, Thomas. 1970. With the National Geographic on its endless, cloudless voyage. *New York Times Magazine*, 6 September.

References

Budd, Mike, Robert Entman, and Clay Steinman. 1990. The affirmative character of U.S. cultural studies. *Critical Studies in Mass Communication* 7:169–84.

Burgin, Victor, ed. 1982. *Thinking Photography*. London: Macmillan.

———. 1986. *The End of Art Theory: Criticism and Post-modernity*. London: Macmillan.

Canaan, Joyce. 1984. Building muscles and getting curves: gender differences in representations of the body and sexuality among American teenagers. Paper presented at the annual meeting of the American Anthropological Association, Denver.

Carbaugh, Donald. 1988. *Talking American: Cultural Discourses on Donahue*. Norwood, N.J.: Ablex.

Carby, Hazel. 1985. "On the threshold of woman's era": Lynching, empire, and sexuality in black feminist theory. In *"Race," Writing, and Difference*, ed. H. Gates, 301–16.

Carragee, Kevin M. 1990. Interpretive media study and interpretive social science. *Critical Studies in Mass Communication* 7:81–96.

Carson, Claybourne. 1981. *In Struggle: SNCC and the Black Awakening of the 1960's*. Cambridge: Harvard University Press.

Cartier-Bresson, Henri. 1979. *Henri Cartier-Bresson: Photographer*. Boston: New York Graphic Society.

Chafe, William. 1983. Social change and the American woman, 1940–70. In *A History of Our Time: Readings on Postwar America*, ed. William Chafe and Harvard Sitkoff, 157–65. New York: Oxford University Press.

Clifford, James. 1988. *The Predicament of Culture: Twentieth-Century Ethnography, Literature, and Art*. Cambridge, Mass.: Harvard University Press.

Collins, Patricia Hill. 1991. *Black Feminist Thought*. Boston: Unwin Hyman.

Davis, James A., and Tom W. Smith. 1986. *General Social Surveys 1972–86: Cumulative Codebooks*. Storrs, Conn.: NORC-Roper Center.

Debord, Guy. 1983. *Society of the Spectacle*. Detroit: Black and Red.

De Lauretis, Teresa. 1987. *Technologies of Gender: Essays on Theory, Film, and Fiction*. Bloomington: Indiana University Press.

Denning, Michael. 1990. The end of mass culture. *International Labor and Working-Class History* 37:4–18.

Devereux, George. 1967. *From Anxiety to Method in the Behavioral Sciences*. The Hague: Mouton.

Dower, John. 1986. *War Without Mercy: Race and Power in the Pacific War*. New York: Pantheon Books.

Drinnon, Richard. 1980. *Facing West: The Metaphysics of Indian Hating and Empire Building*. Minneapolis: University of Minnesota Press.

Dumont, Jean-Paul. 1988. The Tasaday, which and whose? Toward the political economy of an ethnographic sign. *Cultural Anthropology* 3:261–75.

Ehrenreich, Barbara, and Deirdre English. 1978. *For Her Own Good: 150 Years of the Experts' Advice to Women*. Garden City, N.Y.: Anchor Press/Doubleday.

Ehrenreich, Barbara, and John Ehrenreich. 1979. The professional-managerial class. In *Between Labor and Capital*, ed. Pat Walker, 5–45. Boston: South End Press.

Ellsworth, Phoebe. 1975. Direct gaze as social stimulus: The example of aggression. In *Nonverbal Communication of Aggression*, ed. P. Pliner, L. Krames, and T. Alloway, 53–75. New York: Plenum.

Enzensberger, Hans Magnus. 1974. *The Consciousness Industry: On Literature, Politics and the Media*. New York: Seabury.

Etienne, Mona, and Eleanor Leacock, eds. 1980. *Women and Colonization: Anthropological Perspectives*. New York: Praeger.

Ewen, Stuart. 1988. *All Consuming Images: The Politics of Style in Contemporary Culture*. New York: Basic Books.

Ewing, Katherine. 1990. The illusion of wholeness: Culture, self, and the experience of inconsistency. *Ethos* 18, no. 3: 251–78.

Fabian, Johannes. 1983. *Time and the Other: How Anthropology Makes Its Object*. New York: Columbia University Press.

Fanon, Frantz. 1965. *A Dying Colonialism*. New York: Grove Press.

Fiske, John. 1986. Television and popular culture: Reflections on British and Australian critical practice. *Critical Studies in Mass Communication* 3:200–216.

Frith, Simon. 1986. Hearing secret harmonies. In *High Theory/Low Culture*, ed. C. MacCabe, 53–70.

Forbes, H. D. 1985. *Nationalism, Ethnocentrism and Personality: Social Science and Critical Theory*. Chicago: University of Chicago Press.

Foucault, Michel. 1977. *Discipline and Punish: The Birth of the Prison*, trans. A. Sheridan. New York: Pantheon Books.

———. 1978. *The History of Sexuality*. Vol. 1, trans. R. Hurley. New York: Random House.

Fussell, Paul. 1975. *The Great War and Modern Memory*. New York: Oxford University Press.

Gaines, Jane. 1988. White privilege and looking relations: Race and gender in feminist film theory. *Screen* 29 no. 4: 12–27.

Galassi, Peter. 1987. *Henri Cartier-Bresson: The Early Work*. New York: Museum of Modern Art.

Gans, Herbert J. 1979. *Deciding What's News*. New York: Pantheon Books.

Gates, Henry Louis, Jr. 1985. Writing "race" and the difference it makes. In *"Race," Writing, and Difference*, ed. H. L. Gates, 1–20. Chicago: University of Chicago Press.

Geary, Christraud M. 1988. *Images from Bamum: German Colonial Photography at the Court of King Njoya, Cameroon, West Africa, 1902–1915*. Washington, D.C. Smithsonian Institution Press.

Gero, Joan, and Dolores Root. 1987. Public presentations and private concerns: Archaeology in the pages of *National Geographic*. In *The Politics of the Past, Proceedings of the World Archaeological Congress, Southampton, England, September 1986*, ed. Peter Gathercole and David Lowenthals. London: Allen and Unwin.

Gilman, Sander. 1985. *Difference and Pathology: Stereotypes of Sexuality, Race, and Madness*. Ithaca: Cornell University Press.

Gitlin, Todd. 1990a. Blips, bites and savvy talk. *Dissent* 37:18–26.

———. 1990b. Who communicates what to whom, in what voice and why, about the study of mass communication? *Critical Studies in Mass Communication* 7:185–96.

Goffman, Erving. 1979. *Gender Advertisements*. New York: Harper and Row.

References

Gould, Stephen Jay. 1981. *The Mismeasure of Man*. New York: Norton.

Graham-Brown, Sarah. 1988. *Images of Women: The Portrayal of Women in Photography of the Middle East, 1860–1950*. London: Quartet Books.

Gramsci, Antonio. 1971. *Selections from the Prison Notebooks*. New York: Lawrence and Wishart.

Green, David. 1984. Classified subjects. *Ten/8* 8, no. 14: 30–37.

———. 1989. Burgin and Sekula. *Ten/8*, no. 26: 30–43.

Griswold, Wendy. 1987a. The fabrication of meaning: Literary interpretation in the United States, Great Britain, and the West Indies. *American Journal of Sociology* 92:1077–1117.

———. 1987b. A methodological framework for the sociology of culture. *Sociological Methodology* 17:1–35.

Grover, Jan Zita. 1990. Dykes in context: Some problems in minority representation. In *The Contest of Meaning*, ed. R. Bolton.

Grundberg, Andy. 1990. Ask it no questions: The camera can lie. *New York Times*, 12 August.

Guimond, James. 1988. Exotic friends, evil others, and vice versa. *Georgia Review* 42: 33–69.

Hall, Stuart. 1973. The determinations of news photographs. In *The Manufacture of News*, ed. Stanley Cohen and Jock Young, 176–90. Beverly Hills, Calif.: Sage.

———. 1981. Notes on deconstructing "the popular." In *People's History and Socialist Theory*, ed. Raphael Samuel, 227–39. London: Routledge.

Hallin, David. 1987. The American news media from Vietnam to El Salvador: A study of ideological change and its limits. In *Political Communication Research: Approaches, Studies, Assessments*, ed. David L. Paletz, 3–25. Norwood, N.J.: Ablex.

Hammond, Dorothy, and Alta Jablow. 1977. *The Myth of Africa*. New York: Library of Social Science.

Haraway, Donna. 1984/85. Teddy bear patriarchy: Taxidermy in the Garden of Eden, New York City, 1908–1936. *Social Text* 4(2): 20–64.

———. *Primate Visions: Gender, Race, and Nature in the World of Modern Science*. New York: Routledge.

Harding, Vincent. 1981. *There Is a River: The Black Struggle for Freedom in America*. New York: Harcourt Brace Jovanovich.

Harris, Neil. 1978. Museums, merchandising and popular taste: The struggle for influence. In *Material Culture and the Study of American Life*. New York: Norton.

Hellman, Geoffrey. 1943. Geography unshackled II. *New Yorker*, 2 October, 27–35.

Hess, Thomas B., and Linda Nochlin. 1972. *Women as Sex Object: Studies in Erotic Art, 1730–1970*. New York: Newsweek Books.

Higham, John. 1955. *Strangers in the Land: Patterns of American Nativism, 1860–1925*. New Brunswick, N.J.: Rutgers University Press.

Hodge, R., and D. Tripp. 1986. *Children and Television*. Cambridge: Polity Press.

References

Hofstadter, Richard. 1944. *Social Darwinisn in American Thought*. Philadelphia: University of Pennsylvania Press.

Honour, Hugh. 1989. *The Image of the Black in Western Art*. Vol. 4, *From the American Revolution to World War I*. New York: Morrow.

hooks, bell. 1981. *Ain't I a Woman: Black Women and Feminism*. Boston: South End Press.

Hull, Gloria, Patricia Bell Scott, and Barbara Smith. 1982. *All the Women Are White, All the Blacks Are Men, but Some of Us Are Brave: Black Women's Studies*. Old Westbury, N.Y.: Feminist Press.

Hunter, Jefferson. 1987. *Image and Word: The Interaction of Twentieth-Century Photographs and Texts*. Cambridge, Mass.: Harvard University Press.

Hurston, Zora Neale. 1984. *Dust Tracks on a Road: An Autobiography*. 2d ed. Urbana: University of Illinois Press.

Jameson, Fredric. 1979. Reification and utopia in mass culture. *Social Text* 1, no. 1:130–48.

———. 1983. Pleasure: A political issue. In *Formations of Pleasure*, ed. Fredric Jameson, 1–14. London: Routledge.

———. 1984. Postmodernism, or The cultural logic of late capitalism. *New Left Review*, no. 146: 53–92.

JanMohamed, Abdul. 1985. The economy of manichean allegory: The function of racial difference in colonialist literature. *Critical Inquiry* 12:59–87.

Jeffords, Susan. 1989. *The Remasculinization of America: Gender and the Vietnam War*. Bloomington: Indiana University Press.

Jussim, Estelle. 1984. Propaganda and Persuasion. In *Observations*, ed. David Featherstone, 103–14. Carmel, Calif.: Friends of Photography.

Kabbani, Rana. 1986. *Europe's Myths of Orient*. Bloomington: Indiana University Press.

Kaledin, Eugenia. 1984. *Mothers and More: American Women in the 1950's*. Boston: Twayne.

Kessler, Lauren. 1989. Women's magazines' coverage of smoking related health hazards. *Journalism Quarterly* 66:316–22.

King, Michael. 1985. Maori images. *Natural History* 94, no. 7: 36–43.

Krasniewicz, Louise. 1990. Desecrating the patriotic body: Flag burning, art censorship, and the powers of "prototypical Americans." Paper presented at the annual meeting of the American Anthropological Association, New Orleans.

Lacan, Jacques, 1981. *The Four Fundamental Concepts of Psycho-Analysis*. New York: Norton.

Lambert, W. E., and O. Klineberg. 1967. *Children's Views of Foreign Peoples*. New York: Appleton-Century-Crofts.

Lears, T. J. Jackson. 1981. *No Place of Grace: Antimodernism and the Transformation of American Culture, 1880–1920*. New York: Pantheon.

Lemagny, Jean-Claude, and André Rouille. 1987. *A History of Photography: Social and Cultural Perspectives*. New York: Cambridge University Press.

Levine, Lawrence W. 1988. *Highbrow/Lowbrow: The Emergence of Cultural Hierarchy in America*. Cambridge, Mass.: Harvard University Press.

References

LeVine, Robert, and D. Campbell. 1972. *Ethnocentrism: Theories of Conflict, Ethnic Attitudes and Group Behavior*. New York: Wiley.

Liebes, Tamar. 1988. Cultural differences in the retelling of television fiction. *Critical Studies in Mass Communication* 5:277–92.

Liebes, Tamar, and Elihu Katz. 1990. *The Export of Meaning: Cross-Cultural Readings of Dallas*. New York: Oxford University Press.

Lindstrom, Lamont, and Geoffrey White. 1990. *Island Encounters: Black and White Memories of the Pacific War*. Washington, D.C.: Smithsonian Institution Press.

Lipsitz, George. 1981. *Class and Culture in Cold War America*. New York: Bergin.

Livingston, Jane. 1988. The art of photography at National Geographic. *National Geographic* 174:324–51.

Livingstone, Sonia M. 1989. Audience reception and the analysis of program meaning. *American Behavioral Scientist* 33:187–90.

Luhrmann, Tanya. 1989. *Persuasions of the Witch's Craft: Ritual Magic in Contemporary England*. Cambridge: Harvard University Press.

Lutkehaus, Nancy. 1989. "Excuse me, everything is not alright": On ethnography, film, and representation. An Interview with Filmmaker Dennis O'Rourke. *Cultural Anthropology* 4:422–37.

Lutz, Catherine. 1988. *Unnatural Emotions: Everyday Sentiments on a Micronesian Atoll and Their Challenge to Western Theory*. Chicago: University of Chicago Press.

Lyman, Christopher M. 1982. *The Vanishing Race and Other Illusions: Photographs of Indians by Edward S. Curtis*. New York: Pantheon Books.

MacAloon, John. 1987. Missing stories: American politics and Olympic discourse. *Gannett Center Journal* 1:111–42.

MacCabe, Colin, ed. 1986. *High Theory/Low Culture: Analyzing Popular Television and Film*. Manchester: University of Manchester Press.

Macfarlane, Alan. 1987. *The Culture of Capitalism*. New York: Oxford University Press.

McGrane, Bernard. 1989. *Beyond Anthropology: Society and the Other*. New York: Columbia University Press.

Maquet, Jacques. 1986. *The Aesthetic Experience*. New Haven: Yale University Press.

Marcus, George, and Dick Cushman. 1982. Ethnographies as texts. *Annual Review of Anthropology* 11:25–69.

Margolis, Maxine. 1984. *Mothers and Such*. Berkeley and Los Angeles: University of California Press.

Mast, Gerald, and Marshall Cohen, eds. 1985. *Film Theory and Criticism: Introductory Readings*. New York: Oxford University Press.

May, Elaine Tyler. 1988. *Homeward Bound: American Families in the Cold War Era*. New York: Basic Books.

Meltzer, Milton. 1978. *Dorothea Lange: A Photographer's Life*. New York: Farrar Straus Giroux.

Metz, Christian. 1985. From *The Imaginary Signifier*. In *Film Theory and Criticism*, ed. G. Mast and M. Cohen, 782–802. New York: Oxford University Press.

Mitchell, Timothy. 1989. The world as exhibition. *Comparative Studies in Society and History*. 31:217–36.

Modleski, Tania. 1986a. Femininity as mas(s)querade: A feminist approach to mass culture. In *High Theory/Low Culture,* ed. C. MacCabe.

———. 1986b. Woman is an island. In *Studies in Entertainment: Critical Approaches to Mass Culture,* ed. T. Modleski. Bloomington: Indiana University Press.

———. 1988. *The Women Who Knew Too Much: Hitchcock and Feminist Theory.* New York: Methuen.

Moeller, Susan. 1989. *Shooting War: Photography and the American Experience of Combat.* New York: Basic Books.

Monti, Nicolas. 1987. *Africa Then: Photographs, 1840–1918.* New York: Knopf.

Moore, Henrietta. 1988. *Feminism and Anthropology.* Cambridge: Cambridge University Press.

Moorehead, Alan. 1960. *The White Nile.* New York: Harper and Brothers.

Morley, David. 1980. *The "Nationwide" Audience.* London: British Film Institute.

———. 1986. *Family Television.* London: Comedia.

Mulvey, Laura. 1985. Visual Pleasure and Narrative Cinema. In *Film Theory and Criticism,* ed. G. Mast and M. Cohen, 803–16.

Myers, Kathy. 1987. Towards a feminist erotica. In *Looking On,* ed. R. Betterton, 189–202.

Nachtwey, James. 1989. *Deeds of War: Photographs.* New York: Thames and Hudson.

Nader, Laura. 1974. Up the anthropologist—perspectives gained from studying up. In *Reinventing Anthropology,* ed. Dell Hymes, 284–311. New York: Vintage Books.

Nash, Roderick. 1982. *Wilderness and the American Mind.* 3d ed. New Haven: Yale University Press.

National Geographic Society. 1981. *Images of the World: Photography at the National Geographic.* Washington, D.C.: National Geographic Society.

Nead, Lynda. 1990. The female nude: pornography, art, and sexuality. *Signs* 15:323–35.

Ohmann, Richard M. 1987. *Politics of Letters.* Middletown, Conn.: Wesleyan University Press.

Okely, Judith. 1975. The self and scientism. *Journal of the Anthropological Society of Oxford* 6, no. 3: 177–88.

Oliver, Douglas. 1961. *The Pacific Islands.* Rev. ed. New York: Doubleday.

Omi, Michael, and Howard Winant. 1986. *Racial Formation in the United States: From the 1960's to the 1980's.* New York: Routledge.

Ong, Aihwa. 1988. Colonialism and modernity: Feminist re-presentations of women in non-Western societies. *Inscriptions,* nos. 3/4: 79–93.

Ortner, Sherry. 1974. Is female to male as nature is to culture? In *Woman, Culture, and Society,* ed. M. Rosaldo and L. Lamphere, 67–88. Stanford: Stanford University Press.

Parenti, Michael. 1986. *Inventing Reality: Politics and the Mass Media.* New York: St. Martin's Press.

Pauly, Philip. 1979. The world and all that is in it: The National Geographic Society, 1888–1918. *American Quarterly* 31:517–32.

Polan, Dana. 1986a. *Power and Paranoia: History, Narrative, and the American Cinema, 1940–1950.* New York: Columbia University Press.

———. 1986b. "Above all else to make you see": Cinema and the ideology of spectacle. In *Postmodernism and Politics,* ed. Jonathan Arac, 55–69. Minneapolis: University of Minnesota.

Pollock, Grieselda. 1987. What's wrong with 'images of women'? In *Looking On,* ed. R. Betterton, 40–48.

Postone, Moishe, and Elizabeth G. Traube. 1985. The return of the repressed. *Jump Cut* 30:12–14.

Pratt, Mary Louise. 1982. Conventions of representation: Where discourse and ideology meet. In *Contemporary Perceptions of Language: Interdisciplinary Dimensions,* ed. H. Byrnes, 139–55. Washington, D.C.: Georgetown University Press.

———. 1985. Scratches on the face of the country: Or, What Mr. Barrow saw in the land of the bushmen. In *"Race," Writing, and Difference,* ed. H. Gates, 138–62. Chicago: University of Chicago Press.

Preiswerk, Roy, and Dominique Perrot. 1978. *Ethnocentrism and History: Africa, Asia, and Indian America in Western Texbooks.* New York: NOK Publishers International.

Price, Sally. 1989. *Primitive Art in Civilized Places.* Chicago: University of Chicago Press.

Rabinow, Paul. 1986. Representations are social facts: Modernity in anthropology. In *Writing Culture,* ed. J. Clifford and G. Marcus, 234–61. Berkeley and Los Angeles: University of California Press.

Radway, Janice. 1984. *Reading the Romance.* Chapel Hill: University of North Carolina Press.

———. 1988. The Book-of-the-Month Club and the general reader: On the uses of "serious" fiction. *Critical Inquiry* 14:516–38.

Ritchin, Fred. 1984. The photography of conflict. *Aperture* 97:22–27.

———. 1989. What is Magnum? In *In Our Time: The World as Seen by Magnum Photographers,* ed. William Manchester, 417–44. New York: American Federation of Arts.

———. 1990. Photojournalism in the age of computers. In *The Critical Image,* ed. C. Squiers, 28–37.

Robinson, H. 1976. *A Geography of Tourism.* Estover, Plymouth: MacDonald and Evans.

Rosaldo, Renato. 1989. *Culture and Truth.* Boston: Beacon Press.

Rose, Jacqueline. 1986. *Sexuality in the Field of Vision.* London: Verso.

Rosenblum, Barbara. 1978. *Photographers at Work: A Sociology of Photographic Styles.* New York: Holmes and Meier.

Ross, Ishbel. 1938. Geography, Inc. *Scribner's Magazine* (June), 24.

Rostow, Walt. 1960. *The Stages of Economic Growth: A Non–Communist Manifesto.* Cambridge: Cambridge University Press.

Rowe, John Carlos. 1986. Eye-witness: documentary styles in the American representations of Vietnam. *Cultural Critique* 3:126–50.

Rydell, Robert. 1984. *All the World's a Fair: Visions of Empire at American International Expositions, 1876–1916.* Chicago: University of Chicago Press.

Sacks, Karen. 1989. Toward a unified theory of class, race and gender. *American Ethnologist* 16:534–50.

Said, Edward. 1981. *Covering Islam. How the Media and the Experts Determine How We See the Rest of the World.* New York: Pantheon Books.

———. 1989. Representing the colonized: Anthropology's interlocutors. *Critical Inquiry* 15:205–25.

Schaffer, Kay. 1988. *Women and the Bush: Forces of Desire in the Australian Cultural Tradition.* Cambridge: Cambridge University Press.

Schick, Irvin Cemil. 1990. Representing Middle Eastern women: feminism and colonial discourse. *Feminist Studies* 16, no. 2: 345–80.

Schiller, Dan. 1981. *Objectivity and the News: The Public and the Rise of Commercial Journalism.* Philadelphia: University of Pennsylvania.

Schudson, Michael. 1978. *Discovering the News: A Social History of American Newspapers.* New York: Basic Books.

Schwartz, Dona B., and Michael Griffin. 1987. Amateur photography: the organizational maintenance of an aesthetic code. In *Natural Audiences,* ed. T. R. Lindlof, 198–224. Norwood, N.J.: Ablex.

Schwartz, Tony. 1977. The Geographic faces life. *Newsweek,* 12 September, 565.

Sekula, Allan. 1975. On the invention of photographic meaning. *Artforum* 13:36–44.

———. 1981. The traffic in photographs. *Art Journal* 41:15–25.

Shapiro, Michael. 1988. *The Politics of Representation: Writing Practices in Biography, Photography, and Policy Analysis.* Madison: University of Wisconsin Press.

Sider, Gerald. 1987. When parrots learn to talk, and why they can't: Domination, deception, and self-deception in Indian-white relations. *Comparative Studies in Society and History* 29:3–23.

Silverstone, Roger. 1985. *Framing Science: The Making of a BBC Documentary.* London: BFI Publishing.

Simmons Market Research Bureau. 1987. *Simmons 1987 Study of Media and Markets.* New York: Simmons Market Research Bureau.

Slotkin, Richard. 1985. *The Fatal Environment: The Myth of the Frontier in the Age of Industrialization, 1800–1890.* New York: Atheneum.

Smith, Barbara Herrnstein. 1983. Contingencies of value. *Critical Inquiry* 10:1–35.

Smith, Bernard. 1985. *European Vision and the South Pacific.* 2d ed. New Haven: Yale University Press.

Snow, Edward. 1989. Theorizing the male gaze: Some problems. *Representations* 25 (Winter): 30–41.

Sobran, M. J., Jr. 1977. Tariff on truth. *National Review,* 13 May.

Sontag, Susan. 1977. *On Photography.* New York: Dell.

Squiers, Carol, ed. 1990. *The Critical Image.* Seattle: Bay Press.

Stewart, Susan. 1984. *On Longing: Narratives of the Miniature, the Gigantic, the Souvenir, the Collection.* Baltimore and London: Johns Hopkins University Press.

Stocking, George. 1968. *Race, Culture, and Evolution.* New York: Free Press.

———. 1987. *Victorian Anthropology.* New York: Free Press.

Stoler, Ann. 1989. Making empire respectable: The politics of race and sexual morality in 20th century colonial cultures. *American Ethnologist* 16:634–60.

Strathern, Marilyn. 1990. Enterprising kinship: Consumer choice and the new reproductive technologies. *Cambridge Anthropology* 14, no. 1: 1–12.

Strauss, Claudia. 1990. Who gets ahead? Cognitive responses to heteroglossia in American political culture. *American Ethnologist* 17:312–28.

Tagg, John. 1988. *The Burden of Representation: Essays on Photographies and Histories.* Amherst: University Of Massachusetts Press.

Taussig, Michael T. 1987. *Shamanism, Colonialism, and the Wild Man: A Study in Terror and Healing.* Chicago: University of Chicago Press.

Thorburn, D. 1988. Television as an aesthetic medium. In *Media, Myths, and Narratives: Television and the Press,* ed. J. Carey. Newbury Park, Calif.: Sage.

Tiffany, Sharon, and Kathleen Adams. 1985. *The Wild Woman: An Inquiry into the Anthropology of an Idea.* Cambridge, Mass.: Schenkman.

Torgovnick, Marianna. 1990. *Gone Primitive: Savage Intellects, Modern Lives.* Chicago: University of Chicago Press.

Trachtenberg, Alan. 1989. *Reading American Photographs: Images as History, Matthew Brady to Walker Evans.* New York: Hill and Wang.

Traube, Elizabeth G. 1989. Secrets of success in postmodern society. *Cultural Anthropology* 4:273–300.

———. 1992. *Dreaming Identities: Class, Gender, and Generation in 1980s Hollywood Movies.* Boulder, Col.: Westview Press.

Trinh, Min-ha T. 1989. *Woman, Native, Other: Writing Postcoloniality and Feminism.* Bloomington: Indiana University Press.

Truehart, Charles. 1990. The great divide at National Geographic. *Washington Post,* 7 May.

Turner, Terence. 1980. The Social Skin. In *Not Work Alone,* ed. J. Cherfas and R. Lewin, 114–40. Beverly Hills: Sage.

Turow, Joseph. 1984. *Media Industries: The Production of News and Entertainment.* New York: Longman.

van Dijk, Teun A. 1987. *Communicating Racism: Ethnic Prejudice in Thought and Talk.* Newbury Park: Sage.

Vance, Carol. 1990. The pleasures of looking: the Attorney General's Commission on Pornography versus visual images. In *The Critical Image,* ed. Carol Squiers, 38–58.

Vesilind, Priit Juho. 1977. *The Development of Color Photography at National Geographic.* M.A. thesis, Syracuse University.

Walker, Pat, ed. 1979. *Between Labor and Capital.* Montreal: Black Rose Books.

Wallace, Michele. 1990. *Invisibility Blues: From Pop to Theory.* London: Verso.

Wallis, Roger, and Stanley J. Baran. 1990. *The Known World of Broadcast News: International News and the Electronic Media.* London: Routledge.

Weaver, David, and G. Cleveland Wilhoit. 1986. *The American Journalist: A Portrait of U.S. News People and Their Work.* Bloomington: Indiana University Press.

Wescott, Glenway. 1928. *Goodbye Wisconsin.* New York: Signet.

Williams, Anne. 1987. Untitled. *Ten/8* 11:6–11.

References

Williams, Raymond. 1986. An interview with Raymond Williams. In *Studies in Entertainment*, ed. T. Modleski, 3–17.

Williamson, Judith. 1978. *Decoding Photographs*. London: Marion Boyars.

Willis, Susan. 1991. *A Primer for Daily Life*. New York: Routledge.

Wilson, Christopher. 1983. The rhetoric of consumption: Mass market magazines and the demise of the gentle reader, 1880–1920. In *The Culture of Consumption: Critical Essays in American History, 1880–1980*, ed. Richard Fox and T. J. Jackson Lears, 39–64. New York: Pantheon Books.

Wolf, Eric. 1982. *Europe and the People without History*. Berkeley and Los Angeles: University of California Press.

Wolf, Naomi. 1991. *The Beauty Myth: How Images of Beauty Are Used against Women*. New York: Morrow.

Young, Iris Marion. 1990. Breasted experience: The look and the feeling. In *Throwing Like a Girl and Other Essays in Feminist Philosophy and Social Theory*, ed. I. M. Young. Bloomington: Indiana University Press.

Index

Index

Index

Index